T0247600

Praise for

METARACISM

"Tricia Rose has long set the bar for what it means to be a leading public intellectual. Brilliant, astute, and fearless, she has taken on the difficult task of demystifying 'systemic racism' from a catchphrase that merely asserts racial disparities are the result of hidden forces, explaining exactly how systemic racism works in the United States. With great clarity and precision, she moves beyond the shocking story, the point of trauma, or the dizzying statistics to expose the system as a whole; apprehending its operations by revealing each part, policy, and practice, and the myriad ways they conjoin. In the face of relentless attacks on the mere mention of racism, and the nonsense spewing from the new 'anti-racism industry,' *Metaracism* offers the clear-eyed analysis we urgently need."

—Robin D. G. Kelley, author of *Freedom Dreams*

"Rose is one of our most dynamic and thoughtful public intellectuals today, and in her new book, *Metaracism*, she gives us the gift of sight. At a time when terms like 'structural racism' and 'systemic racism' are tossed around in the political fires with little rigor or reflection, *Metaracism* provides a much-needed primer on the real-world meaning of the problem. From housing to education, economic inequality to the criminal justice system, Rose invites us to see that the roots of racism run deep and are pervasive in the traumatic suffering we have witnessed in our time—of Trayvon Martin, Michael Brown, Kelley Williams-Bolar, and so many others. We must not only say their names. We must be able to name the reasons why. In this critical text, Rose helps us to do just that."

—Henry Louis Gates Jr., *New York Times*–
bestselling author of *Stony the Road*

"Rose is a brilliant scholar who has been on the cutting edge of every concept she's touched. I read everything she writes and always learn from her insights and analyses."

—Imani Perry, National Book Award–
winning author of *South to America*

"This book will be the most definitive and comprehensive treatment of systemic racism we have from the academy for the larger culture in America! There is simply no one better equipped to write this magisterial text than Rose! She brings together the best of sociological analysis, cultural criticism, and brilliant prose!"

—Cornel West, *New York Times*–
bestselling author of *Democracy Matters*

"Rose is one of our most powerful and profound public intellectuals. Her work on systemic racism is groundbreaking in its ability to elucidate the myriad ways in which we are still blind to how race operates under the surface of every American encounter. This book will become essential reading for anyone seriously interested in understanding the ways racism is seamlessly reproduced in this culture."

—Michael Eric Dyson, *New York Times*–
bestselling author of *Tears We Cannot Stop*

"Rose shook the ground with *Black Noise* in 1994, calling a field into existence and making rigorous work in the history and rhythms of Black popular culture possible. She wrote the groundbreaking *Longing to Tell*, setting a new standard for how to talk about the sexual lives of Black women. And *The Hip Hop Wars* inaugurated an entirely new generation of students into what it means to critically engage the music we bop to. When Rose takes to her pen, we listen for the record scratch, for the invitation to read closely. We do so because we know things will be different and we will be different after picking up whatever Rose is putting down."

—Brittney Cooper, *New York Times*–
bestselling author of *Eloquent Rage*

METARACISM

ALSO BY TRICIA ROSE

The Hip Hop Wars: What We Talk About When We Talk About Hip Hop—and Why It Matters

Longing to Tell: Black Women Talk About Sexuality and Intimacy

Black Noise: Rap Music and Black Culture in Contemporary America

METARACISM

HOW SYSTEMIC RACISM DEVASTATES BLACK LIVES— AND HOW WE BREAK FREE

TRICIA ROSE

BASIC BOOKS

New York

Basic Books
Hachette Book Group
1290 Avenue of the Americas, New York, NY 10104
www.basicbooks.com

Printed in the United States of America

First Edition: March 2024

Published by Basic Books, an imprint of Hachette Book Group, Inc. The Basic Books name and logo is a trademark of the Hachette Book Group.

The Hachette Speakers Bureau provides a wide range of authors for speaking events. To find out more, go to hachettespeakersbureau.com or email HachetteSpeakers@hbgusa.com.

Basic books may be purchased in bulk for business, educational, or promotional use. For more information, please contact your local bookseller or the Hachette Book Group Special Markets Department at special.markets@hbgusa.com.

The publisher is not responsible for websites (or their content) that are not owned by the publisher.

Print book interior design by Amy Quinn.

Library of Congress Control Number: 2023951775

ISBNs: 9781541602717 (hardcover), 9781541602731 (ebook)

LSC-C

Printing 1, 2023

CONTENTS

Metaracism *(the metaeffect of systemic racism): the dynamic, compounding patterns of racial disadvantage and discrimination produced by the interconnections among policies and practices across society over time. No single policy or practice—nor a linear, additive combination of them—can produce metaracism. Metaracism is an impact greater than the sum of systemic racism's parts.*

INTRODUCTION

I was born in Harlem. We lived on 145th Street between Broadway and Amsterdam Avenue. It must have been a beautiful building in 1905, when its bricks were still visibly red and decorative lintels and elaborate pediments framed its windows. By the time I was born in 1962, it was a decrepit walk-up tenement run by a landlord who did nothing to care for it. Some of my earliest memories are of standing near the oven to warm up because we had no heat. My father paid professional exterminators to keep rats and roaches out of our apartment, and my mother organized rent strikes to force the landlord to turn the heat back on. My parents' efforts worked for a time, but soon enough the heat would disappear, and the rats and roaches always made their way back inside.

Despite the condition of my building and my neighborhood, I was happy. I played with my friends in view of my parents' window, living in a community where neighbors looked out for us and we looked out for our neighbors. Those neighbors included even the most vulnerable like Daddy-O, who appeared to be a homeless alcoholic, who hung out on our stoop. Daddy-O's presence was also a sign: If the door to the vestibule was open and Daddy-O was there, we knew it was safe to go inside. If the door was closed and Daddy-O was gone, we knew there might be something sordid going on. When I think back on it, he was our own personal neighborhood watch.

As the 1960s rolled along, the neighborhood became even less stable. The mayor closed my local library claiming "budget shortfalls." Meanwhile, my mother regularly got into arguments with my all-white teachers about the absence of helpful comments or corrections on any of my homework. These teachers (who lived far away from my block) seemed more concerned with my "unruly" hair than they were with developing my basic math skills, grammar, and punctuation. My father, a lifelong Harlemite except for his time in the Army during World War II, decided it was time to leave, but our options were few. Finally, in 1970 we moved to a brand-new development called Co-op City, an affordable multiracial cooperative for working families, on the outskirts of the Bronx. Compared to Harlem, Co-op City was a haven, with expansive fields of grass, bike paths, playgrounds, and shopping plazas. The plaza nearest my building had a new library. And, most importantly for my parents, the schools were one step better than my Harlem elementary school, P.S. 186, though they still held out hope that even better schools would become attainable.

Then, in 1975, when I was thirteen and a rising eighth grader, my parents' hopes were answered. I was plucked from the financial aid waiting list and admitted to the Dalton School, an elite private school on Manhattan's Upper East Side. Going to Dalton gave me culture shock I can still feel today. It exposed me to a race and wealth gap so great that two New York City neighborhoods separated only by a few miles felt like they were a whole universe apart.

Getting to and from school took over an hour by bus and subway each way. It's a trip I took alone five days a week for five years. These daily subway rides became one of my first research sites, demonstrating just how segregated by race and class New York City really was. Taking the 6 train during rush hour at 86th Street, I quickly realized that all the white passengers would be gone by 125th Street and the rest of the ride would be Black, Latinx, and Asian folk. I was a motivated student and strategized that if I stood by a seated white person when I got on, I'd have a seat in three stops and could spend the rest of my way to Pelham Bay Park, the very last stop on the number 6 train, doing my homework on my lap.

As my high school years progressed, my initial observation about spatial racial segregation thickened. The train's path also illuminated a pattern of targeted neglect and destruction that turned much of the South Bronx into piles of rubble, decimating and displacing whole communities of working-class people of color. These were communities under siege. As I bore witness to the accelerating state of crisis in Harlem and the Bronx alongside the unshakable wealth, immense privilege, and the racial homogeneity at Dalton, I began to ask questions. *Why were things the way they were? And how did they get this way?* By the time I was sixteen, it was clear to me that even though I was a very good student, no amount of hard work and no amount of studying would close the cavernous gap between my Dalton peers and everyone I knew outside Dalton. But I still couldn't figure out why.

Even in a top private school like Dalton, there was no history or social studies class then available that could explain to me how American society had come to be arranged in such a visibly unequal way. Our highly regarded curriculum simply did not include any discussion of the central role of slavery, race, and racism in the development of the United States, nor any African American history. Instead, a key moment here or there—such as a brief consideration of the impact of the civil rights movement—was folded into a larger story about America's commitment to democratic opportunity for all. This high point of Black struggle for freedom was largely severed from a long history of such struggle and from the ongoing and evolving policies that maintained racial inequity. The results of these policies were right in front of me, but their origins were rendered invisible by the fragmented way they were discussed.

At home, my parents encouraged lively conversations and debates around the dinner table about all kinds of social issues, especially racism. Nonetheless, I, like the majority of people in America, tended to notice and recall racism as expressed by individual behavior. When I was in the ninth grade, one of my friends with whom I played on the girls' basketball team invited me over after school. When I arrived at the entrance of her exclusive building on the Upper East Side of Manhattan, I announced myself as a classmate of hers from Dalton. Despite this, the white doorman gruffly sent me around back to the service elevator reserved for nannies, maids, and others in the employ of the building's wealthy residents. I experienced his relegating me to the service elevator as an act of individual/ interpersonal racism, the kind of thing that people did because they were ignorant or hateful or "raised that way."

It wasn't until I took a sociology class on inequality as an undergraduate at Yale that I began to find real answers to my questions. Sociology classes revealed and then connected the pieces that had been separated and hidden from view. At the same time, African American Studies gave me the capacity to see African American history, culture, and politics from the view of the community's vantage point. After a while, the conditions of my childhood were no longer random facts of life, or the product of individual decisions alone, but a system I could study that had reliable and predictable outcomes for the folks I grew up with.

What I couldn't initially understand as a child growing up in Harlem and the Bronx, but would come to understand through my graduate studies, is that a relentless focus on personal or individual racism masked a complicated and durable system. Much of the power of that system was maintained and hidden by the stories we consistently tell about racism, stories that appear to confront racism but instead avoid addressing the systemic forces that continue to produce and maintain inequality. If we want to shed light on and dismantle the system, I reasoned, we would have to find ways to illuminate and personalize it. We need to make much more room for compelling stories that reveal the reinforcing impact of systemic racism on the lived experiences of those who bore the brunt of its effects.

Hip hop dramatically filled this void. Emerging in the mid-1970s in New York City, hip hop gave voice to those who were left to survive in the rubble-strewn lots of the South Bronx. My first book on hip hop, *Black Noise: Rap Music and Black Culture in Contemporary America* (1994), explored connections between the structural and spatial destruction of Black opportunity and community and the electrifying and creative determination of hip hop's earliest progenitors. These "voices from the margins," as I called them, exposed elements of systemic racism that challenged the mainstream idea that such a system was dismantled by antidiscrimination laws and that we had become a colorblind society. Over the next fifty years, as the genre moved to the center of American culture, the stories uplifted by the music industry began to reflect the very mainstream narratives about racism the genre had originally challenged. The relatively few artists who managed to resist the tremendous money and fame offered by the music industry and continued to make a systemic critique of racism were themselves pushed to the commercial margins. What I observed about hip hop was part of a larger process in the broader culture that embraced stories about Black experience while evading system-revealing stories of Black life. This book seeks to bring those stories, their systems-focus, back into view.

Metaracism is an effort to reveal systemic racism for what it is: a network of systemic impediments that works with devastating precision not only to influence our lives but to hide its own operations. The chapters that follow will argue that systemic racism remains the most important but largely concealed and therefore underestimated barrier to creating a racially just society. The repercussions of unaddressed and interlocking past and present policies and practices—some of which are designed to discriminate and others of which are used to generate discriminatory outcomes—work to create a network of mutually reinforcing racial disadvantages. When these connections are illuminated, a context of harm that is much greater than any one policy or institution could produce comes into view: metaracism.

Systemic racism's power derives not only from its interconnections and mutually reinforcing metaeffects, but from its ability to hide in plain sight. The stories we tell about spectacular acts of racism often serve to obscure our view of the systemic racism all around us. In the drama of the singular catastrophic racist act, the workings of the system drop into the background. To see how this sleight of hand works, we need only look at the public reporting on individual acts of extreme discrimination or police brutality. News stories about such outrages regularly generate heightened emotional responses to racist acts few are likely to defend. Yet by focusing on extreme individual acts of racially motivated violence, these stories help reinforce the perception that racism is an obviously and visibly malignant, individual behavior. Such reporting builds a broad, if temporary, consensus against racism—with an almost singular focus on flagrant acts of interpersonal racism. These kinds of stories on the surface appear dedicated to exposing racism. Instead, they are mired in frames that pin blame on aberrant racists while hiding systemic racism.

These stories help create and support a widely held belief that America has ended societal racism. Recent studies show that today, a majority of Americans adamantly deny being racist, express strong belief in racial equality, and understand themselves to be practicing racial equality in their everyday lives.[1] This firm belief in one's personal practice of racial equality extends to perceptions of society itself. Nearly 80 percent of white Americans, for example, believe that "we are already or are almost a racially equal society."[2] These beliefs and perceptions sit quite precariously atop a vast network of interlocking forces and practices that work to create consistent and profound disadvantages for Black people and create and maintain stronger safety nets and enhanced opportunities for white people. This combination of dynamics is so normalized that many conclude that society must be racially just; that people's life outcomes reflect what they have earned.

In many ways, this tension—a strong and broad-based belief in racial equality in a system whose societal institutions and policies maintain racial inequality—reflects a positive shift. For most of American history, the vast majority of white Americans explicitly believed in their racial superiority and deployed this belief to justify their control of resources and institutions, thereby more explicitly defending racial hierarchy. For most of our history, there was no need for systemic racism to be actively compartmentalized or denied; it was simply the publicly dominant social view. This was especially the case during the century-long era of southern Jim Crow racism, when many of the signposts of racial hierarchy and segregation were easily seen, reinforced, publicly supported, and legally enshrined. The civil rights movement, a multiracial push organized and led by Black Americans, is principally responsible for ending legalized racism and fueling the transition to a majority who express support for racial equality. As a result, Jim Crow signs and restrictions, though they were once openly supported, are now legally outlawed and rejected by the public. And yet the arrangements of policies and practices across every facet of society remain and often produce starkly similar racial outcomes as were documented more than a half century ago under the regime of Jim Crow. Racial wealth gaps have remained consistent for over seventy years, and school segregation has returned to 1960 levels.[3] During the 1980s a much expanded and brutal system of mass incarceration, which scholars have clearly shown disproportionately targets Black men and women, gathered steam and exploded pre-1960 levels of incarceration. Legally required discrimination has ended, yes. The signposts of segregation and racial oppression have been taken down, but segregation and policies that reinforce oppression remain and have even expanded in some areas. Public support of explicit racial hierarchy has been explicitly rejected or reduced to a murmur. But the gears of systemic racism continue to turn even so.

Today, systemic racism doesn't need a "Whites Only" sign or an unapologetic racist to keep its wheels turning. Over the past fifty years, a period marked as the post–civil rights era, systemic racism has been an effective, well-oiled machine under liberal and conservative presidents, under Ronald Reagan to Barack Obama to Joe Biden. Systemic racism is not driven only by openly hostile anti-Black forces; it is a powerful driver of Black disadvantage within liberal and progressive communities and among whites who steadfastly claim to believe in racial equality.

In my thirty-plus years of teaching and writing about racism, I have met many people who admit racism exists but reject the notion that today's policies and practices are structured to generate harm on multiple levels for Black people. This is, in part, because we have been socialized to identify Jim Crow–style, explicit domination of Black people as the predominant form racism takes. In the past, this version of history goes, society believed that whites should have greater status and value—and now we don't. This perception hinges on society-wide racism as a waning phenomenon, on the idea that what we see are the vestiges of a past system. This false divide between "then" and "now," the relentless focus on individual racism, along with the inherent stealth of systemic racism itself, combine to make systemic racism invisible to most Americans today.

The idea that today's conditions are simply holdover racist practices from decades and centuries past is not only wrong but dangerous. This illusion makes it very difficult to see how recent and current conditions and policies at once create, enforce, and reproduce to keep the systems of racial discrimination working in the present tense. We are not weathering the bumpy but declining legacy of a racist past. We are, right now, reinforcing and developing new policies that will maintain systemic racism in the decades ahead. The wealth gap has been steady for seventy years, not only because of the bedrock of discrimination that created it, but also because of ongoing and new practices and decisions in policy and practice that maintain it. The long history of excluding Black people from bank loans gave way to various forms of discriminatory inclusion, for example, the practice of allowing Blacks to apply for loans but then disproportionately rejecting their applications and/or targeting them for high-interest loans.[4] School segregation is illegal and very few publicly support school segregation today, and yet our schools are as or more racially segregated than they were in the 1960s. These and other continued, modified, and newly developed policies and practices generate contemporary and future patterns of systemic racism. A systems lens brings into sharp relief the adaptations in policy that nonetheless maintain consistent outcomes, such as significant school segregation, lending discrimination, and a cavernous racial wealth gap. Furthermore, systems thinking draws our attention to the impact of an insidious and evasive network of policies and practices working together to create *metaracism*: the dynamic interconnections between policies and practices that generate effects greater than any one policy could achieve on its own.

Many who oppose racism that is clearly rooted in hate are nonetheless beneficiaries and sometimes defenders of the conditions under which systemic racism flourishes. And, when serious effort to disrupt the impact of systemic racism gathers steam close to home, it is too often white liberals who line up to protect the status quo that maintains white advantages. It can be disheartening to witness liberal parents decry police acts of violence against Black citizens and post "Black Lives Matter" signs on their lawns, and yet attend school board meetings where they fight vigorously to retain a disgraceful, largely segregated, and unequally funded school system that provides advantages for their own children. This contradiction is not new. Martin Luther King, Jr., wrote bluntly about northern white liberals who welcomed him to their cities "and showered praise on the heroism of Southern Negroes." However, when King focused national attention on deplorable northern urban conditions on the South Side of Chicago and elsewhere, he noted: "Only the language was polite. The rejection was firm and unequivocal."[5]

Over the past ten years or so, our public conversation on racism seems to have expanded, and some might even suggest that the dramatic rise in the public validation and visibility of once obscure terms such as "systemic racism" and "structural racism" reflects a collective step forward toward creating a permanent, more level ground.

Some of this shift was the result of the vast reach of social media to distribute instantaneously, to a global audience, recorded incidents of police violence against Black people. Whether recorded on citizens' phones or on police body cams, this footage was now instantly consumed by a mass public. As a result, these incidents became more easily seen as part of something bigger, something structural or systemic. Between 2000 and 2019, usage of the terms "systemic racism" and "structural racism" each saw an eightfold increase in book publication references alone, with the most significant rise beginning between 2012, the year Trayvon Martin was murdered by George Zimmerman, and 2014, when Ferguson police officer Darren Wilson gunned down Michael Brown in the middle of the street.[6] For the year and a half or so following the May 2020 police murder of George Floyd, these two terms were everywhere. Public statements from college presidents, presidential candidates, celebrities, and a number of major corporate CEOs noted that structural and systemic racism are serious problems in our society, and many called for meaningful change. The nation's fifty largest companies and their foundations, including the likes of Apple and Pfizer, pledged to fight racism with a commitment to the tune of billions of dollars to address racial inequality.[7] Celebrities and activists implored their fans and followers to better understand the systemic forces at work in their lives.

We were told that this was a racial reckoning. But what do people really mean when they say "systemic racism"? For as ubiquitous as the terms "structural racism" and "systemic racism" have become, our public conversation around them remains muddled, often confused, and imprecise. We may *think* we know what we are talking about when we say "structural" or "systemic," but I've come to realize that most of us have only the most general and vague idea.

This confusion is not entirely our fault. Clear definitions or explanations of these terms have not been at the forefront of our public talk about them. It is also the case that some of us prefer to be vague. Despite the momentum generated by activists and millions of outraged citizens post–George Floyd, and the heightened attention brought to bear on racism, most books and public conversations referred to systemic racism but rarely exposed with clarity how it works. Most of the mainstream conversations were content to retreat to a well-worn habit of turning inward to expose and eradicate racism in ourselves and others around us. Dealing with the magnitude of systemic racism is harder than a self-improvement-focused approach to ending racism, one person at a time. We were implored to examine the racism embedded in individual attitude, by a cadre of "how-to" guides: how to become good antiracism allies, or how to acknowledge white privilege. It is rare for this conversation to cut through the haze of individual anecdotes to reveal the larger system at work.

I do not think we yet share a meaningful understanding of what systemic racism is and how it works. The more casually used and confused with personal attitudes, the more familiar it seems. But this familiarity is established at the expense of clarity and coherence. In fact, a lack of clarity about what systemic racism is and why it matters, coupled with the tendency to approach racism as a matter of personal reflection on individual belief, has left the term vulnerable to treacherous manipulation.

As I write this, we are approaching the three-year anniversary of the horrific murder of George Floyd. The first eighteen months were heady days buzzing with conversation, reading, reflection, institutional promises, and activism. As time moved on, support for tackling systemic racism receded from public view, fatigue set in, and attacks on the idea itself gained more public attention. As has been the case during many stages in the Black freedom struggle, key phrases around which activists mobilize get twisted and vilified by those who resist such change. Influential terms are intentionally manipulated in ways designed to frighten people from being associated with them. Critical Race Theory, "intersectionality," and "woke" have most recently been the center of such campaigns. The aggressive vilification of these and other terms led the College Board to sharply curtail and remove content for the first-ever Advanced Placement course in African American Studies. The term "systemic" was removed entirely from the course.[8] A central aim of these smear campaigns is to make *the study of racism a threat*. In this case, it is the mere *idea of systemic racism* that threatens us—not its existence and its terrible impact on our society. Mere reference to systemic racism is to be stopped, not systemic racism itself! Efforts such as these not only further muddy the definitional waters, but they also generate fraught conditions that paralyze regular folks, conditions that leave many of us unwilling and unable to figure out how to challenge systemic racism deniers.

This is a book about systemic racism in American society today. Any serious racial reckoning demands that we take a clear-eyed look at what systemic racism is and how it works. The practice of paying close attention to systemic racism as a current-day convention has been deliberately and falsely equated with charges of individual racism. This has led some to conclude that systemic racism amounts to a permanent indictment of society, and of white people. This is not the case. When we focus on how racism works *as a system*, we can better see how the policies and forces organizing our society can and do operate with or without our explicit investment in racism. What a systemic approach to racism allows is an honest, collective reckoning with the forces that shape our outcomes no matter how progressive or antiracist we think we are.

Our best chance of dismantling systemic racism begins with a close examination of how systems work and using systems thinking to identify the discriminatory outcomes. Of course, it is impossible to step completely outside the systems we live in, but some new frameworks and stories can help us begin to see the workings of systems all around us, making connections that were previously invisible to many of us. This involves an urgent focus on interconnection. In a system, the overall outcomes are generated by the multidirectional and reinforcing interactions between parts of the system. The interactions or interconnections generated by systems dynamics are sometimes called "metaeffects." A metaeffect is an impact based on these multidirectional and reinforcing interactions, an impact more comprehensive, more transcending than any one element or policy could create on its own. In society today, the metaeffect of systemic racism is metaracism.

Understanding how racism works systemically changes everything we think we know about racial inequality in America today. Myriad explanations offered for the staggering range of ways that disadvantages and discrimination shape Black life in this country rarely if ever begin with the admission that society is organized actively, and in the present, to generate these outcomes. Part of this absence has to do with *the way we define racism*—as an individual belief in action. But it also has to do with *the way we tell stories about racism*—stories that focus on individual events generally disconnected from the broader context in which they take place. But systemic racism is also made less visible by *the way we silo and compartmentalize our thinking* about race-related social problems. Racial inequality in education is deeply intertwined with housing discrimination, and it will be very difficult, if not impossible, to grasp the full scope of either one if they are approached as separated from one another. Put another way, systemic racism and its metaeffects are much harder to grasp when interlocking issues are not examined relationally. There are many facets to these interconnections and the arrangement of current policies that should be identified and examined, including, for example, the patterns that allow the disproportionate targeting of Black people for punishment *and* the unpunished discrimination of Black people at the same time. Compartmentalization robs us of the ability to see the system as a whole, preventing us from addressing the forces that maintain the profoundly effective, devastating system of racial discrimination.

The vantage point of the collective lived experiences of Black people opens up space for insight about the operations of systemic racism. This vantage point is a hallmark of the rich legacy of Black/African American Studies, a legacy built by many generations of activists, artists, and thinkers who have been tracing, theorizing, defining, documenting, and organizing against various iterations of systemic racism.

At the heart of this project is my desire to document in accessible and clear language what it means and what it feels like to experience life as a Black person in this country today. Refusal to confront the truth about systemic racism has put many Black people in the position of trying to explain it, or prove it, usually in the wake of yet another publicly circulated act of brutal violence against a Black person. Living with this leviathan is hard enough; managing the broader society disbelief and constant repudiation of its existence makes bad matters worse.

I admit that I didn't have a full grasp of the profound interconnections in and between so many key policies and practices until I set about examining them closely and relationally—specifically looking at how an array of policies and practices in key areas worked in concert to compose an interconnected whole. A few years ago, I began in earnest trying to answer the question: How does systemic racism *actually* work? Doing so involved diving into systems theory and learning what makes a system a system. It also involved digging deeper into a broad range of housing, education, criminal justice, and wealth policies and practices. In the end, I explored close to one hundred policies and practices. In every case, I wanted to know not only the general purpose or function of the policy, but also how it impacted Black lives by design and by strategic implementation. The more I examined these policies and studied how they specifically hurt Black people, the more I realized that the compartmentalized, myth-laden story we tell about racism hides and denies a trio of interlocking, and devastating, systemic metaeffects of systemic racism on millions of Black lives: containment, extraction, and punishment. This was when the magnitude of systemic racism, the existence of *metaracism*, began to come into view. It shocked me, it angered me, but it also motivated me to share what I had found.

OVERVIEW OF THE BOOK

We must begin with the building blocks of what constitutes a system. To analyze and see "racism as a system," in chapter 1, I ask readers to think in a way that identifies and examines key connections between the parts of the system, with a focused attention on how interconnections generate outcomes that are different, and often more impactful and long-lasting, than one individual component could produce on its own. The way interconnections compound to create magnified outcomes is an important insight into the impact of systems. Most people learn what racism is (and what it is not) through the public stories we tell. This chapter shows how different kinds of storytelling to a greater or lesser extent either reveal or hide the workings of systemic racism by offering the "same" story told first in a way that hides systemic racism and then in another way that brings it into view.

I then shift to an examination of the wide range of policies and practices whose interconnections create consistent metaeffects. Chapter 2 presents my research into nearly one hundred key policies and practices that drive systemic racism, particularly in *housing, schools, wealth, and criminal justice*, and illuminates how they work as part of a system that generates devastating outcomes for Black people. These systemic effects are produced by the ways that policies are written, enforced, and maintained through the interconnections between them and the larger social contexts within which they all take place. Systems are not fixed. They adapt to shocks and changes, often finding ways to generate arrestingly consistent outcomes over time.

My research illuminated an immense network of policies that despite their vast differences in purported aims share an ominous and strikingly consistent pattern of outcomes and effects. I closely researched a range of policies developed and/ or escalated in the post–civil rights era: from Stop and Frisk to the War on Drugs to Stand Your Ground; from zero-tolerance school punishment policies to perverse new forms of lending practices, land seizures, and voter disenfranchisement; from how we fund public schools to how municipal fines and fees are used in ways that exclude or disproportionately target Black people. Of course, the longer-term impact of earlier and highly influential policies like the G.I. Bill, government-regulated redlining, racial covenants, and Jim Crow weigh heavily on the present and should be accounted for as a crucial foundation for today's racial landscape. But, here in this book, I pay special attention to the more recent policies and practices that enforce, maintain, expand, and deepen systemic racism in America today.

It is through the regularized process of disproportionate impact that the metaeffects of systemic racism gather force. While racist policies and policies practiced in discriminatory ways can have many different kinds of effects, my research shows that a range of important, influential policies and practices that fundamentally shape our society generate systemic racism through three central, consistent, and interlocking metaeffects: the containment, extraction, and punishment of Black people. Chapter 2 shows that policies we think may be mainly about containment can also have important extracting dimensions. The way they interact as a group of influential policies can reveal effects greater than can be measured simply by adding them together. We will see a key feature of a system at work: that the interconnections between system components produce "effects that are greater than the sum of their parts." In systemic racism this generates metaracism.

Stories about racism very often frame collective experiences that result from systemic racism into stories that are disconnected in various ways from the racial system in which they take place. These stories reinforce a perception that racism is a singular event rather than a system that generates a collective set of outcomes. Chapters 3, 4, and 5 expose the mechanisms of systemic racism and the role of public stories about racism by retelling three stories with which many readers are likely familiar: the terrible murders of Trayvon Martin and Michael Brown, and the criminalization and punishment of Kelley Williams-Bolar, the Akron, Ohio, mom convicted of "stealing education" for her two daughters. The primary public mainstream versions of the stories about Martin, Williams-Bolar, and Brown reflected the complicated dynamics of the struggle over illuminating systemic racism and how it is erased from view: how we define racism, the way we tell stories about it, and our compartmentalized approach to racism. In the case of Trayvon Martin, we see a vivid example of a story that completely erases systemic forces by framing Zimmerman's pursuit and murder of Martin as a "chance encounter." This interpretation motivates a lengthy examination of the character and intentions of the key players, their individual behaviors, and the actions of others—to find proof of individual guilt or innocence and very little in the way of systemic context. The public debates about whether Kelley Williams-Bolar was justified in her decision to enroll her daughters in excellent schools in a district in which she did not live revolved around a compartmentalized approach in which educational inequality was the sole issue at hand for her defenders, even though her own explanations suggested a more multifaceted set of motivations that revealed interconnected effects of systemic racism.

In both cases, Martin's family and Kelley Williams-Bolar were strongly advised not to mention the impact of racism at all in court, effectively defining racism as outside the scope of influence and relevance in determining a just outcome. In the case of Michael Brown, initial national news reports were content to present the official police explanation of events, which justified the killing by lying about key elements of what transpired at the scene. The subsequent community uprisings and the militarized, occupation-like police response to Black protest led to the Ferguson Department of Justice report that revealed a staggeringly corrupt police department. Continued activism led to additional exposure of educational segregation and neglect. And yet, even as the evidence of the existence of systemic racism in Ferguson mounted, the depths of the interconnections remained difficult to see and Ferguson itself became a scapegoat; it began to be perceived as an outlier. The many discriminatory patterns that connect Ferguson to regional and national practices were rarely connected. The stories that attempt to expose systemic racism are pushed to the margins or out of the frame entirely.

A systems lens allows us to examine how their lives, extreme punishment, and deaths are deeply connected to, and flow from, the larger social circumstances in which they take place. These retellings will reveal much more about the regularized, hidden, and deeply interconnected forms of discrimination that shaped Trayvon, Michael, and Kelley's lives, families, and communities.

These retellings are designed to do four things: (1) critically contextualize their stories as embedded in systemic racism to challenge the individualistic or single-silo versions; (2) dive deeply into the policies and practices to expose how they impacted the lives of Trayvon Martin, Michael Brown, and Kelley Williams-Bolar; (3) show how these policies are part of a much larger national pattern that extracts, contains, and punishes Black people; and (4) try to offer a tangible sense of what it feels like to be subjected to these conditions. Finally, these chapters shine light on the pivotal role of two racial myths, the myths of Black criminality and Black cultural inferiority, that work to justify the status quo and suggest that Black people are themselves the problem.

All of us are deeply impacted by the social terrain in which we operate. For Black people, this terrain is treacherous and steep. In the face of a massive network of disadvantages, it is, frankly, an act of cruelty to argue that Black people are personally and individually responsible for the conditions they face. Until we adequately examine, confront, and work to dismantle what we have forced Black people to survive, we have little business preaching about Black people's supposed lack of individual responsibility.

How, then, can we break free? It is hard to hear the truth about how society is organized to create and reinforce racial advantages for whites and disadvantages for Black people. A truthful accounting of systemic racism is painful and daunting, and can be overwhelming. The discomfort can distort the issues at hand (aka, isn't systemic racism just a class problem?). Some people get angry, feel guilty, retreat to fantasy; some use the power of silence as a way to impede change-oriented dialogue and action. For others it is depressing and derailing, it gives them little hope for getting ahead, and it diminishes the amazing stories of success of those who "started from the bottom." For still others it generates shame for being associated with those of us who bear the more visible wounds caused by the system. And yet, refusing to deal with systemic racism gives it more power, not less. Even as we ignore it, we won't be free of it.

Chapter 6 explains that understanding what systemic racism is and how it works to perpetuate racism is essential to ending it, but there is more to be done too. The creation of a society dedicated to equity, justice, and belonging depends on our willingness to dig deep, to fully understand the profound effects of the discrimination systems we have built. The terms we use to describe our shared reality and the care with which we use them carry high stakes. Vague generalities only serve to further obscure how the system works and lay the groundwork for those who wish to deny or de-emphasize its powerful effects. Confused and misdirected uses of the terms supply ammunition for pernicious attacks by those who deny the existence and influence of systems to perpetuate racism. Resisting these attacks requires that we fully understand the terms and the realities hidden beneath them, so that we can push back with force when it comes to all the places systemic racism does its dirty work.

Making the workings of systemic racism visible and comprehensible is a crucial part of dismantling it. Right now, it is rendered invisible by the elongated distorting shadows of American individualism, racial mythology, and the separation that segregated living has forged. This book is a call for a paradigm shift. We must expose and deflate the power of systemic racism by asking different questions, building support for the changes that will exert the most leverage, and taking issue with those who perpetuate the myths that Black people created their own conditions and that everyone has an equal chance. We must challenge those who deny society's obligation to correct and repair what it has done and continues to do to Black people—not only for the sake of Black people, though this would be reason enough, but for the sake of us all. It's the only way to break free of the mess we've created.

1

CAUGHT UP IN THE SYSTEM

METARACISM AND THE STORIES THAT HIDE IT

LISTENING IN ON CONVERSATIONS GOING ON AROUND ME growing up, there was a phrase I often heard peppered throughout adult conversations. At a friend's house, someone might ask: "Where is he now? Did he get caught up in the system?" Or an elder in the barbershop might caution: "They keep carrying on like that and they gonna get caught up in the system." That phrase, "caught up in the system," and the worried, hushed tones that accompanied its use got my attention. What was this system, where was it, and how was it so powerful and dangerous that you couldn't get out?

As usual, the practical wisdom and creative speech of Black people was on point: there is a "system." It produces consistent, consistently harsh, comprehensive, and relentless conditions for Black people. Across the country a network of systemic forces exerts profound targeted pressure on millions of Black Americans, causing real and substantial harm to their lives and blocking their opportunities to reach their human potential. This system continues to contain where Black people live; it reduces the quality of their communities, and it limits their access to critical resources. It profoundly shapes Black people's relationships with the police and the criminal justice system, funneling them into conditions of highly punitive, life-threatening police violence and longer jail sentences than others would face for similar charges or crimes. The system suppresses Black people's wages and reduces their access to quality lending and housing. These, along with other forms of significant economic discrimination, have for decades reduced the growth of intergenerational black wealth to a small fraction (roughly 10 percent) of the wealth white Americans pass down to their children, creating economic precarity and increasing the likelihood of financial catastrophe.

This same system shapes our neighborhoods, whether majority white or Black—including who has greater or lesser access to green space, to sources of healthy food and safe outdoor recreation, and to quality doctors, hospitals, and other health care professionals. The environmental conditions created by this system cause extreme physical distress and illnesses that drive many chronic diseases to which Black people are disproportionately vulnerable. It profoundly influences the quality of our schools, including staggering gaps based on race in levels of funding and teacher experience and quality.

Systemic racism is among the most powerful and determinant forces constraining life, opportunity, and freedom in our country today. It casts a wide, flexible, and often invisible net over Black people. It functions more or less seamlessly and largely out of view. The effects of systemic racism are not exclusively or even mainly created by policies that make an explicit announcement of intent to discriminate, but instead by a combination of policies written in race-neutral language whose content is designed in ways that interact with other policies and entrenched practices and beliefs to reinforce negative outcomes for Black people. For example, Stand Your Ground laws, which extend the right to self-defense into any public space, are written in race-neutral language, but, because they hinge on the "perception of threat" to determine their legitimate application, entrenched and heightened white fears of Black people provide enhanced legal cover for whites who shoot or kill Black people. In fact, Stand Your Ground defenses are least effective when Black people shoot or kill whites. Three Strikes laws—laws that require sentences of twenty-five years to life (as in the case of California) for a third felony, no matter how minor the felony might be—have triggered preposterous and nonnegotiable sentences for people who are charged with or commit minor offenses. When the application of Three Strikes laws interconnects with other highly punitive policing behavior, such as the ghetto-targeted application of Broken Windows (discussed further in chapter 3), the combination increases the likelihood that Black people will be disproportionately stopped and charged for low-level offenses, and subjected to disproportionately harsh treatment. This has led to Black people being overrepresented among those receiving extreme sentences such as "fifty years without parole for a man who stole three golf clubs from a pro shop, and fifty years without parole for another man for stealing children's videotapes from a Kmart store."[1]

The collective effect of these kinds of policies and practices is the creation of a normalized, unacknowledged process that produces disproportionately negative outcomes for Black people. Systemic racism functions much like the Southern Strategy offered by legendary Republican political campaign consultant Lee Atwater. In an interview in 1981, Atwater described it as a strategy designed to thwart civil rights efforts while avoiding the direct appearance of racism. He explains the intentional shift away from the explicit language of anti-Black racial hate to a focus on abstract-sounding policies like "states' rights" and "cutting taxes"—policies that sound racially neutral, but as Atwater says, "a byproduct of them is, Blacks get hurt more than Whites."[2] The absence of explicit racial intention, the use of race-neutral language, and the complex interaction between those policies and practices encourage those who most benefit from the system's arrangement to deny and/or refuse to pursue large-scale changes that would disrupt it.

But before we can see systemic racism and how it works, we need to understand the interconnections and metaeffects that make it so pernicious. In order to expose the full complexity of what makes systemic racism such a powerful and durable discrimination system, it is important first to know what a system is and how it works.

WHAT IS A SYSTEM?

A system is an interdependent, interconnected group of components, parts, or elements that work as a whole. The components in a system are dynamically interconnected and coherently organized to achieve stable patterns and consistent outcomes over time.[3] The way the components interconnect over time also produces metaeffects; these are effects that amount to something greater than a "sum of its parts." These metaeffects generate what systems scholars describe as "outcomes that no individual subsystem can produce."[4]

There are many kinds of systems, some found in nature, others produced by humans in societies. For example, the sun and the planets make up the solar system, and hospitals, physicians, medical schools, health insurance companies, nurses, and pharmaceutical companies make up the health care system. Systems feature the following characteristics:

Elements: Elements are the components, or parts, of a system.

Interconnection: One of the most important features that define a system is the fact that its elements are interconnected and function interdependently and simultaneously in myriad, dynamic ways. The interconnections between different parts of a system shape and drive its effects. The outcomes produced by a system, then, are the product of various interactions.

Metaeffects: Metaeffects (also called "emergent" and "uber" effects) are effects that no individual part of the system alone—nor a linear, additive combination of those parts—can produce. These encompass the set of impacts or effects of a system that are different from—and often greater than—the sum of its parts. They include properties or behaviors that emerge only when the parts or elements interact in the context of a greater whole or system.

Outcomes: System outcomes are a product of the interconnections, metaeffects, and other relationships established between parts of a system. Outcomes are what a system actually does; they are the circumstances the system produces—even when those circumstances seem to contradict what one or many parts of the system claim or intend to do.

Award-winning systems thinker Donella Meadows developed a simple four-question test to determine whether something is a system or if it is, as she playfully calls it, just "a pile o' stuff":

1. Can you identify the parts or elements?
2. Do the parts affect each other? (e.g., interconnections)
3. Do the parts together produce effects that are different from each part on its own? (i.e., metaeffects)
4. Do the outcomes over time persist in a variety of circumstances?[5]

As an example, we can try out Meadows's four-question test on American health care, and determine whether it's just a pile o' stuff or a system with interconnections, metaeffects, and persistent outcomes.

Can we identify the parts? Yes: hospitals, physicians, nurses, medical schools, health insurance companies, and so on are among the elements and organizations that comprise health care as we know it. To this list we could add ambulance companies, EMTs, wheelchair manufacturers, pharmacies, and more.

Do the parts affect each other? Yes, they do, sometimes in profound and interconnected ways, visible in the interplay between hospitals and health insurance companies; physicians and pharmaceutical companies; ambulances, EMTs, and other emergency services.

Do the parts together produce effects that are different from or greater than each part on its own? Yes. A network of hospitals, with ambulances, EMTs, nurses, physicians, pharmacies, and hospital administrators interacting with one another toward the goal of managing and attending to health, produces vastly different health effects than any of these health-related elements would produce on their own.

Does the outcome over time persist in a variety of circumstances? Yes. The outcome of our health care system is the profit-driven management of health and the preservation of life. This does not mean that the health care system saves everyone from illness, injury, or death—or that it delivers its services to all people equally. Put another way, a system does not and need not have a perfect track record of preserving life and health in order for it to be understood and function as a health care system. If, however, a health care system is to remain a system, then the outcomes of the health care system—to profitably manage and preserve health—should generally persist over time and in a variety of circumstances.

Multiple systems, especially complex systems, operate simultaneously and relationally with one another. So, to keep the example going, the US health care system also intersects with and is impacted by the criminal justice system and the economic system. And the way this same health care system works in real life—based on the policies, practices, and driving forces that propel its operations across different parts of society and different communities—can contribute to and uphold a racial discrimination system and thus produce significant racial disparities in health care outcomes between white and Black people.[6]

RACISM AS A SYSTEM

Meadows's four questions can help us determine whether anti-Black racism functions as a system with or without individual racial prejudice or interpersonal hatred.

Can we identify the parts or elements? Is it composed of many parts? Yes. More than a century of scholarly research has documented disparities that advantage whites and disadvantage Blacks across every major indicator and all areas of society. Significant racial disparities and evidence of discrimination have been documented in housing, lending, credit and consumption markets, education, criminal justice, insurance, health care access and treatment, and employment. Many of the system's elements take place within seemingly racially neutral policies and practices, while other effects come from clearly discriminatory elements that have been obscured from view or explained as disparities without systemic origin.

Do the parts interconnect/affect each other? Yes. Systemic racism and its powerful effects cannot be observed when we focus on one event, one policy, or one type of discrimination. A single-area focus obscures the details and reach of systemic racism and the ways discrimination in one area intersects and propels racism in another. For example, pervasive racial residential segregation is reciprocally interconnected with educational segregation. Children are assigned to schools based on where they live, the boundaries for which are defined by district and other municipal boundaries. Legal and "in practice" segregation of district boundaries, however, are surveilled and readjusted to protect the rewards given to predominantly white school districts, while at the same time denying those rewards to Black districts.

Do the parts together produce an effect that is different from each part on its own? In other words, do the parts in combination create metaeffects? Yes. The impact of racism as a driving force in residential and school segregation over time results in significant inequality in the value of property based on race, and this in turn generates a racial gap in available property taxes—taxes that are a foundational resource for school funding. Housing discrimination has repressed home values and associated tax revenues in Black neighborhoods, thus producing a school funding gap of $23 billion compared to white districts.[7] The impact of residential segregation on its own would not be nearly as great if it were disconnected from school funding and school segregation. And, if we did not rely on property taxes to fund schools, then the racial gaps in housing values would not be reproduced in cavernous school budget disparities. These factors also interconnect with well-documented lending discrimination, real estate industry steering, significant housing appraisal discrimination, and racially discriminatory enforcement of municipal ordinances. These dynamic interconnections are not linear or additive; they create metaeffects—effects that are greater than any individual part can produce on its own and effects that cannot be measured by simple addition. Metaeffects operate in multiple directions simultaneously and result from an array of interconnections that reciprocate, reverberate, and accumulate.[8] As sociologist Barbara Reskin notes: "In effect, interrelated disparities to which discrimination contributes to some degree comprise a system whose product is societal-level discrimination."[9]

Does the outcome over time persist in a variety of circumstances? Yes. Although the focus of this book is on the elements, interconnections, and outcomes of systemic racism in post–civil rights era America, we cannot fail to recognize that the country was founded as a racial discrimination system beginning with the colonization of Indigenous people and the enslavement of Africans. Throughout US history, the outcome of significant anti-Black racial discrimination and disparity has persisted under a wide variety of circumstances. Systemic racism today is an accumulation and extension of many older discriminatory policies, and it is also the result of a set of ongoing contemporary practices.

What it all adds up to is unmistakably a system. Systemic racism is made up of interconnected policies and practices in key areas, such as housing, education, criminal justice, lending, and wealth, that work together over time to produce metaracism: dynamic, compounding patterns of racial disadvantage and discrimination that no single policy could produce on its own.[10]

SYSTEM VS. STRUCTURE

It is not unusual to hear the terms "structural racism" and "systemic racism" used interchangeably. In fact, in the past I have used them this way. This is understandable as both phrases have key characteristics in common. Structural racism and systemic racism both describe the "built-in" characteristic of racism in society. "Structural" and "systemic" both refer to racism that is identifiable and embedded in the organization of society's institutions and their policies and practices. Neither term refers to individual-level racism, or racism that some people or even some institutions choose to practice. Instead, they each describe the way racism is "manifested in all major societal institutions."[11]

For some, it might seem unnecessarily picky to draw sharp distinctions between structure and system, especially given the important similarities between them. "Structural" remains a valuable framing term and leaves open for consideration the examination of "structures" that are not part of a system. The term "system" invokes systems thinking, an established approach to problem identification and problem solving deployed by biologists, computer scientists, engineers, managers, policy experts, activists, and others.[12] While structure and system share a focus on the embedded quality of racism in all major societal institutions, systems thinking requires that they are interconnected. A systemic-racism approach illuminates the ways that important institutionalized forms of discrimination or disadvantages in one area or institution interconnect with, generate, propel, or reinforce disadvantages in another. In a system, these dynamic interconnections produce effects that are greater than what can be generated by each part on its own.

I have found systems thinking to be especially produc-tive as an approach for identifying the scope and impact of anti-Black racism. In particular, the emphasis on interconnec-tions between parts and the metaeffects generated by them has the potential to expose and articulate the reasons for the more extreme forms of racial disparity. (I am thinking here about the staggering and intractable Black/white wealth gap, for example.) The systems concept of metaeffects encourages an approach to systemic racism that has the capacity to assess the impact of interconnecting, compounding past and present parts of systemic racism—an impact more profound and more pow-erful than that which could be created by a mere tally of indi-vidual acts of discrimination in any one institution. Systems thinking reveals the work of metaracism.

STORIES ABOUT RACISM THAT HIDE SYSTEMIC RACISM

In America, we do not lack for stories about racism. Yet, when we tell them, more often than not we fail to account for the for-midable impact of systemic racism. Most of our stories revolve around incidents of individual-level racism in which a person is caught behaving in a racially discriminatory manner against a Black person. These stories are, in effect, taken out of the cru-cial context of metaracism produced by the racial system in which these incidents take place.

Recall the 2020 story of the white woman (Amy Cooper) who called 911 on a Black man and claimed that "she was being threatened by an African-American man" when in fact, he (Christian Cooper—no relation) had asked her to leash her dog in an area of New York's Central Park where leashes were required. In 2021, the news reported the story of a fourteen-year-old Black teenager and his father being accosted by a twenty-two-year-old white woman who accused the teenager of stealing her phone and demanded he prove it was his. It turns out she left her phone in a taxi.

These are the kinds of stories about racism that predominate in our media landscape, stories in which an often-shocking individual act of prejudice or racism is exposed. A Race Forward content analysis of mainstream media on race-focused media coverage found that "two-thirds of race-focused media coverage fails to consider how systemic racism factors into the story, instead typically focusing upon racial slurs and other types of personal prejudice and individual-level racism."[13] Airing stories that expose personal prejudice has its place, but they do not illuminate or serve as proof of systemic racism. In fact, these stories frequently hide, ignore, or minimize systemic racism, unless they are intentionally crafted to make the connections.

Let's consider another example: the 2020 news story about Sauntore Thomas, an African American Air Force veteran who attempted to deposit checks totaling $99,000 into his bank account at TCF Bank in Livonia, Michigan. The manager refused to cash or deposit the checks and initiated a fraud investigation. Although the manager told Thomas she would need a moment to verify the checks, she instead called the police. Four officers arrived at the bank and questioned Thomas about the checks. Thomas then called his lawyer to verify the origin and legitimacy of the check—but the manager was still not convinced. The manager was immediately suspicious that the checks were fraudulent and began to question Thomas about the source of the checks. The same day, Thomas took the checks to Chase Bank and the checks cleared within twelve hours. What were the checks for? They were the compensation he received as a settlement for racial discrimination at work![14]

This story got quite a bit of media traction; it was carried in the *Washington Post* and by the BBC, NBC News, and the Associated Press, among other major news outlets. Like many media reports on racism, Thomas's thwarted quest to deposit legitimate checks was reported as an example of a Black person experiencing an act of individual racism. The bank distanced itself from any institutional culpability by issuing the statement: "We strongly condemn racism and discrimination of any kind."[15] Although this manager was presented as expressing individual bias and acting entirely alone, her actions reflected patterns that reverberate systemically. The story neglected to connect the manager's actions to the pervasive practice of racial profiling generally and in the banking industry specifically, the immediate criminalization of Black people for a variety of non-criminal reasons, and the inability to be trusted, even when reliable sources confirm what a Black person has reported. A confirming call from Thomas's lawyer was unable to convince the bank manager that the checks were legitimate. In this case the manager rejected the veracity of an otherwise highly credible source to satisfy an elevated standard of proof. These are some of the ways that individual-level stories about anti-Black racism frequently end up severed from the metaracism-producing system in which they take place.

Another prominent form of storytelling about racism endeavors to reveal the racial inequality that exists within a single institution. For example, there are many special reports and documentaries about policing, health care, and school inequality and segregation that provide important information. Consider the 2017 documentary *Teach Us All*, which explores the history of education and racial segregation in Little Rock, Arkansas, covering the sixty-year period since the Little Rock Nine attempted to integrate Central High School in 1957.[16] The film offers a compelling and painful focus on the profound inequality in education that continues in Little Rock, as well as New York City and Los Angeles. *Teach Us All* does draw some important, if brief, links between schools and housing segregation (not only in Little Rock but across the country). And yet the documentary does not help us see how those links are embedded in a wider system of racism in which segregation in schools and housing also interconnects with policies and practices in banking, urban land management, and more.[17]

Because a system is an interdependent/interconnected group of elements that work as a whole, shedding light on a system requires identification of interconnections across and between several different areas of society (and related institutions) not only at one point in time but over time. This approach gives us a way to capture a deeper look at what it means to be caught up in systemic racism. Not only does it tell us about the world around us, it expands what we know about our own lives and our lives in relation to the lives of others. Our individual experiences are better understood when they are systemically informed. Systemic racism has been a profound force in all our lives—including those who have benefited from it and those who have not.

If we are able to identify the differences between a story whose aim is to expose systemic racism and one that does not, we can begin asking the kinds of questions that lead us to the sorts of changes that can make a big difference. As I mentioned, we mostly tell individual stories in ways that fail to connect with the broader social context: and it is this very storytelling practice itself that can make the system's parts and interconnections and effects invisible to us. In anticipation of and preparation for later chapters, which will offer a series of systems-based retellings of widely known stories about Trayvon Martin, Kelley Williams-Bolar, and Michael Brown, I want to use a familiar and yet fictitious story about a Black woman I call Melody and her daughter Ashley to show how systemic forces can be brought to light and what is at stake when we neglect to show them.

Melody Jackson works two jobs to save enough money to move out of the predominantly Black neighborhood where she rents an apartment. Her goal is to buy a small house in a community with better schools for her daughter. She eventually finds a house in a place with schools that are somewhat better, though not by much, than her original neighborhood. The mortgage is costly given her budget, but the bank reviews her finances and approves her for a loan; the real estate agent reassures her that high appreciation rates will swiftly grow her equity. Melody's daughter, Ashley, graduates high school and enrolls in a trade college, which has a local office to enroll students. Tuition is expensive. Because her mom drained her savings to buy their home, the daughter is urged by college recruiters to take out a student loan to pay for tuition. Ashley is reassured that, upon graduation, she will easily score an excellent job placement in a growing sector. That doesn't come to pass. Instead, Ashley has trouble finding a job and is burdened with high-interest student loans. Without sufficient income, she falls behind on the loan payments and applies for public assistance. She and her mom are disheartened, but Ashley vows to keep working hard until the loans are paid off.

This tale may sound familiar. So many mothers try to move their families up, economically and educationally, in the face of many obstacles. Many of us have tried to improve our lot and pass on better opportunities to our children. We applaud the determination of those who struggle against such challenges. But systemic racism has funneled the risks and likelihood that these obstacles are disproportionately placed in Black people's paths. Without knowing this, it is easy to insert an individual explanation (Melody's own financial mismanagement for example) or a universal reason like "It's hard out here for everyone."

This story and countless others like it offer an empathetic portrait of a struggling Black family—yet it hides far more than it reveals about the specific characteristics of their struggles. Far too often such stories draw us in to feeling an emotional connection to the plight of the individual in a way that studiously disconnects their plight from the enormous impact of past and present forms of systemic racism on their circumstances. Melody and her daughter Ashley confront struggles all working people face and, in addition, they are subject to the grinding, yet largely invisible and unacknowledged, workings of systemic racism—a system that created and intensified many of the problems they encountered. Melody and her daughter faced systemic racism that created targeted hurdles at every life transition, a system that placed their dreams even further from reach than would have been the case were they white. What do their stories look like when systemic racism is brought into view?

When we first meet her, Melody lives in a community shaped by generations of racial segregation, economic devaluation, underinvestment, and decapitalization through policies such as redlining, racial zoning, steering, and various means of racial containment engineered by decades of legal housing and urban planning policy. The deliberate, long-term devaluation of property in areas where Black families like Melody's were forced to live was reinforced by lending evaluations that attached "higher risk" to such communities, thus fueling many negative ripple effects, including the perpetuation of a cavernous racial wealth gap; chronic underfunding of local public schools; concentrated psychological and emotional pressures brought on by racially targeted economic discrimination; difficult-to-access sources of healthy food; difficult-to-navigate transportation options; and lower levels of municipal services, including fewer playgrounds and trees, and infrequent garbage pickup. The Black neighborhood Melody is trying to leave is a product of systemic racism.

Key to Melody's move is finding a home and securing a stable, affordable mortgage. What are the lending conditions like for Black people? Black people continue to be disproportionately denied access to good residential or commercial loans. In the United States there is a substantial history of legally protected redlining and associated discriminatory practices, some of which were established by federal policy and some of which were common practice among financial institutions.[18] Although redlining was nominally abolished by the 1968 Fair Housing Act, lending discrimination is not a thing of the distant past. In 1989 the records of ten million applications from every savings and loan bank in the country "reveal a lending gap so pervasive and so wide that in much of the country high-income Blacks are rejected at the same rate as low-income Whites."[19] In fact, while writing this book, the National Association of Real Estate Brokers conducted a study showing that Black applicants are more than twice as likely to be denied a home mortgage as white applicants. In a specific example, Lakeland Bank, based in New Jersey, agreed to pay $13 million to settle Department of Justice charges that it had avoided lending to Black and Latinx customers. Lakeland was found to have discouraged and avoided serving the credit needs of majority Black areas such as Newark, New Jersey, while providing services to white borrowers in majority white areas. Lakeland Bank has nearly forty Lakeland bank branches in New Jersey. All of them are in areas where the majority of the population is white, and none are in majority Black neighborhoods.[20]

Predatory lending is another significant kind of lending discrimination. Rather than outright refusal to lend, or rejecting Black loan applicants at far higher rates, predatory lending targets Black borrowers, including those who qualify for access to lower-interest loans with protective and stable repayment terms, and steers them to high-interest loans with treacherous repayment terms. Black borrowers are also held to standards of creditworthiness that are significantly different from those of white borrowers. For example, one study found that a white borrower with an income that is less than 80 percent of the area median is just as likely as a Black borrower with an income that is 120 percent of the area median to receive a prime loan.[21] When placed at this disadvantage, Black borrowers are more frequently forced to take out subprime loans with terms that guarantee prolonged and higher levels of debt. Low-income Black women are the most vulnerable to subprime lending agreements.[22] Black families at every level of income, however, are more vulnerable to subprime lending than white families. In 2002 the Center for Responsible Lending reported that high-income African Americans were three times more likely to be subjected to subprime terms than low-income whites.[23]

The financial implications of various kinds of racial lending discrimination are significant on their own, but the picture becomes far more devastating when we examine the tight interconnections between lending discrimination and neighborhood segregation together. These interconnections start to shed light on the wide reach and power of racism as a system. For example, not only does today's predatory mortgage lending negatively impact Black wealth, but so, too, does the legacy of past lending exclusions and housing discrimination—because they prevented earlier generations of parents and grandparents from accumulating wealth that could have been passed down. Past discriminatory practices that destroyed wealth-building opportunities have a tangible impact on present opportunities and help lay a firm foundation for future disadvantages. In short, discriminatory practices in a system produce inherited disadvantages that reverberate across generations.

Like many African Americans, Melody's parents and their parents before them were subjected to multiple generations of wealth-extracting policies that made it extremely difficult, if not impossible, to help younger generations meet the costs of buying a home. Melody's parents' limited access to capital grew directly from the creation of the racial wealth gap begun during slavery and then continuously facilitated by legalized racism in land seizures/theft, targeted civil forfeitures, exclusions from borrowing opportunities, job discrimination, and more. In addition, discrimination in Black property assessment continues to reduce the wealth-building capacity of Black property, which continues to reinforce the staggering racial wealth gap.

It is not uncommon for Black people to be steered to look at home purchases in mostly segregated Black communities. Melody was very likely, as is often the case for Black home buyers, asked to pay a higher price than white buyers would for a comparable home in a predominately white neighborhood. She eventually secures a subprime mortgage with higher interest rates than her good credit should have warranted to purchase a home that should have cost less than what she was required to pay, including the requirement of an oversized down payment. In short, lending discrimination, and, in particular, the targeting of higher interest rates to single Black mothers like Melody significantly added to her financial precarity. Despite the realtor's promise of equity accumulation, in practice, Melody's home actually depreciates in value. Depreciation is not unique to her neighborhood. Black-owned property has been shown to actually lose value over time, while white-owned property in segregated white neighborhoods consistently accrues significant value.[24]

The school in the neighborhood Melody moved away from was consistently ranked near the bottom of the state's schools, as far as quality was concerned. This is yet another feature of how systemic racism impacts Black people. Neighborhood segregation (which is reinforced by the strategic placement of school district boundaries) propels and ensures school segregation. Quality schools usually have a higher percentage of excellent teachers and abundant resources. These resources are amply secured by the use of property taxes to fund public school budgets. Homes with higher market value have higher property taxes, and higher property taxes fuel better-funded schools. And, as one might imagine, better-funded schools with better teachers increase property values. This advantage is significantly curated by race. Black neighborhoods are contained and segregated, with homes undervalued, which in turn reduces school funding. This dynamic then reinforces the impact of redlining and other value-extracting practices to which Black communities are subjected. Majority Black districts receive an average of $5,000 less funding per year, per student, than majority white school districts.[25] Black students, especially those in segregated Black schools, disproportionately face harsh disciplinary methods such as zero tolerance for minor infractions. These conditions result in high levels of student suspensions and expulsions. Research also shows that students who are subject to more suspensions are more likely to drop out of school and more likely to end up in the school-to-prison pipeline.

Given these conditions, it should not be surprising that Ashley's new school was not all that much better than the one Melody moved to avoid. Instead, the new school served as more of a feeder to the local for-profit vocational colleges that offered admission with few scholarships and very-high-interest loans, along the way paying little attention to the academic and career potential of students. Studies show that for-profit colleges specifically target African American students who have been trapped in schools that provide few avenues for upward advancement, manipulating the students' hunger for wider opportunity.[26] After attending this for-profit college, Ashley learns that the skills she obtained are not nearly as relevant as the school claimed, nor are there abundant jobs in the field associated with these skills. She now carries high levels of debt, faces very limited job or career options, and her mother, Melody, cannot help offset the debt because of her own indebtedness resulting from the exploitative terms of her mortgage.

Were Melody and Ashley's circumstances the result of a run-in with individual or interpersonal racism? No. No one called them a racial slur, no one said anything explicitly about discriminating against them, and no institution involved had an explicitly discriminatory policy. And yet many of the interconnected factors that most contributed to Melody's and Ashley's difficulties and hurdles were the result of the interconnections that make up systemic racism, and the metaeffects it generates. There is extensive documentation of the ways discrimination in lending, residential segregation, educational segregation, and school funding interconnect and generate persistent, compounding outcomes like the ones outlined here. And yet, rarely are these circumstances depicted as resulting from a system that consistently creates and reinforces disadvantage based on race. Without a story frame that connects Melody and Ashley's environment to a regional and national pattern, the school's low quality is perceived as a singular institutional problem and encourages us to focus on primarily school-based corrective solutions, like establishing more strict school punishment policies, closing the "bad" school and opening a new charter school in its place, or firing the teachers or the principal. By focusing on siloed or single elements of the problem, our ability to see systemic interconnections and outcomes over time is minimized or erased.

A systemic analysis, in contrast, allows us to see the interconnections between educational inequality, housing discrimination, and hypersegregation as key drivers of racial gaps in school quality. A systemic story also makes visible the metaeffects that result from the interconnections that fuel the system. (Remember, metaeffects are effects that none of the system components can produce on their own.) The greater the complexity of the system, the greater the degree of metaeffects. In a complex system such as systemic racism, not only are housing and education interconnected to each other at a national scale, but the interconnections between them and other facets of the system generate metadiscriminatory effects—discriminatory effects that none of the individual practices in any one area could generate on their own. It is the way these elements interconnect that creates metaracism.

Let's think of it in reverse: What happens if we disconnect the parts that drive systemic racism? What if schools were not funded to a meaningful degree by property taxes, and what if property values were not so significantly pegged to the racial composition of the neighborhood and long-standing wealth gaps by race, largely generated and maintained by various forms of housing and lending discrimination. What if excessive policing and arrests that target Black communities were not used as the basis for "future predictions" of where crime will take place? And, what if these arrest records were no longer used to establish insurance rates (based in part on risks associated with race)? How might key disconnections such as these alter the metaeffects of systemic racism?

If we don't do the necessary work to render visible the elements and interconnections that make up systemic racism and its persistent outcome of metaracism, we risk falling victim to familiar mystifications about what systemic racism is and how it works. This in turn feeds the misconceptions that prevent us from seeing systemic racism.

THREE IMPORTANT THINGS TO REMEMBER

One: All Black people don't have to be worse off than all whites.

"He went to Harvard, and I didn't go to college at all."
"He's doing much better than I am! I am broke. How can I 'oppress' Black people?"

Some people think that in order for systemic racism to be real, then all Black people must systemically be at a disadvantage in every way in relation to all whites. This is not true. Systemic racism does not mean that Black people are the most oppressed group or that all Black people are economically worse off than all white people. Nor does it mean that Black people cannot be successful or rich or famous. Systemic racism is not a system of absolute subordination; it is a system that dependably generates discriminatory, or disparate and less favorable, outcomes for Black people that persist over time. Systemic racism truncates expected rewards for Black people and buffers whites against economic disadvantages. Our society is arranged to consolidate disadvantages and punishments for Black people and to consolidate advantages and rewards for whites, in general terms.

The claim "He went to Harvard, and I didn't go to college at all" aimed at defusing claims of systemic racism is the type of assertion that implies that systemic racism results in all Black people having less opportunity than all whites. Put another way, if a white person is worse off than any Black person, it proves that racism isn't a systemic reality. A more accurate way to assess the role of systemic racism in this case would be to ask, if you both went to Harvard, would race negatively impact the white Harvard graduate's employment or other economic and career opportunities after graduation? The answer to the question is no. What about the Black Harvard graduate? The answer to this question is yes. Using carefully crafted resumes, a recent study found that Black graduates of elite schools were as likely to get positive responses from potential employers as white graduates from much less prestigious state colleges. To put it bluntly, an elite education for a Black student gets her as far as a much less prestigious state school degree would for a white student.[27]

This kind of discrepancy takes place in other contexts as well. Stanford researchers found that among Black and white families "with similar incomes, white families are much more likely to live in good neighborhoods—with high-quality schools, day-care options, parks, playgrounds and transportation options. . . . Most strikingly, the typical middle-income black family lives in a neighborhood with lower incomes than the typical low-income white family."[28]

Two: Not every institutional action has to demonstrate discrimination.

"I know a Black person who got a great rate on their home loan."

In a discriminatory system, not everyone in the disfavored group is equally discriminated against, nor are they discriminated against in exactly the same ways. A system of discrimination does not require that every individual have a visible, direct experience with racial discrimination. Absolute uniformity of experience is not required or necessary for a discrimination system to be accurately labeled as such, nor is absolute uniformity of experience required for a system to flourish. No single policy or practice alone (whether equitable or not) stands in for a discrimination system. What makes systemic racism work is the impact of an interconnected network of discriminatory practices and policies that when considered together produce meta-discrimination for the disfavored group as a whole.[29]

Three: Personal support of racial justice doesn't diminish white systemic advantages.

"I marched on Washington."
"My family has all different races of people in it."

A discrimination system generates disadvantages for the disfavored group, regardless of the personal beliefs of an individual from a favored group. The fact that a white person could personally have been an advocate for racial justice, or have Black family members, close friends, or colleagues who are Black, does not negate either the existence of systemic racism or diminish the advantages the system bestows on that person. The implication of claims like "I marched on Washington" or "I marched for Black Lives Matter" suggests that individual effort in support of racial justice repels or nullifies systemic benefits bestowed on white people. In fact, a person can be in solidarity with the disfavored group and yet continue to accrue race-based advantages from the system. Sometimes advantages show up as the absence of certain conditions, such as those that appear as distance from risk, or lower levels of punishment for equal infractions, or freedom of mobility without fear of profiling. These advantages mean that when whites break the law, their race insulates and rewards them with lower levels of punishment when compared to Black people who break the law similarly. Systemic racism is designed to reward the favored group and to do it as part of the normal process of everyday life.

The better we understand systems thinking and systemic racism, the better we're able to distinguish between individual stories and the metaeffects operating in the background. To fully understand how these dynamics function, however, we need to apply our systems lens to recent policy and practice.

2

THE DEVIL IS IN THE DETAILS

SYSTEMIC CONTAINMENT, PUNISHMENT, AND EXTRACTION

"THE DEVIL IS IN THE DETAILS" WAS ONE OF MY father's favorite sayings. He was a methodical person and often said it while guiding me and my brother to pay close attention to the specifics as we worked to complete a difficult homework assignment or learn a piece of music. It was his way of reminding us that even though something may appear simple or quickly comprehensible at first blush, upon deeper investigation, you learn that the specific features or particular dimensions make the thing as a whole much more complicated than it initially seemed. This adage and my dad's insight came rushing back to me as I dug more deeply into the workings of systemic racism.

Over several years, I closely examined policies in four key areas of society: housing, education, criminal justice, and lending. Policies and practices in these areas are critically important in that they can either enhance or deplete stability, opportunity, economic growth, and community well-being. Policies and practices in these four areas go a long way toward determining who does and who doesn't gain access to affordable and safe housing, high-quality, well-resourced schools, public safety designed to protect and respect the community, and fair access to affordable credit for buying homes, building businesses, and other investments, such as paying for higher education.

My initial interest was to consider how important policies and practices in housing, education, criminal justice, and lending either contributed to or depleted individual and community well-being generally and then specifically for Black people. Toward this end, I've researched approximately one hundred policies and practices and focused in more closely on about seventy-five, among them Stop and Frisk, the War on Drugs, the G.I. Bill, redlining, zero-tolerance school punishment policies, "felony" box on job applications, sundown towns, property tax–based school funding, subprime and other loans, loan denials, racial covenants, land seizures, school segregation, Broken Windows policing, bail, school-to-prison pipeline, distribution of teacher quality, urban renewal, Stand Your Ground, home appraisals, steering, and uses of municipal fines and fees.

For each policy or practice, I wanted to know its overall definition and purpose and then what specific impact, if any, each one had on Black people specifically. If these policies and practices were having a specific and negative impact on Black people, then perhaps they could be understood as identifiable parts of systemic racism. For example, what is subprime lending and how does it work? But also, how has subprime lending impacted Black people and communities? Or, in the case of zero-tolerance school punishment policies: What is it and how does it function in schools, and how did it impact Black students and families differently from white students and families? What did I find? In virtually every policy I studied, I found that whites were afforded advantages and Black people were saddled with disadvantages. Even more, Black people were often negative targets of some of the policies and practices, regardless of the colorblind language or expressed purpose of the policy. In other words, these policies and practices were identifiable as parts of systemic racism.

Examining the policies and practices as a group, I returned to Meadows's four-question test designed to establish whether something is a system or not: (1) Can you identify the parts? (2) Do the parts interconnect? (3) Do the parts interconnect in ways that produce metaeffects? and (4) Do the outcomes/effects persist over time?

Sure enough, I began to notice important interconnections between the identifiable parts. As mentioned in chapter 1, residential segregation significantly interconnects with school segregation. Zero-tolerance school punishment policies result in hyperpunishment of Black students, which results in much higher levels of expulsions of Black students and disproportionately supplies the school-to-prison pipeline with Black students.

Not only did the policies and practices interconnect, but they did so in ways that intensified negative effects for Black people in multiple and reverberating directions. For example, Black people, women especially, have been targeted for subprime loans even when they have good credit. These loans have higher interest rates and other terms that reduce equity building. So when a Black person is targeted for subprime loans, they are also simultaneously affected by the racially discriminatory practice of lower appraisal values for Black people's homes (even when located in predominantly white neighborhoods). The combination of and interconnections between these and other practices intensify the reduction of equity Black homeowners would otherwise be able to accrue, which in turn drives and maintains the significant wealth gap between Black and white homeowners.

A number of federal and state postincarceration policies include housing exclusions that prevent formerly incarcerated people from living in subsidized housing or even staying temporarily with family in public housing without triggering their family members' legal eviction. After being incarcerated, many people simply have no resources and nowhere to live; in fact, many rental apartments will not accept applications from the formerly incarcerated. When one combines formerly incarcerated people's postincarceration debt (costs imposed by the criminal justice system for being incarcerated), limited access to jobs and high levels of job discrimination, the overrepresentation of Black people among this group, and the high level of poverty among Black people and the postincarcerated, the impact of policies that exclude the formerly incarcerated people from public housing support becomes devastating. For these and other reasons, although Black people make up only

13 percent of the population, Black people make up 37 percent of the houseless and 49 percent of homeless families with children.[1]

Not only do the policies and practices interconnect in ways that reverberate in multiple directions to produce metaracism—the metaeffect of systemic racism—they persist over time. For example, long-standing patterns of housing and job discrimination significantly contribute to disproportionate Black poverty, leading to disproportionate residence in public or subsidized housing. At the same time, the staggering expansion of mass incarceration fueled in part by a racially discriminatory War on Drugs policy and rampant profiling in Black communities has dramatically expanded the number of Black people who are arrested and incarcerated.

The more I explored these policies and practices, the more I noticed a pattern of negatively reverberating interconnections that generate additional hurdles for and burdens on Black people. No one policy alone could be singled out as *the* source, but by exploring multiple policies relationally, and doing so from the vantage point of how they impact Black people, the depth, breadth, and intricacy of how the policies and practices worked to maintain metaracism came into sharp focus. But this is not all I found.

I discovered that the intricate interconnections across many policies were strikingly consistent and targeted in both focus and impact. The vast majority involved some combination of containment, extraction, and punishment of Black people. Once I recognized how prominently containment, extraction, and punishment shaped the system, it became impossible not to see these processes amplifying one another and thereby creating entirely new metaeffects.

The process could take many forms, but the patterns were familiar. A policy that on the surface seemed to be designed to result in punishment or containment was designed in ways to produce maximum extraction of resources along the way. If those resources were not handed over, the result was often additional punishment and containment. In some cases all three worked in concert, producing extreme effects.

This is metaracism in action. Policies framed in racially neutral language produce targeted outcomes that together intensify the devastating impact of containment, extraction, and punishment. Systemic racism tightens its grip as the metaeffects of its policies and processes amplify one another and evolve. The devil, it turns out, *is* in the details.

CONTAINMENT

Containment is a process that keeps something—often something harmful, for example, a highly contagious virus—restricted in space, under control. In the context of systemic racism, containment restricts Black people within physical boundaries, almost always based on the underlying myth that Black people are dangerous to society. We see it in the constant and disproportionate association of Black people with criminality and in how the perception of Black people as dangerous drives systemic and aggressive policing strategies like Stop and Frisk, as well as the exponential growth of mass incarceration that disproportionately targets and harms Black people and communities.

Containment is likewise a defining feature of neighborhood segregation. Redlining, racial zoning, and steering enabled and maintained segregation, and white flight reinforces it. Research shows that residential segregation is not the outcome of individual choice, but rather has been organized and facilitated by federal and local governments and by the real estate and banking industries to contain Black people—a process that literally sets boundaries to hold Black people in some spaces—and to keep them out of others. Residential segregation is highly interconnected with other areas of society, including educational segregation and diminished access to supportive financial services, quality health care, jobs, affordable housing, and other opportunities.[2]

Containment also describes the pattern of limiting Black mobility in a wide range of contexts and travel. The phenomenon called "driving while Black" or "walking while Black" emphasizes the ongoing surveillance and challenges of being situated in or moving through physical spaces. Similarly, the network of thousands of towns across America called "sundown towns," which "allowed" African Americans within their borders during daylight hours only (usually to work for white families and white-owned businesses) and threatened them to be gone by sundown "or else . . . ," contained Black mobility, shaping where, when, and how Black people traveled and lived—and helped establish contemporary conditions of Black-white inequality.[3]

Highway planning strategies inspired by the "promise of urban renewal" also reveal a pattern of bulldozing and constructing massive highways through Black communities. Promises to rebuild such communities rarely materialize. As a result, highways served effectively as nooses, razing or cutting off Black communities from thriving areas and encircling them with large, air- and noise-polluting thoroughfares. Black communities are also frequently contained by the planned inaccessibility of public transportation.[4]

Black economic advancement is contained by widely documented slower and lower rates of upward mobility in the workplace. Qualified Black workers find themselves underhired even for entry-level positions, or hired into positions that are at a lower level than those for which they are qualified—a process known as "channeling down." Even well-educated Black people find their financial horizons contained when compared with their white peers. As noted in chapter 1, studies show that Black Harvard graduates receive the same kind of job and career outcomes as white state school graduates.[5] Containment is a powerful and persistent feature of metaracism. Most easily visible in the context of neighborhood segregation and incarceration, containment also serves to limit economic opportunity and general mobility, particularly through its interaction with other policies and processes.

EXTRACTION

Extraction is the process of taking away valuable resources from people, places, and things. In the context of systemic racism, extraction describes a consistent pattern of resource removal and value from Black people and communities, including, but not limited to, income, capital, assets, talent, land, knowledge, confidence, self-worth, health, and labor. The removal of these resources drains assets, health, and value from Black spaces and people. It limits Black people's ability to weather difficulties and creates many significant disadvantages especially by producing the racial wealth gap, which rises from the absence of intergenerational transfer of wealth and the preponderance of intergenerational transfer of debt.[6] Of course, slavery was the ultimate practice of resource and labor extraction (as well as containment via punishment), but the coercive extraction of Black labor continued long after emancipation, including into our contemporary moment.[7]

In 2016, the net worth of a typical white family was about $171,000—a full ten times the net worth of a typical Black family ($17,000).[8] While income and other figures fluctuate over the decades, the scale of the wealth gap has remained consistent for more than seventy years.[9] This enduring inequality is not the result of a singular historical force such as slavery alone. Instead, this wealth gap is maintained by an ongoing accumulation of policies and practices, for example, the establishment of Jim Crow segregation; federal government–sanctioned redlining; discriminatory lending and predatory housing contracts and real estate practices; the theft of Black-owned land; the burning of businesses and the slaughter of successful Black communities like the Tulsa, Oklahoma, massacre in 1921, Elaine, Arkansas, in 1919, and Rosewood, Florida, in 1923, among many others. No single policy or action could generate this profound gap on its own; the persistent racial wealth gap is an outcome of multiple multidirectional interconnections crossing many areas of society, interconnections that disproportionately extract or suppress wealth accumulation for Black people over many generations.

Black land seizures (including the seizure of farms) through strategies ranging from outright violence to lending discrimination to technically legal practices have resulted in losses of millions of acres of Black-owned land throughout the twentieth and into the twenty-first century.[10] In 1920, Black people owned perhaps as much as 20 million acres of land. By 2012, the number stood closer to 3.6 million acres.[11] Most of this loss was in farmland; Black Americans represented around 14 percent of the farming community in 1920 but now make up less than 2 percent of it, an 86 percent decrease. Meanwhile, white farmers were once 85 percent of American farmers but are now 95 percent.[12] Many losses accumulate from this massive land seizure. Based on stolen agricultural revenue as well as the value of the land itself, Black people were robbed of an estimated $300 billion. At the same time, primarily white-owned farms have been continuously supported by government subsidies and loans, resulting in the development of extremely profitable industrial farms, especially across the South.[13]

Widespread lending discrimination that first denied qualified Black people access to credit for homes or businesses and then targeted Black people by selling them high-interest loans with unfavorable terms has resulted in an extraordinary extraction of wealth and increase in debt.[14] Recent incidents of racial discrimination in housing appraisals have been shown to result in significant loss of equity. In 2022, some Black homeowners found that when their homes were reassessed with white people posing as the owners, the assessed value increased by as much as 40 percent.[15] Black renters pay more for rent, especially in white neighborhoods.[16] A number of policies that contain Black people (e.g., redlining, racial covenants, and racial zoning) also serve as forms of economic extraction: they concretize and normalize a steep financial penalty for being Black. Over time, these policies and practices have remained crucial for sustaining the consistent deficit in Black household and community resources. Extraction of wealth, land, property, health, security, and other valued resources is a significant and reverberating metaeffect of systemic racism. So, too, is punishment.

PUNISHMENT

Punishment is most evident today in the various facets of the criminal justice system, which disproportionately targets Black communities for surveillance, detainment, arrest, and longer, harsher sentencing. Although drug use was actually declining when the War on Drugs policy was initiated by Richard Nixon in 1971, it established an influential framework for the expansion of America's prison population in general and the Black prison population in particular. In fewer than thirty years, the number of people in prison shot up from three hundred thousand to over two million.

The National Institute on Drug Abuse study of student drug use found that white students were six or more times more likely than Black students to use a range of drugs.[17] Despite this, Black people—including students—are a much more highly targeted group for surveillance, search, and arrest. In 2000, a Human Rights Watch report stated that in seven states, Black people constituted 80 to 90 percent of all drug offenders sent to prison. As Michelle Alexander notes, "When the War on Drugs gained full steam in the mid-1980s, prison admission for African Americans skyrocketed, nearly quadrupling in three years, and then increasing steadily until it reached in 2000 a level more than twenty-six times the level in 1983."[18] Today, African Americans constitute upward of 38 percent of people in jails or prisons but make up only 13 percent of the population.

Sentencing disparities by race also highlight the use of punishment to drive and maintain systemic racism. Due to racial profiling and expanded prosecutorial discretion, in which prosecutors are granted wide latitude to assign the severity of criminal charges, Black defendants often face more severe charges, thereby setting them up to be sentenced more harshly than their white counterparts. Black defendants also face significantly more severe initial charges than white defendants, even after controlling for characteristics of the offense, criminal history, defense counsel type, and age and education of the offender. For example, prosecutors were found to have filed charges carrying mandatory minimum sentences against Black defendants 65 percent more often than for white defendants with similar offenses, thereby increasing the likelihood that Black defendants would be sentenced harshly.[19] Within the federal system, sentences imposed on Black men are nearly 20 percent longer than those imposed on white men convicted of similar crimes.[20] Disparities in sentencing are even more pronounced with extremely punitive sentences, such as life sentences. In 2012, 47 percent of people serving life sentences in federal prisons were Black. In Louisiana, the ACLU found that Black defendants were twenty-three times more likely than white defendants to be sentenced to life without parole for a nonviolent crime.[21]

Punishment drives practices like racialized police brutality, and the constant harassment enacted by Stop and Frisk policing. These tactics were put in place with the purported aim of taking guns off the street and reducing drug sales. In practice, their execution was unmistakably racist. In New York, Stop and Frisk tactics escalated pedestrian stops to the point where, in 2008, the NYPD stopped 545,000 people, 80 percent of whom were African American or Latinx. In that same year, whites accounted for 8 percent of those frisked by the NYPD and Blacks accounted for 85 percent of all those frisked.[22] The targeting of hypersegregated ghettos makes it all the easier to intensify the stopping and frisking of Black people. The *New York Times* found that the greatest density of Stop and Frisk detainments was located in Brownsville, one of the most segregated Black areas in Brooklyn: in an area that measures roughly eight city blocks, Brownsville residents were stopped at a rate thirteen times the city average.[23]

Excessive and targeted punishment is not limited to policing and mass incarceration. The presence of school resource officers—these are regular police officers who are assigned to schools without any special training—has contributed to the transformation of children's behavioral issues or conflicts into criminal infractions. These officers are disproportionately located in majority Black and Latinx schools and reports show a consistent pattern of hyperpunishment of Black students for the most subjective infractions.[24] In the 2011–2012 school year, Black girls in New York City schools were fifty-seven times more likely to be expelled than white girls. Black boys were ten times more likely than white boys to be expelled.[25] Punishment has been an exceptionally destructive and persistent feature of metaracism.

COMBINATIONS

Containment, extraction, and punishment take place in various combinations or all at the same time. For instance, the continued practice of extreme racial disparity in sentencing, as well as policy-driven punishment exacted through a Kafkaesque assortment of postincarceration fines, fees, limitations, and exclusions, continues to disproportionately punish, contain, extract, and burden Black folks for their entire lives.

Interconnections between methods of containment, extraction, and punishment abound. The containment generated by "walking or driving while Black" is connected to a system of racially targeted punishment, which in turn involves the active extraction of resources. Consider for a moment the 2015 Department of Justice report that revealed the Ferguson, Missouri, police department's practice of targeting Black people for minor or nonexistent infractions to generate revenue for the city, and the use of escalating fines and jailtime for the inability to pay for tickets associated with minor infractions. This practice required a particular kind of targeting that was facilitated by the process of containment that I am describing. In this case the targeting created people with criminal records and then used the records as a justification for monitoring. And it thereby extracted resources through fees and heavy fines, and carried serious punishment and threat of punishment for nonpayment.

Or consider the impact of redlining. The practice not only effectively contained Black communities through legalized segregation, but also systematically extracted financial resources and opportunities by denying Black people the ability to amass property at the same rate as whites. This resulted in the devaluation of property in Black communities while simultaneously serving as lenders' justification of higher interest rates. In turn, this dynamic created a racially biased predatory lending market that drove foreclosures and eventually paved the way for gentrification. Finally, redlining was one of the most important factors in creating Black ghettos (which resulted in further containment and extraction). These ghettos, in turn, enabled and justified the aggressive, humiliating surveillance-based policing exemplified by punishing practices like Stop and Frisk, which was not a policy of harassment alone, but also extracted Black people's confidence, sense of safety, and health. Combinations of containment, extraction, and punishment are flexible and layered in ways that are not often easily seen. The single-issue approach often used to analyze discrimination is partly responsible for failing to detect these metaeffects. But systems also manage to escape notice because they are good at adapting.

ADAPTATION

Systems are resilient and durable partly because they readily adapt to changing conditions. They endure not because they're dependent on any single practice but rather because they produce consistent outcomes. In a social system, such as systemic racism, when some policies and practices are legally challenged or become otherwise untenable, new ones emerge and take their place. These new policies may appear to be corrective or a positive modification to the original conditions. Examine their outcomes, however, and more often than not, the new policies will generate the same or similar outcomes that the earlier policies or laws produced. Because of their amazing adaptability, systems are most effectively identified and described based on their outcomes rather than their stated goals. As long as a strategy or policy results in some form of containment, extraction, or punishment, and as long as the ensuing outcomes benefit or do less harm to white folks than to Black folks, the specific means by which these outcomes are achieved can be modified, revised, and/or scrapped in favor of entirely new ones.

The history of lending discrimination is a good example. For most of the twentieth century, systematic exclusion of Black people from stable, low-interest home or business loans was a common strategy that contained and limited Black people from building wealth. Eventually, largely due to the pressures brought to bear by Black activism, this blanket exclusion from the kind of home and business loans that build capital and wealth became politically and socially untenable. Banks then made claims to be practicing fully objective lending evaluation and inclusion. This transition, on the surface, looks like a remedy, an end to discrimination, even. But a closer look reveals continued exclusion through exceptionally high levels of denied loans. For example, nationwide research found savings and loan banks turned Blacks down for home loans twice as often as they did whites. In 1989, the *Atlanta Journal-Constitution* examined the records of ten million applications from every savings and loan in the country and found a lending gap "so pervasive and so wide that in much of the country high-income Blacks are rejected at the same rate as low-income Whites."[26]

In subsequent decades, this pattern of inclusive discrimination was followed by many forms of racially targeted predatory lending, including targeting Black people for higher-risk, higher-interest loans, balloon payment requirements, and more—even when Black loan applicants had credit histories that would qualify them for more favorable loans and terms. This industry-wide deployment of subprime loans extracted millions of dollars in fees from Black people, created more economic instability, and in turn created a pathway to punishment (through higher eviction rates, higher levels of default, penalties, and additional fees associated with tanked credit ratings)— in short, further extraction of resources. Eventually, lending exclusions are replaced by predatory inclusion with excessive subprime lending targeting Black borrowers. Strategies evolve but the outcomes of containment and extraction remain.

Most policies that support systemic racism don't announce themselves as having the explicit intention to contain, extract, or punish. Unlike redlining, which was a legal form of de facto discrimination when put into practice, many other policies and practices that form the dirty details of systemic racism seem to be, on the surface, race neutral or "colorblind." The policies make no mention of any intention to target or exclude Black people—or to disproportionately favor or discriminate against anyone, for that matter. This colorblind approach allows systemic racism to work in an effectively hidden, normalized way—to mask the stable patterns and outcomes that are produced. One important consequence of the "hidden" workings of systemic racism is the validation of stereotypes and myths about Black people—and myths about the inherently fair, colorblind nature of our society. In turn, these myths reinforce and normalize the view that disparate outcomes between whites and Blacks are the logical result of so-called inherent Black deficiencies and, therefore, both are reasonable and acceptable.

Let's take the G.I. Bill as an example of a powerfully influential policy with a colorblind surface that was nonetheless able to perpetuate the effects of systemic racism in housing by stealthily producing stable patterns of housing discrimination against Black people. The G.I. Bill was a sweeping and extensive bill introduced by the Roosevelt administration in 1944 that aimed to provide returning World War II veterans with federal government assistance to support them in their readjustment to civilian life and to help kick-start the postwar economy. The bill provided returning veterans with significant benefits such as unemployment insurance, job training, higher education tuition, and guaranteed, new, low-cost loans for homeownership. While the language of the G.I. Bill was color neutral—it did not explicitly exclude Black veterans—the bill was structured and implemented in a way to ensure very limited access to benefits for the returning 1.2 million Black veterans who fought in World War II. African American veterans were barred at both the state and local levels from receiving certain G.I. benefits, most notably, but not exclusively, in the South.[27] Lobbyists insisted on the requirement that G.I. benefits be administered by the states instead of the federal government, in turn allowing the states, nationwide, to create significant roadblocks to benefits for Black veterans.[28]

The near-total exclusion of Black veterans from the benefits provided by the G.I. Bill was also reinforced by lending exclusions and racial covenants that barred Black people from postwar housing developments. Suburban housing developments funded in part with low-interest, government-backed mortgages were explicitly designed as whites-only via racial covenants. Underwriters of many home loan opportunities, subdivision contractors, and the Federal Housing Administration all advised against and often explicitly outlawed mortgages to African Americans in predominantly white areas, based on the notion of white segregation as the social norm, and the fear of white flight and the threat of a decline in property values should Blacks move in. Only 2 percent of Federal Housing Assistance loans went to African American families in the first thirty years of the G.I. Bill's implementation. In Mississippi, for example, 3,200 white homeowners were supported by G.I. Bill home loans, compared to only 2 Black homeowners. This discrimination also took place in the North: in New York and New Jersey, the racial gap in G.I. Bill–supported mortgages was 67,000 loans for whites versus 100 loans for nonwhites.[29]

The expanded opportunities granted to whites provided by the G.I. Bill are enormous and span generations of families. Access to affordable college education, favorable mortgage terms, and job training literally created a largely white American middle class. Vocational training boosted the skills of workers, who were then more likely to secure good-paying jobs in the skilled trades. Prior to 1940, college was out of reach for most Americans. The G.I. Bill changed that by opening educational doors to first-generation white ethnic immigrants, working-class and middle-class citizens who were now able to attend college and attain advanced degrees. This expanded white middle class attended white colleges, both public and private. African American vets, on the other hand, found it difficult to obtain access to high-quality educational benefits. Instead, they were largely required to attend segregated, underfunded Black colleges (today's HBCUs).

Systemic racism is insidious because the policies that drive the system rely on the metaeffects of the interlocking parts to generate higher levels of Black harm. In this context the veneer of colorblind policy and the scaffolding of antidiscrimination laws help systemic racism adapt by hiding the true impact of a network of policies that on the surface seem racially neutral. Only when each individual policy is viewed in the context of how it interconnects with a range of other policies and practices does it become possible to see how it contributes to the flexibility and durability of systemic racism.[30]

No single policy in one area of society alone can do the level of harm created by a network of interconnected policies. Instead, the metaeffects of the dynamic interconnections between elements of the system are devastating—metaeffects that consistently contain, extract, and punish Black people.

WE HAVE NOW DEVELOPED A BETTER UNDERSTANDING OF systemic racism, a description of how it works, and a sense of how it can nevertheless be hard to see even when it is all around us. Still, for the most part, this has been a journey at thirty thousand feet. There are many more important things to see, and to feel, that only a grounded perspective can offer. *What does it look like and feel like to live with and in systemic racism?* To grapple with this question, we need to look at real people's experiences of life and death in the grip of systemic racism. Let's begin this ground-level journey by looking at the story of how the life of Trayvon Martin was cut short by systemic racism. Only then can we begin to get a sense of what a system that contains, extracts, and punishes looks and feels like.

3

NO CHANCE ENCOUNTER

TRAYVON MARTIN

O N THE EVENING OF FEBRUARY 26, 2012, THE LIFE OF Trayvon Martin was stopped by a bullet to the chest fired from the gun of self-appointed neighborhood watch captain George Zimmerman. Trayvon was unarmed. He had been walking back to his father's girlfriend's house at Twin Lakes in Sanford, Florida, after a trip to a local store where he had bought Skittles and iced tea.

More than a decade on, Trayvon has become a household name, though public familiarity wasn't inevitable. Initially, his death and the manner of dying were of little concern to local police. In the hours after Trayvon was killed, the Sanford, Florida, police did not canvas the Twin Lakes community to find out who Trayvon was, to whom he belonged, where he or his family lived, or whether or not there was a teenager missing in the community. The police acted as if Trayvon couldn't possibly belong at Twin Lakes. It was not until his father went to the police station himself that he learned his son was not missing but dead. That was also when Trayvon's father learned that Trayvon's killer, even after confessing that he had shot Trayvon, was walking free.

Trayvon's death, and the strange, if not suspicious, conditions that surrounded it, did not initially generate any media interest. But the Martin family's anguish and agitation sparked a flame that became a wildfire of public outrage among Black communities and well beyond them. Soon, silent vigils and protests began sprouting up all over the country. The protests grew more intense as Trayvon's killer continued to go uncharged. And then the 911 tapes were released. The recordings touched a nerve: this type of killing is a familiar story for Black folk, a story in which whites can gun down a Black child and go uncharged. Adding to the outcry, George Zimmerman's claims of self-defense were clearly challenged by the 911 call, and overridden by Black lived experience and a fundamental distrust of the criminal justice system. Thus, because of insistent, nationwide protest, the story of what happened to Trayvon became a major news event. George Zimmerman remained uncharged.

At first, news commentary was largely supportive of Trayvon, framed in racially neutral terms. As journalist Mychal Denzel Smith pointed out in 2018, "There was a time in the media where there was sympathy given to Trayvon Martin and the family and that cut across the partisan lines that we're accustomed to."[1] At the time FOX news pundit Megyn Kelly expressed suspicion about the Sanford police's actions, and even Bill O'Reilly said that "every fair-minded American should want justice in this case." Donald Trump said, "Well, it has to be looked into. It is terrible what happened—seventeen years old. And now there are all sorts of stories that just don't feel right."[2] Yet beneath the relatively placid racial surface of race-neutral news coverage was a roiling cauldron of disagreement about racism and the role that racism played in Martin's death.

The story took a sharp turn almost a month after Trayvon's death, on March 23, 2012, when President Barack Obama spoke publicly about the incident. At the end of a White House press conference, a reporter asked Obama to comment on the Trayvon Martin case: "[May I] ask you about this current case in Florida of the very controversial allegations of lingering racism within our society . . . the so-called stand your ground law and the justice impact. Can you comment on the Trayvon Martin Case?" Obama replied:

Well, I am the head of the Executive Branch and the Attorney General reports to me so I have to be careful about my statement to be careful so that I am not impairing an investigation that is taking place right now. But obviously, this is a tragedy. I can only imagine what these parents are going through. And when I think about this boy, I think about my own kids. And I think every parent in America should be able to understand why it is absolutely imperative that we investigate every aspect of this.

And that everybody pulls together, federal, state and local, to figure out exactly how this tragedy happened. So I am glad that not only is the Justice Department looking into it and I understand now that the Governor of the State of Florida has formed a task force to investigate what is taking place. All of us have to do some soul-searching to find out how something like this happened and that means examining the laws and the context for what happened, as well as the specifics of the incident. But my main message is to the parents of Trayvon Martin. **If I had a son he'd look like Trayvon.** And, you know, I think they are right to expect that all of us as Americans are gonna take this with the seriousness it deserves and that we are gonna get to the bottom of exactly what happened.[3] (emphasis mine)

Obama's comments rely on colorblind language in his appeal to "all Americans," especially his entreaty that "I think every parent in America should be able to understand why it is absolutely imperative that we investigate every aspect of this." But one simple phrase disrupted the colorblind-based unity Obama was attempting to forge: "If I had a son he'd look like Trayvon." This sentence hit the public like a bomb.

Immediately, prominent white public figures and in the media changed their position. Instead of the racially neutral support they'd originally declared, their comments became hot with vitriol and indignation. In short, by proclaiming the Black racial connection between himself and Trayvon, Obama not only declared himself as Black; he also suggested—on air with the loudest public mic in the nation—that *what Trayvon looked like mattered.*

This Black racial connection between Obama and Trayvon upset the fundamental but unspoken rule of colorblindness: that whiteness is and must remain the unifying and dominant American identity. In so doing, Obama shattered a cornerstone of the widespread public acceptance of his presidency: unquestioned, unerring racial neutrality. By breaking this rule—even just for a moment—Obama seemed to disavow his implicit promise to uphold colorblind, white-accommodating behavior and priorities.

Colorblindness is an effective rhetorical strategy that evades—if not outright denies—the acknowledgment of racial discrimination. In a colorblind world, the Martin family may expect support if—and only if—they don't mention the central role of race or racism in Trayvon's death and the subsequent trial of George Zimmerman.[4] For many white Americans Obama's racial identification with Trayvon transformed the killing of Trayvon Martin into a racial incident that indicted not only George Zimmerman but all white people. As journalist Joy Reid observes of the response to Obama's press conference, "Black America hears it as a eureka moment, finally having what we've known our entire lives affirmed. White America hears it as this Black president calling each and every one of them racist."[5]

What's more, by referencing race, Obama directly connected Trayvon's death to a broader story about the relevance of racism. He didn't characterize the killing as if racism was a statistical racist outlier; instead, Obama legitimized the demands of Black protesters by suggesting that the case deserved a coordinated, multiagency examination at all levels of law enforcement and social policy. In other words, Obama's very public remark seemed to point a finger toward anti-Black racism as a relevant and important context for the case.

The cauldron cracked. In the media, Trayvon was transformed from innocent victim to menacing thug, George Zimmerman from vigilante to hero. Ensuing coverage, particularly though not exclusively among conservative commentators, retold the story through a set of carefully chosen images— images of Trayvon's face at different ages (preteen, teenager looking tough for the camera), his hoodie, a bottle of soda, and a bag of Skittles. These images quickly became potent symbols in their own right, resonating in simultaneously contradictory ways. Together they reflected the painful and symbolic tension between the imagined threat of the menacing, hoodie-wearing Black man and the harmless, innocent Black boy heading home from the store with candy.

The public story hinged on the question "What happened?" in order to assign individual guilt and innocence—and, by swift association, to judge whether the country was racist or not. Was Trayvon Martin stalked and gunned down or was he acting suspiciously or threateningly? Did George Zimmerman, driven by his racist perceptions and attitudes, attack Trayvon unprovoked, or did he act—at least to some degree—in self-defense? These two versions of "what happened" reflected a bold racial fault line. The public battle over narratives was a proxy for the battle over the existence of racism in America. If Trayvon could be proven to be a thug and criminal, then Zimmerman would be a hero and not a racist, and thus society is not racist. If Trayvon could be proven innocent, then

Zimmerman would be revealed to be a racist and this would prove that society is racist.

Inserting itself between the two competing narratives was the "tragedy of it all" chorus. This framing attempted to unite America by diverting attention away from issues of race and racism toward one cohesive colorblind frame. Rather than attempt to sort through the complex issues of race or racism, the incident was discussed as just a terrible, unfortunate event. How terrible that Trayvon was in the "wrong place at the wrong time."

A quintessential example of this colorblind framing was the April 9, 2012, cover story of *People* magazine. Positioned next to a large portrait of Trayvon, the title reads, "An unarmed 17-year-old is killed in a Florida neighborhood: How a chance encounter turned deadly—leaving a family devastated and a country outraged."

I remember having a strong visceral response to this cover image and its lede. Chance encounter? Really?! The adjective "chance" when used as an adjective is defined as a "meeting or event that is fortuitous, or accidental." The noun "encounter" means: "an unexpected or casual meeting." Taken together the phrase "chance encounter" describes an interaction that was unexpected, casual, and accidental, an event entirely disconnected from its systemic social context.

A chance encounter version of events implies that if Martin had not been walking back to his father's girlfriend's apartment at Twin Lakes at exactly that time, or if he had taken another route, or if Zimmerman had not been on community watch duty that night or was simply in another location of the gated community, this "chance encounter," or this unexpected and accidental incident, would never have happened. On one level, of course, this is true; perhaps they might not have met that night and this particular confrontation may have been avoided.

But the element of "chance" carries with it a dangerous colorblind seduction. While emphasizing the layer of individual experience shaped by chance, it obscures the interconnecting networks of powerful and compounding social forces of systemic racism that shape our lives—and that in this case significantly raised the likelihood that the exchange between Martin and Zimmerman would end in Martin's death. Though systemic forces may seem to operate in the background of our everyday choices and experiences, they nevertheless fundamentally condition individual and collective action and outcomes.

The forces of systemic racism played a large role in Trayvon Martin's presence at Twin Lakes that night, stoked George Zimmerman's zeal as a neighborhood watch captain, distorted his perception of Trayvon, and to a great degree explain his eventual acquittal. A systemic interpretation does not diminish the importance of the individual life of Trayvon Martin. Nor does it suggest that George Zimmerman's individual decisions and actions don't matter. Instead, it allows us to look beyond individual guilt, innocence, and chance to see how systemic racism works. Only by piercing the illusion of "chance" can we see and grapple with the true scope of danger that surrounded Trayvon Martin.

SEEING TRAYVON: A SYSTEMS LENS

All too often individual stories about racism, even when they look like they are revealing something bigger than an individual case, end up leading back to the idea that the problem at hand is isolated, localized—or in the case of Trayvon, an essentially random, if tragic, encounter. Stories that focus on individuals in isolation suggest that society is a backdrop for, rather than a key player in, the action. Who can control "chance"? Stories of individual experiences often neglect to consider the patterns in society that, when considered systemically, offer much greater insight into the factors that drive harm, disadvantage, and risk—the systematically driven factors that made Martin and Zimmerman's collision an inevitably violent and deadly one.

A systemic reading of events invites a larger, more dynamic context for the question "What happened?" A systemic reading enables a focus on how the interconnections among policies, practices, laws, and beliefs shape behaviors and decisions. It shines light on key interconnections that create "metaeffects"—effects that are greater than the sum of a system's parts, effects that none of the system components can produce on their own. A systems approach reveals the inaccurate, misleading "by chance" interpretation of the Martin/Zimmerman case—and instead reveals how systemic racism in housing, policing, laws, and school punishment practices formed the high-risk context of Trayvon Martin's life as well as his death.

Let's begin with place and setting. Martin was shot and killed while walking back from the store, to his father's girlfriend's home at the Retreat at Twin Lakes, a gated community in Sanford, Florida. Zimmerman lived at Twin Lakes, and he founded and served as the captain of the community's neighborhood watch program. What kind of neighborhood was Zimmerman watching, and why was he watching it?

SANFORD, FLORIDA, AND THE RETREAT AT TWIN LAKES

Twin Lakes is a gated community in the city of Sanford, Florida. Sanford is a city of about fifty-four thousand in northern Florida, thirty minutes from Orlando. The city's racial and ethnic composition at the time of Trayvon Martin's death was roughly 50 percent white and 30 percent Black, and 20 percent nonwhite Hispanic.[6] These ratios may suggest more racial integration than was actually the case. A census tract analysis of Sanford shows that most areas include Black, Hispanic, and white residents, but unevenly distributed across neighborhoods. In other words, although Sanford's overall racial demographics suggest racial integration, the actual residential distribution of the races within the city was highly segregated. Most Sanford tracts contain either a clear majority of Black residents or considerably fewer than 20 percent Black residents. This means that the tract is either a predominantly Black (or nonwhite) area or an area with large numbers of white residents and many fewer Black or other people of color. As we will see shortly, this 20 percent threshold for "integration" mirrors a critical marker related to white residential patterns and racial comfort zones well after segregation was outlawed.

Twin Lakes was originally marketed on the aspirational desire for "affordable luxury." A promotional video for the complex boasts an "oasis," and like "living in a resort . . . close to good schools, outlet malls and the magic of Disney World."[7] In 2004, when Twin Lakes was built, a 1,400-square-foot townhouse there sold for $250,000. A few years later, the Great Recession hit. Fueled largely by deregulated lending that exposed homeowners, especially nonwhite homeowners, to bank products that were dependably profitable for the banks yet extremely risky for borrowers, the housing market collapsed.[8] The crash ushered in a national crisis in housing losses, with Florida ranking third in the nation for foreclosures.[9]

By 2012, the same townhouse worth $250,000 in 2004 was worth less than $100,000—a loss of more than half its original value. This sudden and precipitous drop in home values in Twin Lakes drove a spate of bank foreclosures there. During 2012, approximately 40 of the 263 townhomes were left empty, and more than half of the total occupied units were filled with renters like the Zimmerman family and Brandy Green, Martin's father's girlfriend.[10]

Some renters of foreclosed units were able to use Sanford Housing Authority–issued Housing Choice vouchers (aka Section 8 or low-income vouchers) to make their rental payments.[11] This increased rental access to Twin Lakes for low-income families likely increased the number of Black residents (the Black poverty rate in Sanford was about two times higher than the white poverty rate there). These low-income residents would never have been able to afford to live at Twin Lakes prior to the crash.[12]

Taken together, these dynamics brought the Retreat at Twin Lakes to the emotional, economic, and racial edge. By 2012 Twin Lakes had become a fairly diverse place: around 50 percent white, 20 percent Black, and 20 percent Latinx. It's significantly less Black than the overall population of Sanford, which is just shy of 30 percent Black—and that 20 percent Black Twin Lakes resident figure is more important than it may appear. After the 1960s, when the Supreme Court ruled segregation illegal, integration was presumed to be the new American reality. What actually happened, however, was a new process of white flight. Although the laws that had explicitly protected white Americans and ensured for them significant advantages had been struck down, new opportunities for the creation of majority white suburban spaces continued to emerge. These opportunities enabled new patterns of white flight when the percentage of new Black residents reached a key threshold. Researchers Douglass S. Massey and Nancy A. Denton documented a clear pattern of white mobility: if a majority white neighborhood is under 10 percent Black, three-quarters of white people generally continue to move in; once that percentage climbs above 20 percent, though, around 40 percent of whites feel uncomfortable in the neighborhood, about 24 percent of whites try to move out, and 50 percent of whites are unwilling to move in.[13] Unless the percentage of Black residents remains lower than 20 percent, a significant degree of white flight will eventually turn what seems to be an integrated or integrating community into a predominantly Black and racially segregated one. The 20 percent threshold triggers white discomfort and the perception that there are "too many" Black residents; it also stokes the perceived threat of danger and of the devaluation of neighborhood property and reputation. Beyond the 20 percent threshold, white flight accelerates and swiftly produces higher levels of (re)segregation.

The Retreat at Twin Lakes was facing plummeting property values due to the Great Recession. The significant decline in the market value of a townhome at Twin Lakes meant that many of its white residents who might have wanted to move were unable to or delayed in doing so because their mortgage debt was greater than the current value of their property. Owing more than the property's market value, especially during a housing-provoked recession, is frightening for any homeowner. But in a case where the general threat and fears provoked by a sudden economic nosedive were sharpened by an increasing number of renters—specifically more Black and low-income residents—tensions were bound to escalate.

WHITE PROPERTY VALUE(D): GREENLINE, REDLINE

When faced with racial integration, whites resist, and when resistance is forced to give way, most move away to communities that are more white than the neighborhood they're leaving. Often defended as a matter of personal choice or individual preference, this pattern has been a collective choice financed and rewarded by government housing policies, developers, and the real estate industry. White residential community is itself an asset protected by maintaining its homogeneity. The legalization of segregation was not a separate-but-equal arrangement as it has been historically characterized; it was about establishing and protecting the value of whiteness and the assets and social standing associated with it. White homogeneity was a mechanism of de facto segregation that has been widely supported through policies enacted and practiced by banks, real estate agencies, and the federal government throughout the twentieth century.

"Redlining" is shorthand for one of several federally coordinated practices during the early to mid-twentieth century that used the then-existing racial composition of neighborhoods (which were already segregated due to banking and real estate policies and practices) to expand or deny government-backed loans based on race—a practice that reinforced and incentivized the value of future segregation for white Americans. The color-coded system rewarded neighborhoods for being entirely composed of white residents (marked green) and extensively excluded lending in neighborhoods composed of Black people (marked red). These lower assessments and lending exclusions for Blacks were pegged to the notion of lending "risk," which drove high loan denials, further devaluing the property and making it harder for Black people to invest in their homes and businesses.[14]

The economic value bestowed on predominantly white communities because they are predominantly white motivates an investment in white communities. Simultaneously, it enhances the idea that the presence of more than a very small number of Black residents is a threat to white property value and protections that white homeowners expect. The economic value of whiteness is directly related to the economic devaluation of Blackness.[15]

Racially discriminatory evaluations continue today in many forms. Examination of bank-requested property assessments reveals a pattern in which houses owned by Black residents even in predominantly white neighborhoods are assessed at lower values than similar homes owned by whites on the same street.[16] The sheer presence of Black neighbors is often perceived as "stealing" white property value and endangering community stability.[17]

As the economic downturn worsened, crime rose in the town of Sanford. From 2007 to 2011, burglaries in Sanford jumped 42 percent, from 668 to 945. According to resident reports, Twin Lakes itself also experienced a rise in burglaries. In the summer of 2011, the summer before Zimmerman pursued and shot Trayvon dead, the community suffered a wave of burglaries. Most of these were property crimes of opportunity (a stolen bike, etc.) that involved taking items left in clear view inside the home, such as laptops and PlayStations. In the case of one burglary in particular, however, a mother and her child locked themselves in a room while two burglars ransacked their home. The crime escalated fear at Twin Lakes. A narrative soon arose that burglaries were on the rise because of an influx of Black and other "transient" residents.[18]

Residents of gated communities, like the Retreat at Twin Lakes, tend to be especially concerned about conditions that lessen property protections because they threaten to destroy white property values. This concern is exacerbated by a corresponding fear of crime, and an overlapping fear of racial and class social heterogeneity.[19] So, the fears of invasion and Black people "stealing" white property values supported the interpretation that Black people and "other transients" were responsible for the increase in thefts at Twin Lakes.

In September 2011, Twin Lakes residents decided to form a neighborhood watch, and George Zimmerman volunteered to be the captain. In many ways, though, George Zimmerman had already long served as the unofficial watchdog of the gated community. Zimmerman began renting at Twin Lakes in 2009, and between the day he moved in and when he killed Martin, Zimmerman was known to call the police incessantly to report all sorts of things. The transcripts of all his 911 calls from that roughly two-year period filled twenty-eight pages. During the summer of 2011, the focus of Zimmerman's calls to police narrowed significantly—specifically, the *Tampa Bay Times* reported, he started to fixate on Black men he thought looked suspicious. Zimmerman's 911 call transcripts reportedly grew more focused on the association of Blackness with the crimes in the community. Other residents shared a similar assessment of Zimmerman becoming increasingly preoccupied with Black boys and men as criminals. Audio recordings of the six previous calls Zimmerman made to the police before the night he called about Trayvon were preserved; of these, five specifically involved his suspicions of African Americans.[20]

THE APPEARANCE OF DANGER

Why did Zimmerman reportedly fixate on Black boys and men? At the time, some reports claimed that Zimmerman's attitude made sense because the majority of Twin Lakes crimes had been committed by Black people.[21] But this, it turns out, wasn't the case. In the fourteen months before Zimmerman killed Trayvon Martin, there were an estimated forty-five burglaries, attempted burglaries, attempted break-ins, and suspected break-ins. The data available reveal that only "7% (3 of 45) of the reported wrong-doings were confirmed to involve Black males."[22] Despite this small percentage of responsibility, the narrative that emerged about recent break-ins identified Black males as the primary culprits.

So why was Zimmerman singling out Black men when there was no objective reason to do so? And why did his bias, which was largely repeated verbatim by neighbors and in the media coverage, go so underexamined?

The systematic criminalization of Black people, especially Black men and boys, has a long history. The idea that Black people are a criminal class—which emerged not long after the end of slavery—supported and justified various forms of reenslavement such as Jim Crow segregation, helped prevent Black freedom and mobility, and buttressed the logic of redlining and other urban northern forms of segregation. The entrenched stereotype has also been instrumental in justifying a long-standing, destructive pattern of racial profiling, police brutality, police killings, and the emergence of the system of racialized mass incarceration.[23]

Contemporary studies reveal significant, socially reinforced association between Black men and crime that is deeply influential in perpetuating the idea that Black men are criminals. The Sentencing Project report on race and punishment synthesized a large body of recent research showing that when surveyed, white Americans consistently overestimate actual Black participation in crime sometimes by as much as 20 to 30 percent.[24] Implicit bias research also shows that the public as well as police officers apply racial bias when they assess inconclusive and potentially threatening scenarios. A range of implicit bias studies confirm the conflation of Black people with criminality. These implicit association tests (IAT) use techniques that assess rapid-fire associations that happen too rapidly for people to "think" about the "right" answer. In one such test, participants were asked to pair Black or white faces with either tools or weapons. When participants were presented with an image of a Black face (rather than a white one) it increased their speed at identifying guns but reduced their accuracy (they mistook tools for weapons). In another IAT video shooting study, subjects were instructed to quickly identify and shoot armed suspects but to avoid shooting unarmed suspects. Non-Black participants more quickly and accurately decided to shoot an armed target when the target was African American, but more quickly and accurately did not shoot when an unarmed target was white. When images of both the Black men and white men were unarmed, the Black men were more likely to be "shot."[25] Accuracy in these racial/criminal pairings reflects the degree to which the pairings reflect existing associations based on race. To put it bluntly, whites are presumed to be innocent and unarmed and Black people are assumed to be armed and dangerous.[26]

Media narratives, especially since the 1960s, have played a significant role in reproducing and tightening the connection between Black people and criminality while simultaneously overrepresenting whites as victims and defenders of law. Even after controlling for rates of criminal offense, the representation of Blacks as criminal suspects is more likely than such representation of whites; the impact of this finding is magnified by the fact that Blacks appear in more "threatening contexts."[27]

For several decades news media reports on street crime have disproportionately featured African American offenders. The standard crime news "script" focuses on violent crime and associates Black people with crime so reliably that one study reports 60 percent of viewers who were shown a story imagined seeing an image of a perpetrator—even though a perpetrator was not shown on screen—and a full 70 percent of those viewers believed the perpetrator to be African American.[28] The assumption of Black criminalization and the media's reflection of it have had a profound impact on today's policing practices, public policy, and individual perception of Black men and boys.

It was not surprising, then, that when George Zimmerman called 911 about Trayvon Martin, Zimmerman had already convinced himself that Trayvon was an armed criminal. Key excerpts from the recording of Zimmerman's call went as follows:

> **Zimmerman:** Hey, we've had some break-ins in our neighborhood, and there's a real suspicious guy. . . . This guy looks like he's up to no good or he's on drugs or something.
> **Dispatcher:** Okay, and this guy, is he White, Black or Hispanic?
> **Zimmerman:** He looks Black.

Dispatcher: Did you see what he is wearing?

Zimmerman: A grey (dark?) hoodie, like a grey hoodie, and either jeans or sweatpants and white tennis shoes. He's (unintelligible) . . . he was just staring.

Dispatcher: . . . He's near the clubhouse right now?

Zimmerman: Yeah, now he's coming toward me.

Dispatcher: Okay.

Zimmerman: He has got his hand in his waist band. And he's a Black male.

Dispatcher: How old would you say he looks?

Zimmerman: . . . late teens. Something's wrong with him. Yup, he's coming to check me out, he's got something in his hands. I don't know what his deal is.

Dispatcher: Just let me know if he does anything, okay?

Zimmerman: How long until you get an officer over here?

Dispatcher: Yeah, we've got someone on the way, just let me know if this guy does anything else.

Zimmerman: Okay. . . . These assholes they always get away.

(They review directions to location)

Zimmerman: Shit, he's running.

Dispatcher: He's running? Which way is he running?

Zimmerman: Down toward the other entrance to the neighborhood.

Dispatcher: Which entrance is that that he's heading towards?

Zimmerman: The back entrance. Fucking punks. These assholes, they always get away.

Dispatcher: Are you following him?

Zimmerman: Yeah.

Dispatcher: Ok, we don't need you to do that.

Zimmerman: Okay.[29]

The association of Black people with crime has been so deeply embedded and normalized in our culture that it blinds many people to the pure irrationality of its application. In the case of Zimmerman's trial, the fact that a disproportionately small percentage of recent crimes at Twin Lakes were committed by Black people was used to claim Zimmerman's suspicions of Martin (as a Black male) "reasonable." More specifically, Zimmerman's defense team used the Bertalan family robbery (mentioned earlier) in just this way, by presenting a simple syllogism: "Two Black burglars had robbed a house in the neighborhood, Trayvon was Black, therefore, Zimmerman was suspicious of Trayvon, and that suspicion was reasonable."[30] But was his suspicion reasonable? No. Even if many more of the burglars were Black, it wouldn't logically follow that Trayvon was suspect merely because he was a Black male.

This failed attempt at deductive reasoning is consistently used to justify the presumed guilt of Black males. This false logic is then used as a rationale to defend society's negatively biased, severely punitive treatment of Black men and boys. If the same logic is used to explain situations involving whites, its illogical preposterousness would be seen immediately. For example, let's say that two white teenage girls robbed a house in Twin Lakes. And say Trayvon was a white teenage girl; therefore Zimmerman was suspicious of Trayvon because she was a white girl. Would this suspicion be considered reasonable?

Quite obviously not. Not all white girls commit burglaries, so it would be foolish to assume that a random white girl is a burglar. As Lisa Bloom puts it: "Even if all the recent burglaries were committed by Black males, most Black males are not burglars, and it's equally foolish to assume that a random Black male is a burglar."[31]

In general practice, then, white people are presumed innocent until proven guilty; their criminal status must be "earned," so to speak. And even then, sometimes their criminal behavior is minimized. White innocence is the beneficial half of the racial binary between Black and white. White innocence reinforces the idea of Black guilt. The racialization of crime reinforces the idea that white people belong to the community while Black people do not belong (unless it is a majority Black community, which is tainted as having more crime because it is majority Black) and that they are therefore suspicious and dangerous.

Zimmerman's communications consistently reflected this mindset. In addition to his calls to 911, Zimmerman emailed community members repeatedly identifying "suspicious" characters simply as Black—absent any additional details—thereby assigning "justified" suspicion to all Black male residents and all Black male guests. Some Black residents feared being targeted just because they were Black. One Black twenty-five-year-old Twin Lakes resident, Ibrahim Rashada, told a *Miami Herald* reporter: "I fit the stereotype he mailed around. . . . So I thought, 'Let me sit in the house. I don't want anyone chasing me.'"[32]

Research also shows that unconscious links that associate African Americans with criminality extend beyond perceptions of individuals to the association of Black neighborhoods in general. "Residents (especially white but also black residents) of neighborhoods with higher proportions of racial minorities are more likely to overestimate their neighborhood's crime rates. Even after accounting for differing crime rates and other measures of disorder, researchers have found that the percentage of young black men is one of the best predictors of the *perceived* [my italics] severity of neighborhood crime."[33]

Fear of "too many" Black people and the practice of racial profiling are embedded in and reinforced not only by implicit bias and media images but also by the regularized discrimination of Black people in many professional industries. George Zimmerman, it turns out, held key positions in two professions in which the heightened value of white property is reinforced and the criminal profiling of Black people is well documented. Zimmerman worked as a realtor after he graduated high school; he later moved to Florida in the midst of a booming housing market and made $10,000 a month selling homes. Real estate agents are important carriers and practitioners of the key practices that not only encourage racial segregation but are acutely aware of the racial gap in assessed value for comparable property in Black communities. After the market crashed, Zimmerman took a job at a company called Digital Risk, a fraud detection company that "made mortgages safe for banks" by helping banks dispose of toxic, predatory home loans that they'd issued (and which later contributed directly to the financial crisis).[34] This employment history would have given Zimmerman much more than a cursory understanding of the relationship between race, lending practices, and property value. In addition to his experience in real estate and fraud detection, Zimmerman had been a criminal justice major whose application to join the police force was rejected because of his past record of resisting arrest. According to prosecutors, he was known to police as a "wannabe cop."[35]

Now the pieces are all coming together. In Twin Lakes, a predominantly white neighborhood in financial crisis free fall, whose racial composition is approaching the crucial 20 percent Black resident tipping point that triggers white flight, there is a resident who has started to fixate on the presence of "suspicious" Black people. Based on his professional experience in real estate and mortgage risk assessment, this resident understood very well the relationship between fear of Black crime and his neighbors' property rights and value. The resident aspires to be a cop and zealously volunteers to be the captain of the neighborhood watch. Armed with a gun, the resident then sees a Black teenager walking through the neighborhood alone on a Sunday night.

In violation of the 911 dispatcher's clear instructions not to chase Trayvon, Zimmerman pursues him by car and eventually approaches him by foot. According to Zimmerman, the two of them struggle, and Zimmerman shoots and kills Trayvon. He admits to this immediately when police arrive. Trayvon was unarmed, and it's clear from the 911 transcripts that Zimmerman instigated the encounter, against the dispatcher's explicit instructions. And yet, Zimmerman isn't charged with any crime; he is interviewed by a narcotics officer, not a homicide officer, and is not tested for drugs—although both homicide officer–led interviews and drug testing are standard protocol in such situations. Police take his statement and let him go home.

During the six weeks that Zimmerman goes uncharged, the killing becomes national news, due to extensive efforts by the Martin family. It wasn't just that Zimmerman had shot Trayvon; it was that he had pursued him in direct defiance of 911 dispatcher instructions, had killed him, had admitted to it, and yet had been allowed to walk free. Despite Zimmerman's threatening and instigating behavior, Martin's mere presence was interpreted as an appearance of danger.

STAND YOUR GROUND

The legal concept of the inviolability of the home has its roots in the Roman Republic and has been in continual use throughout the history of Western civilization. The legal notion behind Stand Your Ground, which has also been at the heart of the US legal system, is referred to as the Castle Doctrine—as in "a man's home is his castle" (or a person's home is their castle)—which essentially says that if there's an intruder in your home, you're allowed to kill that person, even if it's possible for you to escape instead of killing them or trying to kill them. Under no circumstances are you legally required to flee your home from someone who does not belong there. Stand Your Ground widely expanded the Castle Doctrine. Anyone "who is attacked," the law reads, anywhere he or she is lawfully present, has "no duty to retreat and has the right to stand his or her ground and meet force with force, including deadly force if he or she reasonably believes it is necessary to do so to prevent death or great bodily harm or the commission of a felony." Whereas before Stand Your Ground, the law allowed for lethal force only inside people's own homes; now, in states that have passed Stand Your Ground laws, the use of lethal force is legally permitted anywhere someone is "legally present." Everywhere you are is now your castle.[36]

Stand Your Ground was crafted in 2005 by ALEC—the American Legislative Exchange Council—an organization that brings together conservative politicians, big businesses, and lobbyists to craft "model legislation" that is passed in one state and then promoted to and often adopted wholesale by politicians in other states. In response to extensive and influential lobbying, twenty-seven states developed some form of Stand Your Ground.[37]

The specific way the Castle Doctrine was expanded by Stand Your Ground laws varies across states. Some states justify killing to prevent the commission of a felony on residential property; in these states, one would be legally justified in fatally shooting an unarmed person breaking into a car in the shooter's driveway, for example. In Mississippi, killing is also legally justifiable when trying to prevent a felony on the premises of one's workplace. In Texas, deadly force is justifiable if one believes it is necessary to protect or retrieve property of any value in any place, so long as one believes there is no other way to retrieve the property or prevent "theft during the nighttime." In Florida, deadly force is legally justifiable if one believes it is necessary to prevent felony burglary anywhere, even on unoccupied premises.[38] In six Stand Your Ground states, beginning with the NRA-crafted Stand Your Ground law in Florida, law enforcement is actually prohibited from arresting shooters who claim they should be protected by Stand Your Ground, and may not make an arrest unless they can prove the shooting was motivated by something other than "reasonable fear."[39]

Despite these differences in application by state, states that have passed Stand Your Ground have seen justifiable homicides rise considerably; in states that haven't, justifiable homicides have either remained flat or gone down. From 2005 to 2007, in cases where shooters used "reasonable" self-defense, "the normal average number of legally 'justifiable' homicides increased 200% in Florida, 54% in Texas, 83% in Georgia, 24% percent in Arizona, and 725% in Kentucky." Under Stand Your Ground, racially motivated murders of unarmed Black people and acts of vigilantism have been legitimized and found to be "justified" at staggeringly high rates. From 2005 to 2011, the number of "legally justifiable" homicides of African Americans more than doubled in states that enacted Stand Your Ground laws or similar legislation, while it remained constant in the rest of the country.[40]

More specifically, this law has normalized and legally enabled and essentially sanctioned violence based precisely on the kind of racial profiling and exaggerated fears that led George Zimmerman to pursue and kill Trayvon Martin. As already discussed, a large number of studies have shown that whites perceive Black people to be much more criminal and dangerous than whites. So it makes sense that Stand Your Ground, which allows lethal violence as a response to a "reasonable belief" that such violence is "necessary to prevent death or great bodily harm," would have serious racial implications. And research data confirm this.

The racial dimensions of the application of Stand Your Ground are stunningly consistent. The following chart

In all states—but especially in Stand Your Ground states—white-on-Black killings are exponentially more likely to be deemed justified by law than white-on-white, Black-on-Black, or Black-on-white killings. *Data courtesy of PBS* Frontline, *2012. Graphics designed by Studio Rainwater.*

Justifiable Homicides by Race(s) of Killer and Victim

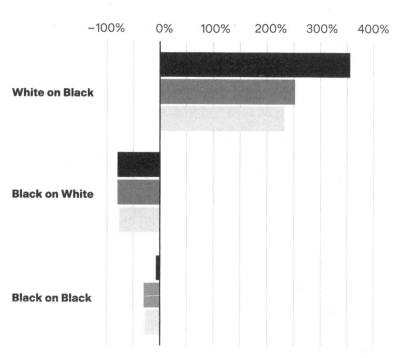

Percentage likelihood that one-on-one killings among strangers will be found justifiable by law, compared to a baseline of white-on-white killings.

All States

Non–Stand Your Ground States

Stand Your Ground States

prepared by PBS *Frontline,* using the results of a study by Urban Institute Fellow Dr. John Roman, shows the likelihood that a killing will be deemed justified based on the race of the shooter and the victim. Using a baseline of white-on-white killings, the chart compares killings between Stand Your Ground and non–Stand Your Ground states. In all states, when a Black person kills a Black person, they have a roughly 25 percent lower chance of being found justified in that killing. In all states, when a Black person kills a white person, the killer is about one-and-a-half times less likely to be found justified than a white person who kills a Black person. But look closely at the data on the right side of the chart. In states without Stand Your Ground laws, whites who kill Black people are two-and-a-half times more likely to be ruled as justified than if they kill a white person. In states with Stand Your Ground, however, white-on-Black killings are three-and-a-half times more likely to be deemed justified, or 40 percent more likely than in non–Stand Your Ground states. In Florida specifically, a state with a particularly expansive version of Stand Your Ground, research has found that controlling for all other variables, Stand Your Ground cases are twice as likely to result in a conviction when the victim is white.[41]

Stand Your Ground was not technically part of Zimmerman's defense at trial, because both sides agreed that the details of the physical struggle between him and Trayvon made the law inapplicable. Even so, the underlying racial perceptual context that motivates Stand Your Ground loomed large and seemed to clearly influence the jury despite the law's technical inapplicability. Despite the fact that both the prosecution and the defense agreed that Stand Your Ground was not applicable, the instructions provided to the jury used the language of the law—including the term itself:

> In deciding whether George Zimmerman was justified in the use of deadly force, you must judge him by the circumstances by which he was surrounded at the time the force was used. The danger facing George Zimmerman need not have been actual; however, to justify the use of deadly force, the appearance of danger must have been so real that a reasonably cautious and prudent person under the same circumstances would have believed that the danger could be avoided only through the use of that force. Based upon appearances, George Zimmerman must have actually believed that the danger was real.
>
> If George Zimmerman was not engaged in an unlawful activity and was attacked in any place where he had a right to be, he had no duty to retreat and had the right to stand his ground and meet force with force, including deadly force if he reasonably believed that it was necessary to do so to prevent death or great bodily harm to himself or another or to prevent the commission of a forcible felony.[42]

In fact, the defense used the phrase "stand your ground" so frequently that it appears jurors became confused about whether the law did in fact justify the killing. After a nearly three-week trial, the jury deliberated for sixteen hours and found that Zimmerman was not guilty. Speaking of the verdict after it was declared, one juror told CNN's Anderson Cooper that the jury did acquit Zimmerman in part because of Stand Your Ground.[43]

What are we to make of an instruction like this: "The appearance of danger must have been so real that a reasonably cautious and prudent person under the same circumstances would have believed that the danger could be avoided only through the use of that force?" If Trayvon was deemed "suspicious" because he was a Black male teenager, then Trayvon's appearance was itself the appearance of danger, is it not? An American Psychological Association study concludes that "perceivers showed a consistent and strong bias to perceive young Black men as larger and more capable of harm than young white men (at least among non-Black participants)."[44] If Trayvon elicited racially motivated, extreme fear in Zimmerman's mind, well, then, it makes sense that Zimmerman might believe that only force would protect him—even though Zimmerman himself pursued Trayvon, not the other way around. Stand Your Ground has turned anti-Black racial profiling into legally protected "common sense."

Stand Your Ground technically extends everyone's right not to retreat from spaces far beyond home when they believe they are being threatened. As one African American Miami police officer put it, Trayvon Martin should have been the one invoking Stand Your Ground as a defense against George Zimmerman. Nevertheless, as the 911 transcript shows, Zimmerman directly disobeyed police dispatcher orders by chasing Martin. One must ask: Who would have believed that Trayvon felt threatened? Who would have confirmed his right not to have to retreat in the face of an armed man chasing him? The data show just how unlikely this would have been. The language of "reasonable belief" and the racial associations of the "appearance of danger" demonstrated by the clearly racially skewed legal outcomes of Stand Your Ground laws confirm the anti-Black idea that it is reasonable to believe that Black people are a grave threat to whites. The racial and legal landscape in which Stand Your Ground exists extends and confirms both the racist perception of Black people as criminals and a fundamental threat to white safety and property. It confirms that whites are granted a wide berth to kill Black people—while Black people are the least justified to kill white people.

The targeted criminalization of Martin by Zimmerman, and the gated, protectionist, and segregated neighborhood logic that made Trayvon so vulnerable in Sanford, Florida, were not an isolated or new situation for him. In fact, Trayvon was at his father's girlfriend's home in Twin Lakes due to another kind of biased criminalization based on race—the one that took place at his high school.

RACIAL PROFILING IN SCHOOL PUNISHMENT

Trayvon didn't live primarily in Sanford—he lived and went to school in Miami Dade County, more specifically in Miami Gardens, a town about four hours south. The night he was killed was a school night, but Trayvon was in Sanford with his father because he had been suspended from school and didn't need to be back in Miami with his mother the next morning.

Trayvon Martin attended Dr. Michael M. Krop High School. The ten-day suspension that led Trayvon to stay in

Sanford with his dad was punishment for committing the third infraction of school policies in that academic year. The first was for tardiness, the second was for writing "WTF" on a locker, and the third was for possessing a bag with marijuana residue on it.

Now, the situation might at first seem cut-and-dried: because Trayvon "broke the rules," he was suspended. The media often cited Trayvon's suspension as proof of his troubled youth. The "simple fact" of the suspension also gave credence to Zimmerman's claims of self-defense. Yet when we look more closely at Krop High School's detailed guidelines for which offenses warrant which type of punishment, the facts become more complex. The following chart that shows the guidelines has three columns: on the left is Trayvon's offense; in the center is the punishment that that offense warrants according to Krop High School's own guidelines; and on the right is the punishment that Trayvon received.

Trayvon's first offense, tardiness, is not listed anywhere in Krop's guidelines as an infraction warranting punishment. The closest match is "cutting classes," which although clearly more serious than being late to class, still doesn't warrant a suspension, according to Krop's rules. The rules state that cutting class should be handled by calling the student's parents, revoking privileges, and other forms of non-suspension-based punishment. Nevertheless, Trayvon was suspended for mere tardiness.

Trayvon's second offense, writing on a locker, is a Level 2 offense, which calls not for a suspension but for a school-based program to promote positive behavior—unless the Level 2 infraction is "serious or habitual." Although Trayvon wrote on

Krop High School declared Trayvon Martin guilty and punished him in excess or to the maximum limit of official school guidelines. *Information courtesy of Lisa Bloom, Suspicion Nation. Counterpoint: Berkeley, CA. 2014. Graphics designed by Studio Rainwater.*

Trayvon Martin's Offense	Krop Punishment Guideline	Trayvon Martin's Punishment
Tardiness	**Unlisted** No punishment	**Suspended**
Writing "WTF" on a locker, once	**Level 2** Suspension only if "serious or habitual"	**Suspended**
Possessing a plastic bag with marijuana residue	**Level 3** Suspension between 1 and 10 days	**Suspended 10 days**

the locker only on one occasion, rather than being enrolled in the school-based program to promote positive behavior (as the rules dictated), he was suspended. Trayvon's third infraction, possession of a controlled substance, was a Level 3 offense for which Krop High School guidelines recommend suspension for between one and ten days. Even if one concedes that residue alone constitutes a controlled substance, Trayvon was punished with the maximum ten-day suspension.

The accumulation of excessive suspensions was not based on official disciplinary guidelines. Instead, Trayvon was first suspended inappropriately for what was falsely labeled a Level 1 offense (tardiness) and then slapped with a second suspension for writing on a locker, in just one instance—even though the school guidelines designated suspension only for "serious or habitual" defacement of school property. And finally, for the Level 3 offense of bringing a controlled substance onto school grounds, while the guidelines allowed discretion to suspend Trayvon for a little as one day—Krop High administrators chose ten.

At every stage of the disciplinary system and for each and every infraction, Trayvon was assigned the maximum punishment or beyond. Trayvon was treated to punishment for behaviors not subject to punishment at all, like tardiness. He was not appropriately reprimanded, but suspended, for it. Why?

Black students are frequently treated to this kind of excessive punishment. In 2009, Black students at Krop High School accounted for nearly half of Krop's 105 suspensions, even though Black kids accounted for just 24 percent of the student body. In Okaloosa County, where Krop High School is located,

50 percent of school arrests involve Black students, even though Black students are only 12 percent of the school population.[45]

Nationwide, these trends reflect a significant pattern of over-punishment and policing of Black students of all age groups. Since the 1970s, the percentage of students suspended from school has doubled, and Black students have been suspended and expelled disproportionately. Today, Black students are suspended at three times the rate of white students and twice as often as Latinx students. The most heavily suspended are Black male students with disabilities. During the 2017–2018 school year, although Black students were 15.1 percent of the overall K–12 student population, nearly 40 percent of all elementary and secondary public school students who received out-of-school suspension—and 38.8 percent of those expelled from school—were Black children. Black preschool children accounted for 18.2 percent of the total preschool enrollment but received 43.3 percent of one or more out-of-school suspensions.[46]

Black students across the United States are disproportionately punished compared to their white peers.[47] This holds true even when controlling for socioeconomic status: Black students from households with higher income are still more likely than white students to be punished for the same infractions. Even in the case of minor infractions and punishments such as office referrals and detentions, Black boys are 1.3 times more likely than white boys to receive punishment. "Black Girls Matter," the African American Policy Forum report on race, gender, and differences in school punishment, compared rates of discipline in New York City and Boston public schools in 2011–2012 and found that in New York, "the enrollment of

Black girls was about twice the rate of white girls but they were subjected to school discipline at ten times the rate of their white female counterparts." Similarly, while the rate of enrollment of Black boys was about twice the rate of white boys, they were disciplined at six times the rate of white boys.[48]

Some have claimed that Black students simply behave more poorly than other children. Research studies, however, have tested and disproved the hypothesis that Black students are more likely to commit subjectively determined offenses than their white peers for reasons of being more poorly behaved.[49] Research has also found that the belief in Black students' "inherent" behavioral differences reflects a significant pattern of racial biases in the perception, not the facts, of Black students' behaviors. It has been shown, for example, that teachers are threatened merely by the way a Black student is perceived to walk. A Black young person's movement through space alone—in the absence of any factually antagonistic or disruptive behavior—is perceived by their instructors as aggressive, low-achieving, and a mandate for removal from classes that teach general (standard, age-appropriate) education curricula.[50]

Black students are not only overly punished in general; they are especially overrepresented among students who receive exclusionary punishment in the form of out-of-school suspensions or expulsions. As the African American Policy Forum reports: "Black boys were expelled at a rate ten times higher than white boys in New York, and six times higher than white boys in Boston." In New York, "ninety percent of all the girls subjected to expulsion were Black." No white girls were expelled, but if one had been expelled, the ratio would be

53:1.[51] Exclusionary overrepresentation begins as early as pre-school and elementary school. Black elementary students were found to be close to four times more likely than white students to be suspended from school. In other words, teachers and administrators disproportionately suspend or expel Black children between ages six and thirteen years, even when age-appropriate, more supportive, and connection-focused alternatives are available.[52]

Exclusionary punishments deeply impair student academic performance and affirming relationships in school. Suspensions are associated with increases in high school dropout rates,[53] decreases in the likelihood of obtaining a high school diploma and bachelor's degree,[54] and even increases in being held back.[55] Even a single suspension can double the odds of a student dropping out, and with each additional suspension the likelihood of graduation becomes a more distant possibility.[56]

Worse still, the negative consequences of school suspensions extend to children's overall health and development. Suspensions isolate and keep students away from their peer community, making it harder to maintain a positive connection with their peers. Exclusionary punishments also put students at an increased risk for moderate to severe depression.[57] The impact of exclusionary punishment is known by medical professionals to be so damaging to the broader health of young people that, in 2013, the American Pediatrics Association officially discouraged suspension and other harsh "zero-tolerance" policies as a practice, and asked its member pediatricians to inquire whether a child has been suspended from school during routine checkups.[58]

SCHOOL-TO-PRISON PIPELINE

These patterns of hyperpunishment of Black students also propel children down a vicious pathway that funnels kids from schools into the criminal legal system.[59] High out-of-school suspensions and other harsh school punishments increase the likelihood of students being arrested or put on probation within twelve years of exiting high school.[60] In other words, suspensions feed a phenomenon known as the school-to-prison pipeline.

The system of school punishment at Krop High School operated very much like a scale of criminal infractions rather than a set of guidelines designed to correct and support adolescent development. There is a striking similarity between Krop High School's application of punishments and the aggressive pattern of policing strategies known as Broken Windows. Broken Windows is a theory and practice of policing based on an unproven hypothesis that aggressive punishment for low-level offenses prevents more serious crimes.[61] The resulting accumulation of arrests for minor anti-nuisance infractions or arrests, based on expanded police discretion to conduct stops, creates a police record that works to prove the criminalization it has itself created.

Trayvon's punishment at Krop High School follows a similar path: he was punished for tardiness as a Level 1 offense, even when it wasn't reflected in the rulebook; Trayvon was suspended for writing on a locker, rather than being offered the recommended referral to a school-based program to promote positive behavior; and finally, Trayvon was given the longest recommended suspension of ten days for a baggie with pot residue on it as an end result of extreme and excessive punishment along the way. School officials built a case for excessively punishing Trayvon by targeting and branding him with a more serious disciplinary record than the school's own guidelines required. Contrary to the unproven but widely accepted hypothesis that aggressive punishment of minor infractions prevents more serious ones, research shows that this Broken Windows–style school punishment for minor disruptions actually increases the likelihood that students will offend again. Perversely, this pattern has been found to be strongest for students who have greater attachment to school in the first place.[62]

Trayvon and thousands of Black students like him are racially profiled as criminals and excessively punished in schools. The same systemic pattern of racial profiling put Trayvon in the path of harm's way that fateful night. But there was more: Trayvon's daily life in Miami Gardens was likewise shaped by an extensive and aggressive practice of racial profiling by the police.

"STOP AND FRISK ON STEROIDS"

At the time Trayvon was killed, his hometown of Miami Gardens had about 107,000 residents. Sixty-seven percent of its residents were Black in a county that overall is less than 16 percent Black.[63] In 2014, the Miami Gardens Police Department was briefly exposed by news reports claiming that it was practicing extreme racial profiling and harassment of Black youth, particularly in and around a neighborhood Quick Mart, a convenience store. Initial reports focused on the egregious treatment of Earl Sampson, whom the Miami Gardens police stopped and questioned a mind-boggling 258 times. The police arrested him for trespassing 62 times at Quick Mart, which, as it turns out, was in fact his place of employment. Sampson was searched more than 100 times and arrested and jailed 56 times. The Quick Mart's owner, who had initially agreed to cooperate with the police to help reduce crime in the area, was so disturbed by the way his employee Sampson and the store's customers were being treated that he installed cameras around the store—not to record criminal behavior, but to document police behavior. The videos became a vital source of evidence in a federal civil rights lawsuit being filed by the store's owner.[64] But the problem of extreme policing, as it turns out, was far more widespread than the Quick Mart lawsuit revealed.

Investigative journalists Alice Brennan and Dan Lieberman of Fusion TV conducted a six-month investigation that included more than 100,000 records from the Miami Gardens Police Department. Their analysis documented an invasive and very aggressive Stop and Frisk strategy. One local public defender dubbed it "Stop and Frisk on steroids." Between 2008, when the police instituted a "zero-tolerance" policy, and 2013, "police have stopped and questioned 56,922 people who were not arrested. There were 99,980 total stops that did not lead to arrests, and 250 individuals were stopped more than 20 times."[65]

Two police officers came forward as whistleblowers and told Brennan that they "were given orders from the top to stop any Black male from the ages of 15–30." This policy was heavily monitored and adherence to it was rewarded: officers who made the most stops were given coveted assignments and promoted, and those who did not "suffered the consequences."[66] While young Black men were targeted for the most vehement treatment, the entire community was terrorized by the constant threat of hostile policing. Fusion's painstaking investigation and analysis of more than 30,000 pages of police field contact reports reveal an extensive pattern of aggressive targeting. They uncovered multiple incidents of police officers providing false information on official field reports, including claiming to stop and question people who were actually already in county jail. "Some residents were stopped, questioned, and written up multiple times within minutes of each other, by different officers." Eight thousand kids were stopped during this five-year period; many were young children playing in playgrounds. Thousands of "senior citizens were stopped and questioned, some near their retirement home, including a ninety-nine-year-old man deemed to be 'suspicious.' Officers even wrote a report identifying a five-year-old child as a 'suspicious person.'"[67]

In practice then, the entire community of Miami Gardens lived under suspicion: They were stopped, frisked, and routinely and systematically denied basic civil rights. Thousands of citizens, especially young Black men in Trayvon's age group, were treated as criminals and subjected to humiliating and frightening "stops," searches, and verbal and/or physical intimidation—or worse. This type of arbitrary aggressive targeting has been shown to have lasting and deep effects on the psychological health of Black people and communities. Living in an aggressively policed environment is a substantial risk factor for mental health issues, especially for people who experience frequent negative or abusive encounters with police. An accumulating body of evidence shows that, on a community level, the need to live on high alert in fear of arbitrary intrusions by police can cause "deep and lasting" psychological trauma. Continual exposure to the conditions of control and intimidation in Black communities over the span of decades has been found to produce poor health effects for the targeted community as a whole.[68] Earl Sampson, the Miami Gardens resident and Quick Mart employee who was stopped 258 times, described his experiences with the police this way: "I feel like I ain't got no rights, no say so. Every time they stop me, every time they take me down, it hurts. I feel like I'm just a nobody."[69]

These stops also have deep and lasting legal and broad social effects in the short and long term. As Alexandra Natapoff's book *Punishment Without Crime* demonstrates, the misdemeanor system is the frontline mechanism through which many people of color, especially Black men, are shunted into the criminal corrections system in the first place. It is through Stop and Frisk and related policing strategies that Black people are initially stopped, become logged in the system, and subsequently are arrested for low-level offenses such as disorderly conduct, trespassing, vagrancy, and other minor order-maintenance infractions. As Natapoff argues:

This is how the petty-offense process actively marks thousands of African-Americans as "criminal," a corrosive dynamic with both immediate and historic effects. The criminal marking prevents people from getting jobs, housing, education, and loans, derailing major aspects of their lives. It sets some people up for the more serious felony convictions that have created our current mass incarceration crisis. And, it insidiously fuels the racist stereotype that Black men are criminals. . . . Arrest by arrest and case by case, the misdemeanor process forcibly connects Black people to the criminal system, arresting them, convicting them, and labeling them criminal for minor conduct, and sometimes for no good reason at all.[70]

At Krop High School, Trayvon Martin was surveilled and hyperpunished in ways that mirror nationwide patterns of oversuspension and other exclusionary punishments for Black students. The excessive use of suspensions (especially unjustly) significantly increased the likelihood of Trayvon dropping out, developing serious emotional and mental health problems, and being funneled into the prison pipeline. The "Stop and Frisk on steroids" tactics deployed by the Miami Gardens police were used to mark, target, and officially label young Black men like Trayvon—and the entire community—as criminal. The high level of targeting made them vulnerable to being arrested for misdemeanors, which, despite their seeming insignificance, serve in practice as the critical gateway into the criminal system. Misdemeanors also have devastating effects on other aspects of life: they reduce access to affordable housing, jobs, and loans—often sending people's lives irreparably off course. The fear and distress associated with such targeting, especially when perpetrated by the police with their virtually unregulated power and authority, heighten anxiety; the fear ripples through the entire community and destroys a sense of safety, self-worth, and belonging.

When Trayvon arrived to visit his father in Sanford, Florida, he was already racially profiled as a criminal because society has allowed to flourish the overassociation of Black people with crime, as well as policies that affirm and deepen that association. Trayvon was thus destined to be perceived as a threat to the gated community, a "retreat" whose design and name had been motivated, at least in part, to keep Black people out. Even full-time Black residents of the Retreat at Twin Lakes were afraid to go outside for fear of being targeted. Zimmerman may have expressed his anti-Black fears in extreme fashion, but he was not alone in his perceptions of threat stimulated by the presence of Trayvon and other young Black men. All the dangerous fantasies Zimmerman falsely observed ("he's on drugs, up to no good, he's suspicious") fueled Zimmerman's armed pursuit of Trayvon and reflect a dangerous and consistent pattern in society. The terms of their interaction were set in motion and had already been profoundly defined by a well-established, ingrained—and therefore largely normalized—set of race-specific social pathways, including the criminalizing racial perceptions of young Black people, the hyperpunishment in schools that push them out of education, and the range of material risks that whites associate with Black "encroachment" on white property.

IN SUMMARY, THE RANGE OF AND INTERCONNECTIONS among policies produce metaracism, the metaeffect of systemic racism. Metaracism produces targeted outcomes that contain, extract, and punish in various, long-lasting configurations. School suspensions and expulsions are punishments that extract and contain. Young Black people are punished and contained through removal (extraction) from the social community of which they are a part, either temporarily or permanently. Stop and Frisk is enacted as a form of punishment and also serves as a form of containment and extraction: it uses state authority to physically contain another person from moving in space. School suspensions and aggressive Stop and Frisk policies extract resources, both personal and financial, such as the benefits of education and life opportunities, and they also extract health and well-being. Stand Your Ground adds legal cover to a pattern of "justified" racially disproportionate killing of Black people.

Media narratives and the George Zimmerman trial itself rarely made any references to how these interconnected factors work as elements of a complex discrimination system. Instead, Trayvon's suspensions were discussed ad nauseam in the media, primarily as an examination of his character rather than an exploration of the punishing and racially targeted characteristics of his circumstances. Twin Lakes was depicted as a community on edge without discussion of why and how that was. George Zimmerman was depicted as less guilty—and, in many ways as the victim—because Trayvon was a Black teen, and the defense was able to weaponize Stand Your Ground without accounting for any of the underlying racial profiling at play. The public heard about Trayvon's suspensions but not about whether they were fair or just. These are some important ways that systemic racism, though unacknowledged and hidden in popular accounts, operated in the life and death of Trayvon Martin and in the wider social conditions in America.

Well-meaning people try to prove that people like Trayvon Martin or George Zimmerman didn't deserve their fate or try to root through the killer's history to find proof of individual bigotry. Yet, when we focus on fate or personality at the expense of a systemic inquiry of racism, we hide and legitimize the very mechanisms that set the stage for the confrontation. When systemic racism is erased from the scene, we imagine that the collision was, in essence, random, a tragic stroke of circumstances. But this was no chance encounter.

An individual chance encounter might create just one Trayvon. Systemic racism creates the conditions for thousands of Trayvons.

4

STEALING EDUCATION

KELLEY WILLIAMS-BOLAR

I n late January 2011 a story out of West Akron, Ohio, made its way into the national news cycle. A forty-year-old African American mother had been arrested for "district hopping" by enrolling her two elementary school–age daughters in adjacent Copley Township from 2006 to 2008. For her actions, which in practice amounted to claiming residency at her father's Copley Township residence, she was charged with two felonies: tampering with records and grand theft. Judge Patricia Cosgrove sentenced Williams-Bolar to the maximum sentence of five years and then suspended all but the nine days she had already spent behind bars, leaving her with two years of probation and eighty hours of community service.[1]

This story became a protracted feature on local, national, and, however improbably, international news. In the twelve months following her trial and arrest, the *Akron Beacon Journal* alone published over one hundred articles and many letters to the editor about Williams-Bolar's case. The headlines and letters from local residents and commentary from various locations near and far from Akron were strongly worded and polarized. Those critical of Williams-Bolar used phrases like she "got what she deserved" because "she lied, cheated, and stole." Bob Dyer, a prominent well-respected journalist at the *Akron Beacon Journal*, wrote many articles criticizing Williams-Bolar. These articles scrutinized her false statement, dug up details aimed to justify the portrait of her as a criminal, and supported the prosecutor's decision to bring charges. Many others defended Williams-Bolar, saying that the punishment was "unduly harsh," with many noting that they would do the same and more for their own children.[2]

Vigorous public debate and intense media scrutiny ensued. There was even a *Dr. Phil* talk show episode featuring Williams-Bolar, Bob Dyer, and Reverend Al Sharpton. Not only was there extensive media coverage, but many news stories were accompanied by pictures of Williams-Bolar walking down a prison hallway wearing a worn, faded, gray-and-white, horizontally striped jail uniform, and followed by a Black female prison guard. Others included a "mug shot" photo of Williams-Bolar looking tired, worried, and with her hair disheveled.

Growing up in New York City, I had witnessed firsthand the epic battle over access to good schools. The strategy and the moral complexities inherent in Williams-Bolar's story were familiar to me from my many peers whose parents had done the same thing. But charges of felony grand theft seemed an extreme outcome.

Until 2011, this very punitive approach to preventing access to schools had been very rare. But between 2011 and 2016, a nationwide shift occurred. Penalties increased in severity from informal investigations and quiet resolutions between individual families and school districts to the active surveillance of children by private for-profit firms that videotaped kids suspected of "stealing education" as they traveled to and from school. The surveilled behavior was then used as evidence to support en masse expulsions of "district hoppers." Felony-level charges such as grand theft began to be filed against families on a regular basis. Similar charges were brought against Tanya McDowell, a homeless, unemployed single mother from Bridgeport, Connecticut, and states such as New York, Michigan, Oklahoma, Illinois, and Missouri have adopted laws that include the possibility of jail time. This kind of treatment for district hoppers represents a new strategy intent on criminalizing the borders between high-ranked and low-ranked schools.

As public attention surrounding Williams-Bolar's prosecution intensified, so, too, did the conflicts over defining her motivations. Although Williams-Bolar explained her reasons for sending her daughters to Copley Township as a combination of physical safety, educational quality, and afterschool supervision, the public debates separated these issues into distinct and often-competing factors. Those who defended

Williams-Bolar focused only on the educational system, indicting it for its extreme inequality. Prosecutor Sherri Walsh and her supporters labeled Williams-Bolar as a criminal whose sole motivation was to defraud Copley Township. In this compartmentalized form of racial storytelling, Williams-Bolar could not possibly have been capable of simultaneously seeking to enhance her daughters' physical safety, educational quality, and afterschool supervision. Instead, discrete arguments that artificially separated the valid, interconnected justifications for Williams-Bolar's decisions camouflaged the larger systemic issues that produced them.

CRIMINAL PARENT VS. CRIMINAL EDUCATIONAL SYSTEM

The Copley Township school system deployed a notably aggressive program for identifying and punishing the families of students who attended their schools without residing in the township. Not only did the district hire private investigators (PIs) to follow and document suspected out-of-town school attendees, they went so far as to create a campaign to reward parents with $100 if they turned in people who they suspected did not live in the district. In fact, according to Williams-Bolar, she recalled "receiving a post card in the mail announcing the reward to families throughout the district." Before and during her trial, Williams-Bolar's place of residence was challenged using evidence gathered by PIs hired by the school district who filmed her taking her daughters to the Copley school from her Akron apartment.

When confronted with the evidence, Williams-Bolar responded with the claim that her daughters lived with both her and their grandfather and that they spent a significant time at their grandfather's home in Copley. She says this was particularly true during the years in question because for some of that time she was a primary caregiver for her father after he had had a stroke. Her father, she explained, was a highly involved grandparent whom she considered a coparent. The school district officials responded to this explanation by instructing her to get a "grandparent affidavit," but then rejected the affidavit in June 2008, apparently because the form did not include the approval signature of the children's biological father. Williams-Bolar explained that she had full legal custody of her daughters and therefore their father's signature would not be legally required, but nevertheless ended her daughters' enrollment in Copley Township schools at the end of the 2007–2008 school year once the grandparent affidavit was rejected. In January 2008, two-and-a-half months after a contentious hearing on her residency, she received an Ohio Department of Education letter saying: "The Department is considering the matter closed at this time."

Eighteen months later, in November 2009, Kelley was indicted on two felony counts of tampering with official records, claiming that records showed that she lived in an Akron public housing development. She was also charged with grand theft for stealing what the Summit County prosecutors claimed was $30,500 in educational resources. The cost of one year of school per child in Copley Township is $6,895. In January 2011 Kelley served nine days in jail. The grand theft charges were dismissed, but the felony counts for tampering with records remained. Judge Patricia Cosgrove sentenced Williams-Bolar to the maximum sentence of five years and then suspended all but the nine days she had already spent in jail, leaving her with two years of probation and eighty hours of community service.

There was little doubt that Williams-Bolar had falsified documents and told several lies related to her effort to get her daughters enrolled in the Copley schools. For these reasons the case may have seemed straightforward to Summit County prosecutor Sherri Walsh and her supporters. As journalist Bill Dyer said, "Fraud is fraud."

Yet an outpouring of sympathy and outrage from a diverse group of moms and confessions from accomplished Black people interrupted the prosecutor's effort to turn Kelley into a criminal parent. Supporters focused on the issues of legalized inequality in education—basically defining the school system, and the residency laws that protect it, as criminal.[3] This became a heated and protracted battle between two single-issue interpretations of the problem.

Nine separate Facebook pages—all but one in support of Williams-Bolar—offered the opportunity to comment frequently on posted articles. As one Facebook supporter said, "I actually don't think she made a bad choice, but rather a forced choice unfortunately. More times than not the underprivileged are expected to accept their situation as just that; . . . theirs. I still commend her choice to go out and change what was a bad educational experience for her children the best way she could." Another supporter from Savannah, Georgia, said: "Kelley, I love you! I am here 110%. The system doesn't always work for us so we have to take matters into our own hands to protect our children! If only all parents cared so much for their kids to risk everything! Now, how can we, as a country, get them to remove your charges? Let me know if I can help!"[4]

Two separate petitions in support of Williams-Bolar were established, and within twenty-four hours each had garnered nearly 8,000 signatures. The first, a Facebook petition grew to 7,292 signatures in less than a day. Petition leader Deborah Price of Washington, DC, told the *Beacon Journal*: "The ladies are so enraged. . . . All the women that have come online have related. It's a living reality for parents."[5] Massachusetts mother Caitlin Lord set up the second petition on Change.org. According to various sites, organizations such as Color of Change and Moms Rising collaborated on this petition—which by August 2011 had over 165,000 signatures—that was scheduled to be sent to the governor of Ohio requesting that he pardon her, which would remove the permanent felony label on her record.[6]

In addition, a number of well-known and accomplished Black people publicly admitted that their parents had made similar calculations in the face of similar circumstances. Celebrities like actor Danny Glover and musician Questlove spoke out in support of Williams-Bolar on Tumblr and Twitter. Michael Lomax, president and CEO of the United Negro College Fund, told the story of his own family providing a different home address so that he and his sister could attend rigorous academic high schools and avoid the L.A. Manual Arts High School, which is notorious for tracking students into trades rather than college.[7] As Jamilah King, writing for ColorLines

News for Action, argued: "At the heart of the matter was the fact that Williams-Bolar was convicted for doing what many reasonable parents have done for decades: cleverly manipulating an already rigged educational system to work in (the) best interests of her children."[8]

Some of Kelley's defenders and even some of her critics were upset over Summit County prosecutor Sherri Walsh's decision to prosecute Williams-Bolar with felony charges when lower-level misdemeanor records-tampering charges would have been appropriate. Walsh found herself in a defensive crouch when the story went public, and she responded by intensifying the rhetoric against Kelley. In public court documents, Walsh depicted Kelley as a criminal whose actions were guided by her attempt to defraud the county and government rather than a parent trying to protect or better the lives of her children:

> Kelley Williams-Bolar was not prosecuted and sent to jail because she wanted a better life for her children. She falsified documents, engaged in many different acts of deception to four different governmental agencies, and continued to do so over a two-year period. When the school district confronted her she continued to lie and created further deceptions, resulting in being charged with a felony.[9]

The vast majority of those public commentators who were critical of Williams-Bolar echoed Walsh's description of Williams-Bolar as motivated by criminal intentions rather than protective parental instincts. They offered support for Copley Township's decision to elevate the matter to the level of the prosecutor's office. A February 2, 2011, Akron News Now.com article by Tina Kaufman stimulated a series of comments of this type from readers. For example, Cruisemeister said: "She lied and manipulated the system, now she is paying the consequences. Just another person who feels that they are entitled to everything and screw the system." Make Sense said: "She is a liar and abused the system, under the guidance of her father." debbilous said: "She is a real piece of work . . . she should be prosecuted for lying on the other government paperwork. She should lose her ability to teach, live in AMHA housing and all the other perks she has received!" who cares said, "People need to learn that they can't just go and TAKE better things . . . they have to earn them. They have to work for it."[10]

These comments and prosecutor Walsh's justification rely on a familiar story of the "undeserving poor" who cheat and take without earning, a story often trotted out to demonize low-income Black mothers. These posts and many others are full of vitriol and insult. They painted Kelley as amoral, selfish, dishonest, criminal, greedy, and lazy. Not content to simply support Walsh's position, the critics rallied for Kelley to lose access to everything: her job, her so-called perk of public housing, and "all the other perks" she has received.

Prosecutor Sherri Walsh and others critical of Williams-Bolar defended the prosecution by presenting arguments that allow for only a single motivation. Walsh attempted to paint Kelley as being motivated by defrauding government agencies as if this was her primary agenda and therefore entirely separate from wanting to protect her daughters. What about safety and school quality? Did she fear for her children's safety or did she want them to attend a better school, as most of her public supporters emphasized? If fears for her children's safety were Williams-Bolar's primary motivation, then the story shouldn't be about getting her children a better education, critics argued. If improving the education for her children was her motive, then she should simply pay for that education; afterschool home break-ins shouldn't matter. Supporters were also single-minded in their defense of Williams-Bolar. Although she herself was consistent in describing her motivation as wanting to protect her daughters from neighborhood crime, defenders were single-minded in their focus on educational inequality as the important issue. Although some commentators made passing reference to school inequality more broadly, school inequality was largely discussed independently from the deep systemic interconnections that created the situation in which Williams-Bolar found herself.

Safe environments for the children of a working mom, the benefits of afterschool family oversight, and the value of attendance in excellent schools were linked together as Williams-Bolar made her decision to enroll them in Copley schools. The safety of her children was the catalyst, but as would be the case for most parents, she took a number of relevant factors into account when making her decision. The arguments against Kelley continued to separate physical danger from educational quality and afterschool supervision. Peeling these factors apart reflects a fundamental denial of the interconnected nature of the forces working against Williams-Bolar and many like her. Systemic racism has created conditions where concentration of risk and lack of social support and resources work together to increase economic precarity and reduce neighborhood safety and school quality and limit access to affordable afterschool childcare. These are deeply intertwined interdependent factors that disproportionately impact Black low-income communities. Dealing with them as separate matters—to "prove" that Kelley Williams-Bolar didn't have a laudable reason to make quality education her goal—denies the very interconnections that make systemic racism a system.

WEST AKRON, OHIO

Central among these denials is the refusal to acknowledge the depth and breadth of the impact of containment on Black people, especially poor and working-class Black people. Containment is the product of a century's worth of systematic discrimination, spatial containment, punishment, and targeted extraction of community resources. The spatial dimension of racism generates powerful forms of interconnecting discrimination by reinforcing, compounding, and exacerbating categories of social, familial, and community instability.

Racial segregation is a form of spatial containment that produces overcrowding, significantly fewer city services, higher concentrations of poverty, underfunded local schools with a more distressed student population, lower-quality educational environments, and fewer childcare and other family support services and networks for working parents. As George Lipsitz notes:

People of different races do not inhabit different places by choice. Housing and lending discrimination, the design of school district boundaries, zoning regulations, policing strategies, the location of highways and transit systems and a host of tax subsidies do disastrous work by making places synonymous with races. The racial meaning of place makes American whiteness one of the most systematically subsidized identities in the world.[11]

Not only have Black people been contained in designated areas where housing values were discriminatorily underevaluated, but as more Black people moved to cities, whites took their racially supported resources out of cities. This white flight preserved and consolidated their advantages and simultaneously repressed the opportunities of Black households and communities. As middle-class whites took their tax bases to predominantly white suburbs, job and other economic forms of discrimination against Blacks reduced the Black community's tax base and added to increasingly concentrated segregated poverty. This racialized pattern created highly concentrated Black communities that are structurally disadvantaged, a pattern that continues today. Such neighborhoods show losses in private businesses, political power, and medical facilities, as well as environmental discrimination, deteriorating buildings, and loss of revenue for public schools.[12]

Kelley Williams-Bolar's life and the lives of her daughters were fundamentally shaped by these conditions. Williams-Bolar was employed as a teacher's aide in an Akron public school at a salary of $19,400 per year—a salary that hovers around the federal guideline threshold for poverty for a family of three.[13] Williams-Bolar's poverty-level wages qualified her for public housing assistance; she lived in subsidized housing on Hartford Avenue in the West Akron neighborhood.[14] Her children faced living conditions that are consistent with many Black kids in Akron and other Black children around the country. In America as a whole, 34 percent of Black children are born into poverty, as compared to 11 percent of white children. At the time Williams-Bolar was sending her girls to Copley schools, the ongoing Black unemployment rate was roughly double the national average of 8 to 10 percent. (It's worth noting that an 8 to 10 percent unemployment rate is considered dangerously high with regard to the health of the overall economy and of society.)[15]

In Akron, the overall unemployment rates were similar to the national average of 8 to 10 percent.[16] In 2011 when the Willliams-Bolar case was in progress, the statewide unemployment rate for Black people reached around 20 percent, about 3 percent higher than the national Black average.[17] In Akron, white unemployment was at about 5.5 percent and Black unemployment was just over 13 percent.[18] In 2018, a major study on racial opportunity in Akron ranked Akron among the ten worst metro areas for Black employment and among the five worst for Black earnings.[19] By comparison, Copley Township had an unemployment rate of 2.1 percent and a poverty rate of 6 percent.[20]

Akron's population in 2012 was 63 percent white and 29 percent Black.[21] A closer look at neighborhood maps reveals a pattern of highly racially and class-segregated arrangements.

The vast majority of African Americans lived in West Akron. However, a demographic map of the west side of Akron (the neighborhoods that abut the Copley Township) also revealed high levels of racial concentration and segregation. Along the western border of Akron, there are five areas that are all significantly segregated. West Akron, where Kelley Williams-Bolar lived, is a significantly larger neighborhood immediately adjacent to Copley Township that was 85 percent Black and 12 percent white. The two smaller neighborhoods north of West Akron were predominantly white: Fairlawn Heights, at 92 percent white, and Wallhaven, at 79 percent white. In the two neighborhood districts south of the West Akron neighborhood, both are yet again disproportionately white: the smaller neighborhood of Rolling Acres is 67 percent white, while the larger Kenmore neighborhood is 95 percent white.[22] Copley Township is itself 86 percent white and 8.5 percent Black.[23]

The current pattern of racial segregation, higher levels of poverty, and higher unemployment in Akron is not simply a holdover from the first half of the twentieth century when Black migration from the South transformed northern cities. Beginning in the late 1960s and continuing for several decades, highway construction projects in Akron were routed directly through Black communities. Under the banner of "urban renewal," Black communities that had already been redlined were labeled blighted and were displaced by three major projects in and around downtown Akron: Grant/Washington, Lane/Wooster, and Opportunity Park. These projects displaced significant portions of the Black population and disrupted stability for those who remained. During this time, the Innerbelt highway project contributed to these displacements but did very little to enhance traffic routes. A director of Planning and Urban Development called it a "blight removal" tool that "was literally a road to nowhere."[24] An Akron Department of Planning and Urban Renewal document from 1975 indicated that during the first two phases of the Innerbelt construction, 737 households were displaced.[25] Later construction phases increased this number. Other estimates suggest that about a dozen intact Black communities were destroyed. Black homeowners' property lost considerable value, the effects of which endure today. Whole swaths of Black homeowners found that their homes in fact depreciated over time, largely due to this urban renewal project. When similar transportation projects were considered in areas that were predominately white, such as Fairlawn, white communities were able to use their significant racial leverage to insist on relocation to other (majority Black) neighborhoods. These displacements pushed Black families westward into West Akron, which prompted white flight into the adjacent suburbs of Copley Township.[26]

SCHOOLS IN WEST AKRON AND COPLEY TOWNSHIP

Kelley Williams-Bolar repeatedly stated in court and in various media outlets that a significant catalyst for deciding to enroll her daughters in the Copley Township schools was her heightened concern over safety. According to Kelley, her Akron Public Housing Authority–subsidized apartment had been robbed several times. The last time was particularly disturbing, Williams-Bolar says, because it occurred during a school day when one of her daughters had almost stayed home from school. That last robbery was cited by Williams-Bolar as a significant factor in her decision to enroll the girls in the Copley Township school and they would be watched by their grandfather after school. Williams-Bolar's attorney described her neighborhood this way during the trial: "During the daytime, it's a pretty nice-looking neighborhood," O'Brien said. "But she doesn't find out until she's living there for a while that, once the sun goes down, look out! There's gunfire. There's home break-ins." During the first two years Williams-Bolar lived there, from 2004 to 2006, O'Brien said, she filed about a dozen Akron police reports about neighborhood violence "and strange people being in and around her house."[27]

Before the frightening break-in, Kelley Williams-Bolar's daughters had attended Schumacher Elementary School and Litchfield Middle School in West Akron. These schools were pretty much polar opposites of the schools in Copley. Both Schumacher and Litchfield were highly racially segregated, were attended by children of families at or near the poverty line, and consistently ranked near the bottom of the state ranking system. Schumacher Elementary is ranked 3,272 out of 3,532; is 83 percent African American and 4 percent white; and 75 percent of the students qualify for free or reduced lunch. Litchfield Middle School is ranked 2,877 out of 3,532; is 63 percent African American and 21 percent white; and 63 percent of the students qualify for free or reduced lunch. Eighteen percent of the students at Litchfield have achieved math proficiency (as compared to the Ohio state average of 50 percent).[28]

In contrast, the two schools in Copley Township that Kelley's daughters briefly attended are both much more highly ranked and score far better on the key indicators of a highly performing school. Copley-Fairlawn Elementary is ranked 120 out of 3,532, and Arrowhead Primary School is 661 out of 3,532. The student populations are about 70 to 75 percent white and 9 to 14 percent African American. Fewer than 15 percent qualify for free or reduced lunch. Math and reading proficiency for Copley is in the top 20 percent and Arrowhead is in the top 5 percent.[29]

How far apart physically are the Copley schools from where Kelley lived in West Akron? Two miles. Kelley wasn't driving her daughters long distances to district hop; she drove a shorter distance to Copley schools than I have ever driven from home to a "local" grocery store.

And yet, the schools are worlds apart in access to resources and funding, overall ranking, reading and math levels, and proportion of students struggling with the effects of poverty and racism. Two worlds right next door to each other; one community flourishes, while the other struggles with joblessness, high poverty, lower budgets for student education, lower property values, aggressive policing, and so on. As different as each is from the other, they share the same roots; both worlds are created relationally by systemic racism. The boundaries of the districts were designed to produce these stark differences. An EdBuild.com report, "Fault Lines," puts it this way: "When a high-need district is next-door to a much better-off school system, it is clear that the area has the capacity to do better by its neediest children— but is isolating them instead."[30] One of the most effective ways to maintain these segregated arrangements is the substantial use of property taxes to fund public school budgets.

PROPERTY TAX–FUNDED PUBLIC SCHOOLS

Local property taxes are a primary funding source for public schools in most states. On average, states raise a third of their public school revenue through property taxes, though for some states this figure is much higher, like Connecticut at 61 percent and New Hampshire at 55 percent.[31] These taxes support school expenses and educational resources, from facilities maintenance and building construction to classroom resources, enrichment opportunities like technology, and teacher salaries.

Property tax school funding is allocated based on the property values within a given school district. The size of school districts in the United States varies considerably, ranging from massive districts that encompass hundreds of schools to small, fragmented districts including relatively few schools. In many cases, school district boundaries do not follow clear city, county, or neighborhood lines. The placement of school district boundaries often has the effect of consolidating the benefits of high property tax revenue in some areas and consolidating the disadvantages of low property tax revenue in others.[32]

The use of property taxes to fund schools, along with the consolidation of resources in certain districts, perpetuates major disparities in educational funding. Schools in districts that have higher property values generate more property tax income, which enables them to execute higher educational budgets. Schools in districts with fewer homeowners and less valuable homes generate less property tax income, and therefore smaller educational budgets.[33]

Black communities receive significantly lower public educational funding than white communities. A 2019 study found that school districts that predominantly serve children of color continue to receive $23 billion less in funding than predominantly white school districts that serve an equal number of students.[34] Key findings from the Century Foundation study show that districts with higher than 50 percent Black or Latinx students face an average annual funding gap of more than $5,000 per student.[35] This gap in property tax resources arises from a long history of redlining, segregation, gerrymandered districting, and economic inequality and reduces the available funds for school resources, teacher salaries, and educational opportunity in Black communities.

The long legacy of housing discrimination against Black Americans has resulted in property values in Black neighborhoods being artificially repressed. Homes in these neighborhoods often have lower market values and appreciate less over time and, in fact, are far more likely to depreciate over time. On the whole, therefore, school districts that serve Black communities tend to have much lower property tax revenue at their disposal.

Disparities in school funding based on property taxes have been determined by the creation of racially segregated school districts. "Gerrymandered" school districting generally separates wealthy white areas from adjacent poor areas with large populations of people of color, thus sequestering elevated property tax revenue within white and more prosperous communities. A 2019 study found that across nearly one thousand American school districts that had substantially different racial makeup and revenue from their neighbors, the average district on the whiter, wealthier side of the line received more than $4,000 more funding per student annually than the district with fewer resources and more students of color. For 132 borders that marked at least a 20 percent difference in revenue and a 50-percentage-point difference in race, the average disparity was more than $6,500 per student. There are 8.9 million students in the disadvantaged school districts this study tracked, making one in five of American public schoolchildren a victim of these gerrymandered funding inequalities.[36] This means that by allowing property taxes to play such an instrumental role in determining school budgets, society reinforces and endorses the disproportionate economic advantages expressly created for white homeowners in white communities.

The use of local property taxes to fund public schooling is widely viewed as a key element in the maintenance of unequal educational spending and opportunities based on class and race nationwide. Towns with excellent and well-funded schools are closely aligned with towns that have higher property values, thus cementing both additional educational and financial resources for wealthier homeowners and their children. Children who live in towns and districts where property values are higher have access to schools where families with higher incomes can use these resources to enrich learning, sports, and other student success support networks.[37] The system of property tax–dependent education largely supports and reinforces wealth and income advantages for whites and enables what Robert Reich describes as "the secession of the successful" from civic life: "In many cities and towns, the wealthy have in effect withdrawn their dollars from the support of public services and institutions shared by all and dedicated the savings to their own private services."[38]

This systemic problem is central to the Kelley Williams-Bolar case. At the heart of Copley Township's justification for aggressively prosecuting Kelley Williams-Bolar for falsifying residency records is that doing so gave her daughters "unauthorized" access to free, very well-funded, public Copley Township schools. But exactly how "unauthorized" was her access?

To understand the way systemic racism in public schooling in Ohio shapes this story and what makes the prosecution of Kelley and her father particularly disturbing, we have to dig into the weeds of how Copley and other wealthy districts used their influence to evade multiple Ohio Supreme Court rulings that demanded the end of the use of property taxes to fund public schools on the grounds that they created a fundamentally unequal education system. The takeaway is that if the Ohio State Supreme Court rulings had been strictly implemented, if the law had actually been followed, then Kelley Williams-Bolar's daughters would have been allowed to freely attend any schools they wished in the state of Ohio, including Copley schools. But how those with the power to do so prevent the law of the land from being implemented and get away with preserving their advantages requires that we go beneath the surface. This is a master class in how systemic racism works. Remember, "the devil is in the details"!

"OPTING OUT" OF EDUCATIONAL EQUITY

Ohio's property tax–based educational funding system was deemed unconstitutional by the State Supreme Court of Ohio in a series of cases, *DeRolph v. Ohio*, I, II, III, IV, and V, over the course of the 1990s. The first *DeRolph* case was filed in 1991, spanned over a decade of legal debate, and produced four Supreme Court decisions. The court continued to reiterate that the Ohio funding system was unconstitutional and systematically flawed, particularly because its overreliance on property taxes created an imbalanced system that did not provide equal education in a "thorough and efficient manner." The court issued instructions to the Ohio General Assembly to create a new statewide system of funding.[39] This ruling has largely been resisted and ignored. Education scholar Sandra McKinley describes the ongoing resistance to the court's rulings and instructions as having created a *"state of siege where the mandates of the court have been ignored. . . . In short, the rule of law had not been obeyed in terms of enforcement of a remedy under DeRolph, yet, the system had been declared unconstitutional no less than four times"* (emphasis mine).[40]

Despite the multiple Ohio Supreme Court decisions that declared this funding system unconstitutional and thus outlawed this practice, Ohio continues to rely heavily on property taxes to fund education. School funding in Ohio is nearly evenly split between state funds and local taxpayer funds, each contributing 46 percent of the overall school budget, with the remaining 8 percent coming from the federal government. Allocations are determined mainly by a cost-per-student figure called the "foundation" amount. This amount is provided to districts based on the number of students enrolled in the district. In 2009, the foundation amount was $5,732 per student. According to the organization School Funding Matters, "Ohio's aid formula assigns a responsibility to each local school district to pay a portion of the foundation amount. Generally, this local share equals the amount of money that the school district would raise with a 23 mill (2.3% property tax).[41] This amount will vary from district to district depending on property values."[42] This funding system creates wide disparities between property value–rich districts and those with lower property values. In fact, for those districts with high property values and thus with high property taxes, their local share based on 2.3 percent of those districts' property tax might exceed the foundation amount they would receive from the state. In other words, the amount these wealthy districts contribute would be higher than the state "foundation" amount. This means wealthy districts would owe the state money.

During this standoff, some legislators attempted to create greater access to a wider range of schools across districts for Ohio's children by establishing the Ohio Department of Education statewide open enrollment program, which "allows a student to attend school tuition free in a district other than the district where his or her parents reside."[43] This policy does not reduce or end property-tax school funding, but it does enable more access to a range of schools by legalizing the flow of students between schools across districts. However, the fundamental concept of "open enrollment" has been undermined by the creation of an "opt out" loophole. Towns can opt out of the open enrollment system and bar students who live beyond the district's boundaries from attending unless they pay tuition. Of the 663 school districts in Ohio, 429 have open enrollment, 144 have opted out of the open enrollment program, and 90 have an "adjacent districts only" policy for accepting out-of-district students tuition-free. According to the Ohio Department of Education, nearly a third of all public schools in Ohio have opted out, in all or in part, of the open enrollment program. Copley Township was one of the towns that had chosen to opt out.

The opt-out loophole is most valuable for property-rich towns as it allows such towns to retain the advantages of existing property tax–based funding. Copley-Fairlawn's tax base is so asset rich that if they contributed their 2.3 percent property tax to the foundation formula, it would override the state/district shared resource-allocation program and require them to reimburse state funds. The *Fairlawn-Bath Patch*, a local internet newsletter, published an article defending Copley-Fairlawn's decision to opt out of the open enrollment with the following argument:

> The Copley-Fairlawn School District has rational (and non-racist) reasons for refusing to offer open enrollment. Copley-Fairlawn schools have real and practical reasons for opting out of open enrollment. Ohio's school funding formula

provides money to each district based on the number of students enrolled, then deducts from that allocation a local share calculated from the local tax base. The tax base in the Copley-Fairlawn district is *so valuable that the local share is greater than the state allocation would be. If the formula were strictly followed, the school would owe the state money.* Instead, the state provides to the district a flat guaranteed allocation. But when the district on the guarantee (allocation) gains students, it does not receive additional funds. So while most districts gain state money when enrollment increases, a district like Copley-Fairlawn gains only expenses without additional money to offset those expenses.[44] (emphasis mine)

By opting out, the Copley Township district pockets its flat guaranteed allocation from the state. And because it does not receive the funds for its student enrollment, new enrollments do not generate additional state funds for the district. Thus, the district saves its property tax–generated funds that would otherwise be due to the state based on the funding formula. The opt-out loophole entitles wealthy districts to continue to receive state funds that augment their own education budgets, but permits them to avoid returning anything to the state for the privilege of hoarding higher tax-bracket-based educational funds. Once the opt-out provision is exercised by some districts, it creates a higher demand for better schools in property tax–rich districts that do not opt out. In turn, this may encourage the districts that experience a higher influx of students from other districts to join the ranks of districts that close their schools to students outside the district. The open-enrollment program maintains the appearance of open exchange of students across class and racially bounded districts, while the opt-out loophole in open enrollment allows those districts with the greatest assets and wealth to retain their most important privileges.

Copley-Fairlawn defended their decision to opt out by interpreting this substantial advantage as a disadvantage: if Copley Township and Fairlawn didn't opt out, they would have expenses without additional resources if and when "outside" students enrolled. School superintendent Brian Poe confirms this logic: "And if we have two more students or five more students that come to us, we don't receive any additional state funds for that. Our state funds are set per year. And so, if two, five or ten more students come to us, we don't get an increase in those funds."[45] This rationale makes it look like they are just "playing by the rules" when in fact, they have rigged them in their favor. Their ability to save and control locally what should be their proper contribution to the cost to educate all children in Ohio is brushed to the side along with the advantages resulting from racially financed support from banks and the federal government. Superintendent Poe puts it this way: "If you're paying taxes on a home here . . . those dollars need to stay home with our students."[46]

The local newsletter describes the town's decision as "rational (and non-racist)." But as we have seen over the course of the preceding chapters, systemic racism creates "rational" behavior that generates racist outcomes without saying anything about race at all. Poe and the local newsletter are invoking an implicitly racialized "defensive localism" that allows the residents of Copley Township to defend its accumulated privilege on embedded racial terms while appearing completely absent of racial motivation. The basis of this "defensive localism" is constructed as "rational" and even virtuous because it saves the district money while providing excellent education to its children. Yet the wealth, property, and other material and social rewards the town benefits from and is adamant to protect were gained through racially discriminatory forces. The language of community preservation replaces any explicit talk of race, even though the boundaries of community and the resources being protected are themselves significantly based on race. Implicit in the defense mounted by Superintendent Poe and other supporters of the town's opt-out decision were the unquestioned assumption and the "right" to defend racial advantages and privileges as if they were entirely "earned." This logic, in turn, self-interestedly distorts as "disadvantage" the very advantages white communities hoard by refusing to share those same advantages with others. Why should their taxes help other people's children? Perhaps because other people's parents' economic disadvantages based on race fueled and funded their children's advantages?

Residents and officials of Copley Township can openly discuss this rationale in what they claim are purely financial terms while ignoring, yet simultaneously benefiting from, the racialized consolidation of resources they seek to protect. It supports a system that is set up to produce and maintain racial privilege in the form of economic rationalism. As George Lipsitz explains, the maintenance of racialized space allows "the advocates of expressly racist policies to disavow any racial intent. They speak on behalf of whiteness and its accumulated privileges and immunities, but rather than having to speak as whites, they protect themselves as racially unmarked home-owners, citizens, and taxpayers whose preferred policies just happen to sustain white privilege and power."[47]

WHY DON'T YOU MOVE TO COPLEY?

To suggest that racism played no role in the case or in the judge's ruling, officials and their defenders have argued that Williams-Bolar had the "option" to move into the district. Many bitter online retorts to articles picked up this point, claiming that Williams-Bolar's seeming unwillingness to move into the district proved that her goal was to defraud the district.

Could Williams-Bolar have simply relocated to Copley Township? Given the prevalence of significant discrimination against African Americans seeking apartment rentals in pre-dominantly white areas, this would certainly have been diffi-cult. But even if we set this obstacle aside, economic and racial segregation is maintained by zoning and other policies that block construction of rental units and affordable housing in the first place.[48] A map of the locations of the Akron Metro-politan Housing Authority (AMHA) public housing buildings shows no public housing in Copley or Fairlawn but shows sev-eral public housing buildings in West Akron—an area that is over 85 percent Black. For voucher-supported privately owned apartments like Kelley's, the AMHA lists 127 possible hous-ing voucher apartments priced between $400 and $800 per month in the West Akron neighborhood, while Fairlawn listed 3 and Copley listed only 1 available unit. The monthly rental price for the Fairlawn apartment was $1,300, a full 62.5 percent higher than the highest-listed apartment in West Akron.

As a divorced, single mother of two young girls, Williams-Bolar relied on her father to help her with after-school childcare while she worked. Critics, however, viewed her as a selfish mother for having her father so involved in the care of his grandchildren. Notwithstanding the upside-down logic this critique represents—family networks of care are consistently idealized over paid childcare—access to affordable and high-quality paid childcare is limited, especially for nonwhite parents in low-income communities. According to childcare experts Edward Zigler and Katherine W. Marsland, "Formal child care is less frequently available in low income neighborhoods, and informal care may be less readily available than previously thought. A 1995 study found that nearly two thirds of families receiving welfare had no friend or relative who could provide child care and that their access to formal arrangements was limited by cost and transportation."[49] The larger context of hyperpunishment places these families at much higher risk for state surveillance and punishment. Dorothy Roberts's book *Torn Apart* demonstrates that child welfare services are actually "family policing" units designed to hypersurveil Black families, disproportionately separating children from families, placing them in foster care, and driving many to juvenile detention and prison.[50]

Kelley Williams-Bolar initially contested the charges leveled against her by submitting a grandparent power of attorney (POA) on the grounds that she and her father shared parenting duties. This POA was rejected by the district and

then subsequently by a judge who upheld the district's decision. While other factors may have played a role in the court's
decision, researchers have shown that when a child's family
structure or living arrangements do not square with the idealized nuclear family (e.g., a family headed and controlled by two
parents in a single dwelling), this can influence legal decisions
related to defining "home," such as determining legal custody,
shared parenting, and residency requirements. The nuclear family ideal holds a great deal of sway in the American imagination, despite the fact that, in reality, many children are cared for
by a network of caregivers; children regularly shuttle between
parents, relatives, and paid childcare workers. As legal scholar
LaToya Baldwin Clark notes, by "refusing to consider other
family forms as sufficient to establish residence—residency
requirements not only impede access to educational resources
for those who are most in need but also entrench a race-class-
gender-specific ideal of the family and ignore the reality of how
many families actually function."[51]

REMORSELESS WELFARE QUEENS

The stigmas associated with single-female-headed households are especially severe for lower-income Black single
mothers. Public opinion continues to rely on the Ronald
Reagan–spawned myth of the Black "welfare queen," resulting
in Black mothers on public assistance often being viewed as
scam artists who use their children to illegally obtain money
and services from the state.[52] Not only are Black mothers on
assistance criminalized but their economic and social fragility

is reimagined as advantage. This myth turns Black vulnerability on its head. As Jordan-Zachary notes, "Welfare use no longer represents a state of poverty, but rather, a life of luxury."[53] This explains how an online critic, quoted earlier in this chapter, can come to the conclusion that Williams-Bolar's access to "perks" like public housing should be revoked.[54]

Many supporters of the prosecution of the Summit County Prosecutor's Office and the policies of the Copley Township School Board used language heavily associated with the long-standing story/narrative of Black criminality, reinforcing the notion that Black people represent the undeserving poor, and that poor Black mothers game the system for personal gain.[55] Foxnews.com issued stories with headlines like "Education Scam Gives Ohio Woman a Lesson in Jail Time," furthering the state perception of Williams-Bolar as a cheater who deserves her comeuppance. The presiding judge, Patricia Cosgrove, made explicit her desire to punish Williams-Bolar in order to deter other potential wrongdoers. She said: "I felt that some punishment or deterrent was needed for other individuals who might think to defraud the various school districts."[56] Punishment aimed to serve as a deterrence plays a significant role in justifying higher sentencing for Blacks, and avoiding application of similar hyperpunishment for whites, who can be treated as individuals rather than exemplars of criminality. Judge Cosgrove's comment is also notable for her reference to the potential threat of defrauding "the various school districts," which suggests that she was concerned with protecting not only Copley Township but also those districts that had chosen to opt out of open enrollment. "Deterrence" only makes sense in the context of protecting the privileges of the higher-property-tax districts that the legal opt-out loophole also enabled. This justification by Judge Cosgrove is contradicted by the fact that the Copley-Fairlawn district elected not to punish the Ebners, "a White family that switched houses with extended family members to enroll their children in the same Copley-Fairlawn district that expelled Williams-Bolar's daughters."[57]

Prosecutor Walsh created a special "Williams-Bolar Frequently Asked Questions" link on the Summit County Prosecutor website. The answers to these "frequently asked questions" all revolve around explaining and justifying the charges and the decision to prosecute the case as a felony. For example, government records tampering is deemed by state law to be a felony, but in practice the crime is often reduced to a misdemeanor. The charges were not reduced in Williams-Bolar's case. Walsh provides a lengthy explanation for the decision not to reduce the charges in this case, emphasizing two key reasons:

> 1) If there is evidence to support a felony charge but there are concerns that a jury might not convict. For example, when a key witness is not cooperating or has disappeared.

> 2) There is sufficient evidence to support the felony charge but the defendant has no prior felony record, has expressed remorse for her conduct, and has accepted responsibility for her conduct. Also, in a theft case, we consider the efforts or desire to repay the money (County of Summit).

Walsh's justification suggests that she is not concerned with needing more evidence or problems convincing a jury. Rather than request more evidence or take into consideration that Williams-Bolar had no prior felony record—two actions that Ohio law permits as justification for a reduced charge and/or sentence—Walsh presents the decision to prosecute as hinging entirely on the prosecutor's judgments about Williams-Bolar's supposed lack of remorse, her refusal to accept responsibility, and her unwillingness to repay the money:

> Ms. Williams-Bolar had no prior felony record. However, at no time did she express remorse or accept responsibility for her actions. Nor did she agree to make any restitution for her crimes (a payment plan was offered numerous times). In fact, her behavior was the exact opposite. She knowingly and repeatedly violated the law. She ignored all requests and attempts to resolve her crime with the school system unlike the other families who were similarly situated and chose to do the right thing. A prosecutor cannot, in good conscience and in fairness to all law abiding citizens, offer a "plea bargain" to a person who has no regard for the law.[58]

Walsh's defense of her refusal to offer Williams-Bolar a plea bargain—her intransigence and consequent unworthiness—appears to differ from typical practice in criminal law. Prosecutorial discretion provides wide latitude for determining which crimes will be pursued, settled, or brought to a jury for criminal prosecution. Plea bargains are made for many reasons, even in the case of multiply convicted hardened criminals who have repeatedly shown a lack of regard for the laws that protect citizens from violence and harm.

Walsh's emphasis on demanding that Williams-Bolar express a desire to repay, show remorse, and take responsibility functions as a public and symbolic demand that Williams-Bolar display submission to the laws and rules that work to protect systemic racism. Walsh frames Williams-Bolar's rejection of payment plans without regard for her actual financial circumstances. Her attorney, David Singleton, said that at that point, Kelley was completely incapable of fulfilling the requirements of the payment plan that was offered.[59] The district had requested repayment of $6,895 tuition for each girl for each of the two years they had attended Copley Township schools—a total of $27,580. This figure amounts to well over a year and a half of Williams-Bolar's gross annual salary as a teacher's aide, a draconian penalty that would have been impossible for her to fulfill.

Nationwide, well-supported petitions strongly urged Governor John Kasich to grant clemency. Together, petitions from Change.org, MomsRising.org, and ColorofChange.org garnered over 180,000 signatures. These petitions were reinforced by Color of Change's follow-up telephone campaign in September 2011 to encourage Governor Kasich to pardon Williams-Bolar. On September 7, 2011, despite a unanimous recommendation by the Ohio parole board to deny Williams-Bolar a pardon, Governor Kasich used his executive clemency to override authority to reduce the felony charges to first-degree misdemeanors. He deemed the penalty "excessive for the offense" and publicly thanked all petition signers.

Still, he took the opportunity to carefully couch his decision in terms amenable to a law-and-order mandate, defending the current system and the laws that protect it by stressing that "no one should interpret this as a pass—it's a second chance."[60]

Advocates were successful in mobilizing public pressure to win a significant reduction in Williams-Bolar's charges from felonies to misdemeanors. This achievement made an enormous difference in Kelley Williams-Bolar's life—and in the life of her daughters, too—as a felony conviction on her record would have severely limited her employment opportunities. For example, she would have been barred from receiving her teaching certificate and other licenses the state bars to felons. In the end, though, the compartmentalized single-issue framing of the story shaped the terms of her victory. Legally speaking, Williams-Bolar continued to be defined as a criminal parent, and systemic racism interconnections that significantly shaped her circumstances and options were legally invalidated and remained largely hidden from view.

Kelley Williams-Bolar dared to transgress a district school boundary that worked to contain her daughters in underperforming schools designed to extract opportunity rather than provide it. For this, she was heavily punished. Her decisions were inseparable from her concerns for her daughters' safety, caring afterschool supervision, and her desire for them to receive a great education at a school only two miles away from her home, yet technically out of reach. When the Ohio Supreme Court attempted to remedy the containment and extraction of Black students and their opportunities, a legally implemented loophole meant that the open enrollment mandate was compromised from the outset. And yet, at every turn, Copley denied that race played a role whatsoever. Kelley was consistently advised never to mention race or racism as being relevant in any way. Attorneys and other advisors warned her that to do so would likely turn sympathetic jurors against her. This, despite myriad interconnections between containing and extracting residential segregation, intentional creation of Black-concentrated poverty in West Akron, limited affordable childcare, the continued use of property taxes to fuel unequal school funding via opt-out work-arounds, and rigged, racially segregated district boundaries.

The interconnections that drive systemic racism may have left fingerprints all over this scene, but Kelley Williams-Bolar and many others like her continue to suffer the consequences. As we will see in the next chapter, even when the evidence of systemic racism becomes overwhelming, the system can still manage to evade detection as long as a scapegoat can be found.

5

MANNER OF WALKING ALONG ROADWAY

MICHAEL BROWN

EVERY TIME I PONDER THE DEATH OF EIGHTEEN-YEAR-old Michael Brown, I imagine the scene, which seemed oddly familiar to me, though for a long time I could not discern why. It was noon on a hot summer day in 2014 when Brown and his friend, Dorian Johnson, were walking down the center of Canfield Drive. Canfield Drive is a twenty-five-mile-per-hour, narrow, local two-way street in Ferguson, Missouri, with narrow, broken, and uneven sidewalks. The pedestrian walkway on Canfield, and in many other parts of Ferguson, is narrow enough that two larger adults would have to touch shoulders to remain on the sidewalk and not be forced to walk in the grass.[1] Both sides of the street are lined with low-rise apartments. Michael lived on Canfield Drive, and his home was just up the road. He did not make it home, however, because Officer Darren Wilson shot and killed him.

That eerie sense of familiarity accompanied the scene every time I thought of it. The reason why didn't occur to me until I impulse-watched the movie *Good Boys*, a 2019 comedy about a posse of friends traversing various middle-class settings on a quest that involves a series of comically rendered criminal acts. The film features its "good boys" in a range of typical white suburban antics. At one point they try to cross a high-speed, two-way highway after one of the characters steals some liquor from a corner store while a policeman looks on kindly and knowingly. All the while, the main plotline plays out and the boys scheme to steal back some drugs from a few older teenage girls. For the entire movie, the boys are presented as harmless—just boys "coming of age." Then it hit me—a scene with boys riding their bikes three-across, clear down the center of a two-way suburban road in swagger-enhancing slow motion. This is a signature trope in the familiar American male coming-of-age story. A small group of boys using their familiar neighborhood street as a place to practice that hallmark strut that signifies their transition to manhood. I recalled the iconic image of James Dean strolling up the middle of 68th Street in New York City and realized that my imagined vision of Brown and Johnson fell in line with these fictitious, idealized visions of young American boys to men, sometimes comic, other times rebellious, or a bit of both, struggling to grow up and claim their place in society.

The script for Michael Brown and Dorian Johnson was different. While strutting down the street, blocks from home, they were noticed by a cop—not the friendly variety, but an officer named Darren Wilson. Wilson drove his squad car parallel to the boys and admonished them to "get the fuck on the sidewalk." When they didn't immediately comply, Wilson pulled his patrol car ahead of them aggressively to block their path. Wilson initially tried to open his car door and reached out of the window to grab Brown by the throat. After a scuffle, the details of which are disputed, Wilson shot through the open window of his cruiser and struck Brown. Both boys ran away, Johnson hiding behind a car and Brown running down the road. Wilson followed Brown on foot and fired a second shot, hitting the youth in the back, then ten more shots, hitting Brown six times total, twice in the head at close range. Other officers arrived and hustled Wilson away.[2]

For the next four hours, Michael Brown lay dead in the street, his blood running "in a wide ribbon several feet down the hill."[3] People living on Canfield Road and the surrounding community grew increasingly upset as Brown's lifeless body remained unattended, like a dead animal carcass. It was, in the words of Jelani Cobb, "an undignified wake."[4] The police apparently had the coordination and resources available to have rushed Wilson away from the scene, but no such sense of official speed and purpose attended to the teenager's dead body, nor to the immediate needs of his family, neighbors, and community. Under optimum conditions, leaving a human being lying dead in the street while a darkening rivulet of blood dries in the hot sun would be an egregious breach of professional protocol. In this case, however, many Ferguson residents considered the incident symptomatic of the hostile disrespect that characterized Black life in the city. As one observer noted, "Leaving him in the street this way says we can do this to you and make you look at it and there ain't nothing you can do about it."[5]

The first national new reports presented the official police explanation of events uncritically: "At a news conference on Sunday morning, the St. Louis County police chief, Jon Belmar, said that a man had been shot and killed after he had assaulted a police officer and the two had struggled over the officer's gun inside his patrol car. At least one shot was fired from inside the car, Chief Belmar said." Later, the *New York Times* quoted Chief Belmar as explaining that the confrontation was initiated by the officer who "approached Mr. Brown and another man." As the officer began to leave his vehicle, one of the men pushed the officer back into the car and "physically assaulted him, according to the police department's account."[6] At the same time, the Ferguson chief of police falsely stated that Brown was stopped because Wilson was looking for someone in connection with the theft of a handful of cigarillos from a local convenience store. This statement, which seemed designed to justify Officer Wilson's actions, had to be walked back later, when others reliably reported that Wilson did not know about the stolen cigarillos when he initiated the confrontation with the two young men.[7]

In the ensuing days, intense social media campaigns were followed by larger and more intense protests in Ferguson. The vigorous protests and the militaristic and terrifying police response forced the national media to begin reporting on the event. Media reports then began to shine a brighter light on the anger and frustration that had long been expressed by many Black people living in and around Ferguson and St. Louis. Residents said their complaints about violent and unjust treatment at the hands of police had fallen on deaf ears. Many Black residents who were interviewed by news media in the wake of the protests described the killing as a tragic and triggering example of a pattern of racial discrimination at the hands of the police. Their statements often sounded as if residents across the region had been living in something like an occupied military territory. Donnell Johnson, forty-four, a Black resident of North St. Louis County for twenty-five years and an Emerson Electric technician, said he had been pulled over by the police, without any pretext, more times than he could count and sometimes even roughed up. Thirty-one-year-old Belinda Tate said, "It's been hard and racist my whole life here. And it is not just Ferguson, it's the whole North County area. They just beat up, they kill Black people." Annie Caine, an African American woman in her sixties, said: "They arrest our boys and our men. It's set up that way and it's been that way for years."[8] Resident experiences were confirmed, in 2015, by a Department of Justice report. The investigation unearthed a coordinated and egregious discrimination system that is documented in a publicly available one-hundred-page report conducted by the Department of Justice under Attorney General Eric Holder. The report's official name is *Investigation of the Ferguson Police Department* and was released on March 4, 2015, seven months after Michael Brown's death.[9]

Police brutality is frequently the most visible face of systemic racism. Individual and community trauma and fear resulting from aggressive encounters with police often leave more official and identifiable scars than other elements of the system. It is much harder to see or describe what the scholar Rob Nixon calls "slow violence," the kind of violence that unfolds over time, gradually and often invisibly. In Ferguson, and in other towns and cities, the police did not operate as peacekeepers or public safety–driven crime stoppers. Instead, as discussed previously, police were given expanded discretion to liberally apply a pretext of "suspicion" and a non-evidence-based technique called Broken Windows policing to stop, frisk, ticket, and harass people. Racial profiling is also highly active during most Black people's initial point of contact with the police. The Ferguson report is an impressive documentation of the ways that a range of policies and practices related to law enforcement and the municipal courts created oppressive and discriminatory conditions. It exposed the workings of the kind of normalized daily violence that unfolds over time and shined light on some key interconnections that for years had negatively impacted Black people in Ferguson.

Continued activism and journalism led to more insights into Ferguson Police Department (FPD) behavior as well as reports on racial segregation and school quality. Even as evidence of interconnected facets of racism in Ferguson mounted, several factors prevented a more comprehensive picture and analysis of the system at work. First, most reporting remained relatively narrow in scope, focusing only on the police and municipal corruption, educational inequality, and segregation. Second, the focus was, for the most part, only on Ferguson. These limitations reduced the visibility of the larger social system of which Ferguson was a part. Ferguson was one small municipality in a county in which police and municipalities in surrounding majority Black towns deployed similarly abusive practices. School segregation and massive gaps in school quality were also present in these adjacent areas. In fact, similar practices have been documented in majority Black towns and cities around the country. Illuminating the many discriminatory patterns and consistent forms of racial profiling that connect Ferguson to regional and national practices allows us to see and analyze Darren Wilson's actions as part of a coherent, nationwide pattern of anti-Black systemic racism. Third, the isolated treatment of Ferguson turned the town into a scapegoat for systemic racism. Once so positioned, the town has paid the price for national racial sins.

Positioning Ferguson as an outlier draws our attention away from the regional and national systemic racism practices of which it is a part. Thus, the individual behavior story frame continued to play a dominant role in public discussions. As we saw with Trayvon Martin and Kelley Williams-Bolar, Michael Brown was frequently portrayed as a criminal. In his case, Brown was described as possessing menacing, superhuman strength. Under oath, Officer Darren Wilson portrayed him "as 'bulking up' with the impact of each bullet, as if 'Big Mike' were gaining in size and strength, not weakening and, inevitably, slowly dying."[10]

THE FERGUSON REPORT

The Ferguson report found that the targeting of Black citizens in Ferguson was a common police practice that went beyond the questionable legitimacy of the pattern of extensive stops. The aggressive stops were just the visible edge of a staggering, interlocking, and reinforcing network of abusive police practices. These included police racial profiling, harassment, threats, and the heavy-handed use of minor and non-public-safety-related, penalty-dense citations with financial and criminal consequences for Black citizens—a net from which it was nearly impossible for people to escape. What may have appeared from a distance to be an individual cop out of line, or a police force simply issuing legitimate tickets to maintain order, was shown by US Justice Department investigators to be a vast network of minor ordinances designed to ensnare the Black population in a largely unconstitutional system that operated to contain, extract maximum resources from, and punish them.

"Manner of Walking Along Roadway" is an order-maintenance misdemeanor that makes it a crime to walk in the street or to walk along the roadway in a way deemed subjectively problematic to an officer. Manner of Walking is the Ferguson ordinance that gave Officer Wilson the legal pretext to order Mike Brown and his friend to "get the fuck out of the street." This seemingly innocuous ordinance claims to ensure that people do not block a roadway or impede traffic. The language of the law is extremely vague, thereby maximizing police discretion to stop, interrogate, disrespectfully order/demand, and issue one or more tickets as they see fit.

Manner of Walking Along Roadway and Failure to Comply are two examples of a suite of fuzzily constructed, flexible ordinances that can be used in this way. These ordinances and others like them around the country (similar to Stop and Frisk) are widely used to "stop people, to implicate them in a crime, harass them or stop them from being in the area."[11] These order-maintenance offenses are "designed to regulate unwanted conduct, to move disfavored people in and out of certain places, and to give the police flexibility. . . . They target unpopular people and groups who are deemed unpleasant or inherently risky, not individuals who have harmed someone else or done something morally wrong."[12] The face of the ordinance is race neutral and the language is colorblind, yet its application in practice targets "disfavored people," a group that in Ferguson and other municipalities around the country means Black people. In Ferguson, where the population is 68 percent Black, African Americans accounted for 95 percent of individuals charged with Manner of Walking Along Roadway, and 94 percent of those charged with Failure to Comply.

Many people call the Manner of Walking Along Roadway charge "Walking Black." If you are Black and simply walking through space, the Manner of Walking ordinance serves as a pretext for being stopped and questioned. A thirty-year-old Ferguson resident, Kevin Seltzer, told the *Los Angeles Times* that people feared leaving their home to go to the store and not making it back. "They'll stalk you and stop you. They will say, 'Hey, what's your name? Got any warrants? Why are you strolling through the neighborhood? Come here, you look suspicious.'"[13]

Although many Ferguson residents had long complained about police harassment and the crushing debt and criminalization imposed on them by persistent ticketing, Michael Brown's death, the Ferguson protests, and the explosive report by the Department of Justice (DOJ) clarified a much deeper and interconnected discrimination system. As it turns out, the killing was not an isolated abuse of a single municipal ordinance by a solitary rogue cop. Instead, it was the tip of a massive iceberg of containment, extraction, and punishment.

Ferguson's vigorous issuance of fines and extreme fine schedule for minor citations were shaped significantly by the city's focus on generating revenue versus ensuring public safety. Racial bias was evident in the overwhelming and disproportionate impact of law enforcement on African Americans, a reality corroborated by interviews with many citizens. The municipal court did not function as a neutral legal mediator of the law but rather used its power to pressure the payment of high fines and fees designed to advance the City's financial interests. The city's obsessive abuse of citations for budgetary gain motivated rather than prevented unlawful police conduct.

The aggressive use of citations to fill city coffers had, as the Ferguson report noted, "a profound effect on FPD's approach to law enforcement."[14] They measured police productivity—and therefore evaluations and promotions—by the number of citations issued. Citizens, especially African American citizens, were pervasively and intentionally perceived as potential offenders who, once cited, served as the means to meet financial performance goals, gain promotions, and provide the city with revenue. This rapacious behavior created a long-standing distrust of the Ferguson police by the public it was purportedly designed to serve and protect, resulting in "patterns of unnecessarily aggressive and at times unlawful policing; [which] reinforces the harm of discriminatory stereotypes; discourages a culture of accountability; and neglects community engagement."[15]

The DOJ report revealed multilayered, mutually reinforcing municipal and police practices and policies that worked at every stage of law enforcement and in multiple interactive ways to harass, criminalize, contain, and further impoverish Ferguson's citizens, especially its African American citizens. These interlaced practices operated at every point of interaction between law enforcement and Ferguson residents and were designed not only to generate revenue but to ensure that ticketed citizens would be constantly indebted, fearful of greater punishment, and thus contained. The driving mechanism for the system was the development and hyperenforcement of Ferguson's municipal fines and fee schedule.

MUNICIPAL FINES AND FEES

Municipal fines and fees are a system of monetary collection imposed on residents by municipalities. Municipal fines are monetary punishments imposed for infractions of local ordinances that are not considered severe enough to require jail time. They are compulsory and issued in response to a municipal ordinance violation or a misdemeanor charge, whether it be illegal parking, public intoxication, letting the grass grow too tall in one's yard, putting out unsecured trash bins, barbecuing in one's front yard, or, as mentioned above, one's manner of walking along a roadway. In contrast, "fees" are not technically intended to punish people for wrongdoing or illegal activity. Rather, they are intended to generate revenue by requiring residents to pay at certain points in an administrative legal process. For example, a fee might be attached as a Public Safety charge on a traffic ticket, or as a surcharge when a person is convicted of a crime.[16]

At the discretion of the municipal courts, overdue fines and fees can result in arrest and incarceration, especially if a person fails to appear in court when payment is due. A multitude of further charges can crop up, including fines for late payments and fees associated with arrest and incarceration. People who lack the resources to pay the initial fine or fee are penalized with more monetary charges that they still cannot pay, as well as a requirement to appear in court on specific inflexible days and times that may be difficult due to limited transportation and set work schedules. These people can subsequently be imprisoned or face an arrest warrant, thereby further cutting off their mobility and ability to keep a job, which makes them even less able to pay while, at the same time, late fees continue to compound and accumulate.[17] Government debt collection remains significantly underregulated, leaving many citizens who are subjected to excessive fees and aggressive tactics with little to no recourse.[18]

As some municipalities have increased their dependence on fines and fees, they have outsourced collection to private debt collectors. Because private collectors are not subjected to even the sparse laws that regulate government debt collection, they often employ more aggressive tactics and charge citizens astronomical fees for their collection services. In some cases, collectors add fees that more than double the original charge.[19] Private debt collection companies, although not technically law enforcement, are nonetheless often anointed with the power to issue arrest warrants or foreclosure lawsuits during the collection process. Thus, a sum that was initially issued as either a fine for a minor offense or an administrative fee for generating revenue can easily lead to incarceration and long-term debt for those who cannot afford to pay.[20]

FERGUSON FINES AND FEES: SQUEEZING "BLOOD FROM A TURNIP"

The leaders of Ferguson prioritized the maximization of revenue from fines and fees in consistent patterns over several years, with escalating annual goals to satisfy ever more ambitious revenue targets. Although Ferguson's population is roughly twenty-one thousand people, between 2010 and 2014, Ferguson issued approximately ninety thousand citations and summonses for municipal violations. In 2014, the city issued close to 50 percent more citations than they did in 2010, even though charges for serious offenses consistent with the municipal code remained relatively constant. The plans for "revenue growth" enabled by FPD citations were explicitly anticipated in the city budget. Ferguson budgeted for, reached, and continually heightened the goals for revenue increases by writing tickets and collecting fees and fines generated by them.

In 2010, the total budget for Ferguson was $11.07 million, $1.38 million of which was collected from fines and fees. By

How municipal fines and fees escalate, while simultaneously reducing a person's ability to pay them. *Graphics designed by Studio Rainwater.*

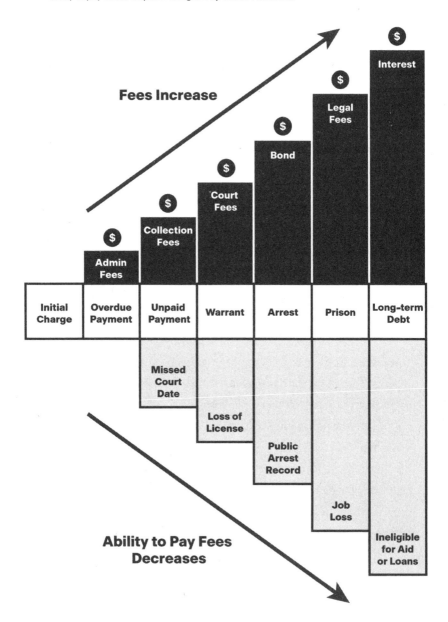

2013, the amount collected from fines and fees had risen to $2.11 million, and by 2015 the projected amount to be collected from fines and fees was $3.09 million. In five years, the dollar value of the revenue generated by collection of fines and fees increased by 124 percent ($1.71 million). Together, increases in the number of citations issued and revenue from those citations, along with new mandates for court appearance related to minor infractions, magnified the size of the court docket. Between 2009 and 2014, the number of traffic and non-traffic cases doubled. The increase in numbers of people needing to appear perversely exceeded the amount of time set aside to hear cases, which resulted in long lines and appearance dates stretching as far as six months after a ticket was issued.

The ongoing growth in budgetary projections based on issuing additional tickets created the need for more court staff, which encouraged the city manager to request new hires in court staff positions, which, the manager noted, "will be more than covered by the increase in revenues."[21]

Think about this for a minute. The city planned on issuing more tickets to grow the budget, which required more court staff to manage the larger volume of tickets and also required new court appearances that further increased the volume and value of fines and fees charged. It was a purposefully designed, cyclical, and self-fulfilling system of expanding the number of paid court positions to process court dockets, which in turn created pressure to expand city and FPD mandates to issue more tickets in order to grow the city's budget, which was structured to pay for the new court positions with citations.

At every stage of the enforcement process, Ferguson officials worked to squeeze the most revenue out of the people they fined. For example, the fine schedule in Ferguson was disproportionately high compared to that of surrounding municipalities, a fact that seemed to delight Ferguson officials. Ferguson's finance director drafted a report on maximizing collections that "favorably" compared Ferguson's fines with its neighbors, boasting that Ferguson's fines are "at or near the top of the list." For example, a citation for "Weeds/Tall Grass" cost as little as $5 in one area town, but ranged from $77 to $102 per citation in Ferguson. The fees were so high, in fact, that even a member of the Ferguson Police Department's command staff questioned the value of such high fines given the income of residents, quoting the old adage: "How can you get blood from a turnip?"[22]

Police were pressured intensely by both city and police leadership to meet citation "productivity" goals to fund the city budget. Not only were citation goals entirely unconnected to public safety concerns, but the pressure to meet current-year citation goals was connected to annual plans to explicitly increase collections. As the finance director noted in correspondence to Chief Thomas Jackson in March 2010: "Unless ticket writing ramps up significantly before the end of the year, it will be hard to significantly raise collections next year. What are your thoughts?"[23]

Municipal court practices in Ferguson disincentivized officials and staff to answer people's questions about or inability to pay fines and avoid extra fees. On the contrary, they "function[ed] to impede a person's ability to challenge or resolve a municipal charge, resulting in unnecessarily prolonged cases and an increased likelihood of running afoul of court requirements."[24] When citizens failed to meet such court requirements, the court imposed penalties that included additional fines and fees, as well as arrest warrants that, as the DOJ report emphasizes, actively contradicted public-safety objectives. The use of arrest warrants to secure collection when someone missed a payment or a required court appearance significantly compounded and increased the harm inflicted on Ferguson residents. As the DOJ report put it, "Once issued, arrest warrants can, and frequently do lead to arrest and time in jail, despite the fact that the underlying offense did not result in a penalty of imprisonment."[25]

The DOJ investigation found "overwhelming evidence of minor municipal code violations resulting in multiple arrests, jail time, and payments that exceed the cost of the original ticket many times over. One woman . . . received two parking tickets for a single violation in 2007 that originally totaled $151 plus fees. Over seven years later, she still owed Ferguson $541—after already paying $550 in fines and fees, having multiple arrest warrants issued against her, and being arrested and jailed on several occasions." In another case, a "90-year-old man had a warrant issued for his arrest after failing to timely pay the five citations FPD issued to him during a single traffic stop in 2013." A sixty-seven-year-old woman told the DOJ that "she was stopped and arrested for an outstanding warrant for failure to pay a trash-removal citation." The court charged the senior citizen, who was unaware of the warrant until her arrest, $1,000 in fines, which, because of her fixed income, she could only repay in $100 monthly increments.[26] Sometimes the court refused to accept partial payments at all, which resulted in additional fines and fees and provoked arrest warrants and the fees associated with those warrants.

Ferguson also liberally used the threat of arrest and jailing: "In 2013 alone, the court issued 9,000 warrants on cases stemming in large part from minor violations such as parking infractions, traffic tickets, or housing code violations. Jail time would be considered far too harsh a penalty for the great majority of these code violations, yet Ferguson's municipal court routinely issues warrants for people to be arrested and incarcerated for failing to timely pay related fines and fees."[27]

In addition to the disproportionate pedestrian and traffic stops, Ferguson increased its issuance of property violations in ways that continued the pattern of disproportionately targeting Black residents. Many of the property violations are mind-bendingly petty and fully lacking in criminal or rational justification, for example, leaving toys or wading pools in the front yard, playing in the street, having basketball hoops or barbecues in front yards, drinking alcohol within fifty feet of a grill including on one's own property, installing mismatched curtains, letting a pet dog pee on its owners' front lawn, and having individuals not listed on occupancy permits spend the night. Labeling such banal, family-centered activities "infractions" extracts from people the ordinary, joyful daily experiences of socializing comfortably with family and friends, playing, and feeling safe and in control of one's own privacy and home.

FERGUSON AND NORTH ST. LOUIS COUNTY

As shocking and extreme as Ferguson's system of policing, court practices, and municipal fining was, the city was not in any way an exception among its peers in St. Louis County. Scholar Jodi Rios conducted lengthy and detailed research on suburban St. Louis; her interviews and data collection showed that municipalities across the county had been practicing and refining similar operations for quite some time. Rios shows that, for years before Michael Brown's death galvanized Ferguson protests, in North St. Louis County, where the vast majority of St. Louis County's Black residents live, "residents consistently described a geography of local legal systems designed to criminalize and entrap people in a web of seemingly endless fines and fees for routine traffic and nontraffic ordinance violations that disproportionately impact poor Black residents."[28]

St. Louis County consists of eighty-eight towns and cities of vastly different sizes. Most Black residents are located in North St. Louis County, where forty-six of the eighty-eight municipalities are located.[29] Rios's chart of demographic, policing, and rates of poverty for all eighty-eight communities shows a county of highly segregated tracts, many of which are tiny hamlets with very few residents and encompassing less than half a square mile of space. Greendale, for example, is home to 651 people, .21 square miles in size, 69 percent Black, with an 18 percent poverty rate. Hanley Hills, with 2,101 people, is .36 square miles in size, 85 percent Black, with 26 percent of its residents living below the poverty line. Beverly Hills is miniscule, at .09 square miles in size, has 574 residents, is 93 percent

Black, with a 29 percent poverty rate. Her research also found that these small communities, with high Black populations and relatively high poverty rates, were significantly associated with municipal budgets funded by fines and fees issued against local residents.[30]

Rios's interviews with people who lived in or traveled through municipalities (other than Ferguson) in St. Louis County reveal the exceedingly harsh consequences of revenue-focused, racially discriminatory practices. A Black man from Hazelwood reported that he had "horrible experiences driving in North County." The police did not ticket him: "They just pulled me over and harassed me." A Black woman from University City was walking with her grandson to day care in their church in North County; the child was wearing rain boots. After dropping him off, the grandmother asked herself, "'What if he wants to play outside and needs his shoes instead of boots?' So [she] turned around in the church parking lot to return home and get his shoes." An observing police officer stopped her under the pretext that she had made a "sudden move." A Black woman from Vinita Terrace said: "My boyfriend used to come over and he would get tickets constantly for parking too often in the community. We went to court and they told us that he would continue to get tickets and he should stay in a hotel. We're still paying for those tickets. I wanted to do community service but I couldn't because I was working a job. . . . There's only certain hours you can do (community service)."[31]

North St. Louis County's patchwork of small-scale, segregated municipalities that share the practices of citizen surveillance and revenue-driving traffic violations often results in people being charged multiple citations for similar infractions over the course of a single journey. Rios recounts residents' experiences of being pulled over for a broken taillight or faulty muffler in one tiny municipality, and then "cross[ing] over into another [town] and in five seconds get[ting] the EXACT same [type of] ticket as you just did." Another tells: "In the county you can get pulled over almost every other day. I have tickets from municipalities I didn't even know existed. Turns out I was driving through five different towns when I thought it was all one—because they are literally the size of a football field."[32]

Activists dubbed the long and expensive journey resulting from these multiple mutually reinforcing municipal fine and fee practices "the muni shuffle." A legal aid group, the ArchCity Defenders, filed a lawsuit against Edmundson and its neighboring towns, claiming that they had "created a calculated and torturous cycle: By over-policing low-income communities of color, law enforcement is able to use excessive citations for minor traffic and municipal code violations, which are then followed by added charges and interest rates that poor residents cannot afford to pay. As those debts pile up, arrest warrants are autogenerated by the municipal court system. And so a person who failed to pay a fine for a broken taillight often ends up in jail because he or she could not pay the initial charge."[33] This lawsuit refers to behaviors that continued for five years after Michael Brown was killed, after the DOJ investigation of the Ferguson Police Department was published, and after the state and many St. Louis County leaders promised reforms.

SYSTEM REMINDER

As we saw earlier in this book, a system is an interdependent group of elements that are dynamically interconnected and coherently organized to achieve consistent, persistent, and stable patterns and outcomes over time. These effects are delayed and can reverberate at a distance. Metaeffects are effects produced not by a single practice but rather by many elements operating interconnectedly.[34]

The Department of Justice report on Ferguson provided clear evidence that the Ferguson Police Department's actions disproportionately impacted African Americans. While African Americans make up 67 percent of Ferguson's population, 2012–2014 records show that Black residents experienced 85 percent of vehicle stops and received 90 percent of citations, and made up 93 percent of arrests. African Americans were also much more likely to receive multiple citations during a single stop. From 2012 to 2014, "FPD issued four or more citations to African-Americans on seventy-three occasions, but issued four or more citations to non-African Americans only twice."[35] But these disparities paint only a surface portrait of the ways that FPD and the municipal courts created a system in which the risks to African Americans were heightened, mutually reinforced, and interconnected in ways that create metaeffects.

It is important to stress that metaeffects of systemic discrimination cannot be captured solely by calculating percentage of stops, citations, and arrests by race. Metaeffects are effects produced not by a single practice or element in a system but by the reciprocal and other kinds of interconnections in a system. How are people treated by police when stopped? What are the long-term health and material effects of frightening encounters with unjust displays of authority? What are the long-term economic effects caused by the interconnections between past forms of economic discrimination and the present? What are the microelements built into the system that work together to beat people down financially, emotionally, and spiritually?

Further findings presented in the Department of Justice report on Ferguson reveal some of the ways that meta-effects are embedded in a network of discriminatory practices. Not only are African Americans much more likely to be stopped, and more likely to be stopped for bogus, arbitrary, and questionable reasons, they are also much more likely to receive multiple citations during one stop. Black people are more likely to be issued bench warrants for unpaid fines and fees. These multiple citations and greater odds of bench warrants being issued generate economic and other effects. Being stopped and cited can be a frightening and traumatic experience, especially when such stops are arbitrary and hyper-punitive. Long-term consequences of various types flow from these encounters as well, including the financial, employment, and employability consequences of having a "record" and high levels of debt. The DOJ investigation revealed that "African-Americans made extraordinary efforts to pay off expensive tickets for minor, often unfairly charged violations despite systemic obstacles to resolving those tickets."[36] Black people in Ferguson were living every day, year after year, under the threats, fears, and economic precarity generated by these practices. Ferguson didn't just hand out extra tickets to Black people; the town leveraged the impact of extreme ticketing to concentrate and interconnect elements of punishment, extraction, containment, humiliation, and fear.

Municipal and law enforcement practices in Ferguson and North St. Louis County reflect a remarkably efficient racial discrimination system. The interconnections and interdependence among the system's parts disproportionately contain, extract resources from, and punish Black people. They contain people by generating fear of crossing boundaries—or even barbecuing in one's own front yard. They contain through surveillance, arrest, and extracting resources under threat—including loss of money, jobs, justice, and a sense of safety and security. They punish through threat, criminalization, force, and imprisonment.

White Ferguson residents defended Ferguson as a great town. They claimed that it was a town that didn't have racial "tensions," a town where whites labeled themselves as "colorblind." Many whites expressed shock about the protests and worried that all the bad publicity would reduce their property values. The mayor said: "There is no racial divide in this city," and he began an "I (heart) Ferguson" campaign to promote positive perception. Some residents, mainly white, expressed frustration that they were being singled out unfairly, noting that "this could have happened anywhere in America."[37]

Indeed, Ferguson and the surrounding North St. Louis County are not exceptions nationally. The defensive residents were correct: systemic racial discrimination and harm not only could have happened anywhere in America, it does happen. In North Sacramento, California, where Blacks are about 15 percent of the population, half of all jaywalking tickets are issued to Black residents. Black residents make up 29 percent of the population in Jacksonville, Florida, but account for 55 percent of all pedestrian tickets and 68 percent of all people who were issued tickets for "failing to cross the road at a right angle, or shortest route."[38] Municipal fines and fees form part of a nationwide misdemeanor system that Alexandra Natapoff describes as the "frontline mechanism" for ensnaring people of color in the criminal justice system: "It is here at the bottom of the pyramid that the criminal process first aims broadly at people of color, mostly Black men, arresting them for disorderly conduct, trespassing, drug possession, and other minor order-maintenance offenses."[39]

"THEY DON'T KNOW HOW TO ACT IN THE SUBURBS"

Ferguson city officials and the FPD consistently defended their enforcement practices, blaming Black people for bad behavior. The Ferguson report notes that the city officials and officers defended their practices and "nearly uniformly asserted that individuals' experiences when they become embroiled in Ferguson's municipal code enforcement are due not to any failings in Ferguson's law enforcement practices, but rather to those individuals' lack of personal responsibility."[40] The concept of "personal responsibility" is often invoked specifically to deflect criticism of unjust treatment and criminalization. This claim hearkens back to long-standing paternalistic racist beliefs that Black culture is "inferior" and requires correction and intensive policing to teach Black people how to behave properly because "they don't know how to act." The conditions of urban ghettoization, this logic goes, are a creation of Black people's "inferior" behaviors, not the product of systemic racism. So, when Black people move to Ferguson or Florissant from the urban ghettos of St. Louis, they bring their Black urban ways and need to "learn how to live in the suburbs" in order to make them "good," compliant suburban citizens.

The so-called moral underdevelopment of Black people, which lies at the core of the claim that they're incapable of taking personal responsibility unless guided—forcibly or otherwise—by whites, is a heavy anchor for the entrenched myth of Black inferiority. This has been used since the early development of racialized slavery to justify and normalize the enslavement and violent control of Black people. Slavery was, under this argument, an improvement, as it provided an opportunity for "civilization" through controlling, punishing, and extracting dehumanization. Prominent religious, political, and social leaders believed slavery was doing Black people a favor by helping advance an "inferior" people. The expression of this idea has evolved over time, but the core of the concept—that Black people are inferior and in need of control by whites—remains a potent source of denial of or justification for an evolving racial discrimination system today.[41]

In the aftermath of Michael Brown's death and the extensive protests and investigations that ensued, racist explanations regarding Black people's lack of "personal responsibility" were commonly emphasized—and rarely challenged publicly by people (municipal leaders, faith leaders, elected representatives, reporters, and others) in positions of authority. In so doing, public narratives directed attention away from the pattern of unjustified use of force exposed by the Ferguson report—and focused it instead on theories of Black incapacity and misbehavior: "They just don't know how to follow the law."

In a lengthy interview with Officer Darren Wilson in the *New Yorker*, Wilson rehashed this justification by claiming that "some Black people are wrapped up in the wrong culture, everyone has to start at the bottom and with personal initiative work their way up." In attempting to make the case for the notion that "good values should be learned at home," Wilson narrated a bizarre tale intended as a cautionary warning, in which the teenage children of a Black single mother who was physically disabled and blind, as Wilson put it, "ran wild," breaking into cars, shooting guns, dealing drugs—and then concluded that the children just didn't respect her. "They're so wrapped up in a different culture than— what I'm trying to say is, the right culture, the better one to pick from." When asked if the absence of jobs was the main problem in Ferguson, reporter Jake Halpern says Wilson responded this way: "'There's a lack of jobs everywhere,' he replied brusquely. 'But there's also a lack of initiative to get a job. You can lead a horse to water, but you can't make it drink.'" Wilson admitted that jobs available in Ferguson offered very low wages, but added, "That's how I started. You've got to start somewhere."[42] Embedded in Wilson's retort are several fallacious assumptions and myths:

* *People have the same or similar starting points in life.* In reality, white male advantages in the workplace, the

intergenerational resources secured by systemic white advantages, higher levels of white opportunity and white social networks combined with the absence of discrimination because of Wilson's race and gender belie an equal starting point.

+ *Starting "somewhere" is a sufficient, reliable path to upward mobility.* The presumption here is that if a person summons enough initiative, they will not only get a job but advance into better positions. Wilson started in low-wage positions, but now, here he is in Ferguson, having advanced into a job as a police officer. Wilson failed to mention that Ferguson is close to 70 percent Black with a fifty-four-person police force that includes only four Black officers. Why is Black citizen representation not paralleled in FPD officer composition? What factors contribute to hiring and promotion practices? Wilson skirts such matters.

+ *Lack of jobs is a problem equally felt "everywhere."* This is not the case. Nationwide, Black workers remain unemployed at twice the rate of white workers.[43] Job scarcity is not evenly distributed in all areas, nor are entry-level positions equal to one another. One of the hallmarks of segregated Black areas is an absence of jobs and the concurrent disproportionate number of dead-end, low-wage jobs. These conditions are further exacerbated by racial discrimination in hiring and additional hurdles that an arrest or low credit ratings confer.

‹ *Black people lack initiative, which explains the cavernous, disparate outcomes they experience.* This racist claim endures despite the many studies that show how white applicants, when compared to equally qualified Blacks, receive much higher percentages of callbacks for entry-level jobs. The advantage gap is so great that whites with a criminal record get called back for entry-level positions at the same rate as Black candidates without a criminal record.[44]

The claim that an absence of personal responsibility explains the racial gap is taken to extremes in *What Killed Mike Brown?*, a documentary film written and narrated by Black conservative Shelby Steele. In it, Steele argues that Mike Brown's death was not a symbol of racism in America but rather a symbol of the decline in Black personal responsibility, the downward trajectory of Black people's investment in their own "development." And that the Ferguson protests erupted because too many Black people are gripped by an inaccurate, "poetic" truth that relies on the tyranny of past racism rather than "objective" truth that racism no longer affects Black people's chances and that equal opportunity is available for those who really want to move up and succeed.

In the film, Steele interviews Bishop Giovanni Johnson, an African American minister identified as part of "Clergy Action During Ferguson Unrest." In the interview, Bishop Johnson conflates residents' concerns about fines and fees with a motivation for personal gain: "We want to know the real story from Mike Brown, we do. Everybody does, ok. But right now the story is, he shot my son. That's the story, ok. But here's the thing. It went from there to personal gain." Bishop Johnson later says, "The sum of stuff people be asking is unreasonable." When the off-camera interviewer asks, "Like what?" Johnson retorts: "We want you to expunge all our tickets!" Someone off-camera can be heard chuckling dismissively and sympathetically. Johnson mimics the protester in a way that makes this demand sound greedy and absurd. As if to say, is that all you can come up with to prove there is real racism today? Don't you have examples of real racism? Bishop Johnson continues, implying that the protester is demanding a free ride because he wants to avoid taking personal responsibility for paying tickets he deserved. In symbolic retort, Bishop says derisively: "This ain't got nothing to do with your ticket, this got something to do with a Black boy being killed!"[45]

Yet the evidence shows that tickets were indeed at the heart of the matter. The discrimination system in Ferguson was held together by an extreme use of ticketing, which served as the hook to extract, contain, and punish Black residents. Residents' and their supporters' outrage and activism were never just about Michael Brown. The intense protests resulting from Brown's death and his corpse being left in the street for four hours were about saying "No more!" to the traumatic, disrespectful, and financially crushing system of ticketing and criminalization under which Black people in Ferguson and surrounding St. Louis County communities had labored and lived for years. Brown's death became a symbol for a pervasive, relentless system of entrenched discrimination and a corrupt criminal justice system.

Some of the positive changes achieved by the protests in Ferguson included a new state law restricting the percentage of Ferguson revenue generated by court fines and fees to 12.5 percent of the budget, and the mandate that all fines and fees collected beyond this percentage were to be given to local schools. This meant that the municipal budget could not be expanded and used with unrestricted discretion to extract unlimited resources from residents at the expense of public services.

What happened after the new law was passed? Within a year, citations for traffic and non-traffic-related infractions dropped by 75 percent and 69 percent respectively for 2014–2015.[46] If the motivation for the volume of previous years' ticketing efforts was legitimate, why did the number drop so massively and precipitously? If we follow the standard explanation—that the level of fines and fees was justified because Black people didn't know how to act—I guess folks learned real quick.

"DO YOU KNOW HOW HARD IT WAS FOR ME TO GET HIM TO STAY IN SCHOOL AND GRADUATE?"

In the public storytelling battle over Michael Brown's innocence or guilt, his guilt was regularly suggested or confirmed by a photo of him raising his middle finger. A starkly different image of him was offered a few weeks later. In a picture of him taken just days prior to his fatal encounter with Darren Wilson, Brown is wearing a bright green high school graduation cap and gown with a red sash. Not only had Michael Brown graduated high school, but he was, according to his family, going to attend college in the fall.[47] High school graduation and admission to college: the hallmarks of a young person's achievement, upward momentum, opportunity, and promise. Yet neither his high school graduation nor the college to which Brown was admitted were designed to facilitate opportunity or upward mobility for him and his peers. Instead, they were both prime examples of how systemic racism extracts opportunity, promise, and resources. The story of his attending college and the difficulties his mother had finding ways to keep him interested relied on the illusion that his schools were the answer, when, in fact, they were a big part of the problem.

Spike Lee's documentary *NYC Epicenters 9/11→2021½* features a brief but unforgettable scene: gut-wrenching footage of Leslie McSpadden, Michael Brown's mother, standing in a small crowd only a few feet from the paved surface where her son was shot down. She is held upright mainly by the support of someone else's arms wrapped around her waist from behind. Speaking intensely and with palpable grief, she says to no one in particular—or perhaps to everyone, to all of us: "This was wrong, and that was cold-hearted. . . . You took my son away from me! You know how hard it was for me to get him to stay in school and graduate? You know how many Black men graduate? Not many!"[48]

In this raw moment of grief and loss, Michael Brown's mother connects her son's death directly to his fragile and precarious school experience—and the victory she'd believed his graduation from Normandy High School represented.

Getting one's children through school to graduation is, for many parents, an important but routine milestone, an achievement that lays basic groundwork on the way to larger, more important opportunities that a good education is expected to facilitate. For Leslie McSpadden, however, her son's graduation from high school was a nearly unattainable achievement, something that took incredible will and focus. Why? What was going on?

Normandy is a town adjacent to Ferguson with about five thousand residents. The population is 70 percent Black, while the public schools are closer to 90 percent Black. Nearly 25 percent of Normandy residents live below the poverty line.[49] The Normandy School District (NSD) serves students from a patchwork of small, predominantly Black municipalities with one high school, which Michael Brown attended, one middle school, and five elementary schools. In the year Michael Brown graduated from Normandy High, roughly 61 percent of the students graduated, compared to Missouri's overall high school graduation rate of 87 percent. Moreover, the Normandy district was, by nearly every standard, an abysmal failure.[50]

THIS IS NOT HYPERBOLE. THE MISSOURI DEPARTMENT OF Elementary and Secondary Education releases an annual report on the quality of education in each of the 520 school districts in the state. This report assigns points to criteria that measure the quality of education: academic achievement, graduation rates, and how well the school prepares students for college. The report released in 2014, the year in which Michael

Brown graduated, shows so few points for Normandy School District that it seems like a misprint:

Points for Academic Achievement in English = 0
Points for Academic Achievement in Math = 0
Points for Academic Achievement in Social Studies = 0
Points for Academic Achievement in Science = 0
Points for Academic Achievement in College Placement = 0

For eleven out of the thirteen measures, Normandy School District did not receive a single point. In fact, Normandy's entire score was 10 out of a possible 140 points.[51]

Normandy scored at the very bottom of the state's overall academic performance scale and was assigned with "provisional accreditation" status, which, as the name implies, was characterized as a probationary or temporary status. And yet Normandy District had been "on probation" for fifteen years running. In other words, there were students in the district who had proceeded from kindergarten to high school graduation—the entire scope of their early childhood through adolescence—without ever attending a school that met the state's accreditation standards for education.

Near the end of 2012, Normandy finally lost its "provisional accreditation" status. Two years earlier, in 2010, the State Board of Education decided to merge Normandy District with nearby Wellston District. Wellston School District had achieved failing status for the five previous years. Wellston's student body was 100 percent African American, with

98 percent qualifying for free lunch. The decision to join two segregated, meagerly funded, academically failing school districts serving children growing up in concentrated poverty contradicted all available evidence for environments that nurture student growth and build good schools.

Based on these abysmal failures and lack of investment toward any improvements whatsoever, angry parents logically concluded that Normandy School District was set up to fail. As Rios notes: "Given the overwhelming data regarding the performance of impoverished Black children in highly segregated and underfunded schools it is difficult to imagine that the board actually believed that combining two failing districts composed of poor Black children was going to improve the educational opportunities for the children involved or help the Normandy School District (NSD) reach accreditation. Many would later argue that the board was fully aware that the NSD would not survive the merger."[52] Dr. Stanton Lawrence, a former superintendent of the Normandy School District, said, "My understanding is that this has never happened anywhere else in the country. There was a much-higher performing district adjoining Wellstone, but there would have been an atomic explosion if the African American students had been sent to University City School District."[53]

Although its status was now officially "unaccredited," Normandy High School remained open. At the same time, the Missouri "transfer law" allowed students in an unaccredited district to attend an accredited school in a nearby district, with no fee charged to the transferring students or their families. The transfer law did, however, require the unaccredited school district to provide free transportation to only one district at a time, and it required the unaccredited district to pay the accredited district, on a per-student basis, for receiving and instructing transfer students. The transfer law allowed the receiving district to set tuition costs, which enabled those accredited districts to extract high fees from unaccredited districts.[54] For reasons that remain unexplained, the Missouri State Board of Education chose the high-performing Francis Howell District, with an 80 percent white student population and location thirty miles away, as the Normandy transfer district. The choice meant skipping over a similarly high-performing district just five miles away, for which transportation would have been far less costly for NSD to cover. Instead, NSD was required to pay both sixty-mile-per-day round-trip transportation costs and per-student fees, including tuition fees, to Francis Howell. Despite the lengthy journeys to and from school, four hundred of the one thousand students who transferred from Normandy to accredited schools signed up for the transfer to Francis Howell.[55]

While some parents and students at Francis Howell welcomed the students from Normandy, a great number, especially parents, were openly enraged and hostile. The transfer law did not allow them to reject Normandy students, whose presence was perceived as a threat to Francis Howell's children's safety, educational privileges, and well-being. Some parents suggested ways to discourage Normandy students from transferring by making it too difficult to get there, perhaps by "changing our school start times? Moving up start times . . . making it a little less appealing?"[56] Parents' outraged comments and demands deployed a complete palette of anti-Black racial fears, stereotypes, and negative associations—all without referring to Black people explicitly. Their response was, in many ways, a seminar on how to use the rhetorical power of colorblind racism to preserve racial advantages for one's own (white) children.

One mother, whose officially recorded comments were punctuated by wild cheering from her peers, demanded of district officials:

This is what I want to know from you. In one month, I send my three small children to you, and I want to know, is there going to be metal detectors? . . . We are talking about violent behavior that is coming in with my first-grader, my third-grader, and my middle schooler that I'm very worried about. And I want to know. You [referring to the elected school board] have no choice, like me. I want to know where the metal detectors are going to be, and I want to know where your drug sniffing dogs are going to be. And I want—this is what I want. I want the same security that Normandy gets when they walk through their school doors, and I want it here. And I want that security before my children walk into Francis Howell. Because I shopped for a school district. I deserve not to have to worry about my children getting stabbed, or taking a drug, or getting robbed. Because that's the issue. I don't care about the taxes.[57]

These white parents' reaction made crystal clear what Dr. Stanton Lawrence meant when he said he feared an "atomic explosion" should children from Normandy be permitted to attend predominantly white, accredited schools in other districts. The hearing displayed an entrenched sense of privilege and entitlement to hoard for their families alone their good schools, plentiful resources, and all the educational and social benefits that racial and racialized class segregation confers on whites. Despite impassioned claims that their concerns were not about race, Normandy students were painted with the brush of criminalized racial profiling: robbery, stabbings, drugs. In other comments, the presence of Black children was directly associated with a drop in school status and ranking. Some parents explicitly said that they would prefer and would choose to move out of the district immediately rather than share it with children from Normandy.

Because of the high tuition fees legally levied on Normandy by Francis Howell and other top-ranked school districts, combined with the legal cost of the lengthy journeys to and from school for one thousand motivated NSD pupils, it was not long before Normandy District was on the brink of bankruptcy. As Nikole Hannah-Jones reported: "By the fall of 2013, the impoverished Normandy District was sending more than $1 million a month to Whiter, wealthier ones. Back at the height of the St. Louis desegregation program in the 1980s, they had a term for this—Black gold."[58] Wealthier white school districts were given large sums of money, much of which was generated by unregulated tuition fees legally established by these districts.[59] Although the funds were nominally intended to cover the costs of the influx of out-of-district students, as of February 2014 receiving districts reported that this so-called Black gold was not being "spent on additional staff or other services to address any academic deficits of transfer students."[60]

During this time period, then, not only was Normandy paying high tuition costs extracted by Francis Howell and other districts, but it also had to maintain schools within its own unaccredited district, as well as cover the costs of the majority of the students who remained in NSD. Thus, the decision was taken to close a school and cut staff. District and Missouri state administrators then made a drastic move. The state assumed direct control of Normandy School District and renamed it the Normandy School Collaborative, which officially dissolved the former district and its unaccredited status. The new district was given an entirely new, as in "never-before-heard of," accreditation status: nonaccredited. Not un-accredited: nonaccredited.

Renaming the district and inventing its nonaccredited status out of thin air did not change the quality or performance level of Normandy schools. What it did achieve, however, was disqualification of the Normandy School Collaborative from participation in the transfer program. State-mandated transfer options were for unaccredited schools only. So now, by virtue of the district's new brand and accreditation status, Normandy students were no longer permitted to attend school in Francis Howell or in any other accredited, high-ranked district as part of the transfer program. Thus, the new status restored in full the segregated and profoundly unequal schooling arrangements that were so stridently demanded by Francis Howell parents at the public hearing. The one thousand transfer students who had been trying to get settled in and learn at Francis Howell and elsewhere all had to return to Normandy.

Education scholars have long argued that the emphasis on school performance gaps should be more accurately understood as opportunity gaps.[61] Schools that are fundamentally unequal in a negative sense should be expected to generate some degree of performance impairment. Impaired performance results from many causes, but especially from the absence of funding: the more money a school district spends on its students, the better those students perform academically.[62] Black students in underfunded schools miss out on the resources necessary for academic growth, social development, and achievement: high-quality teachers, rigorous curricula, advanced learning tools, mental health support, elective classes, environmentally safe outdoor play areas and sporting fields, afterschool programs, and so on. All these benefits are sacrificed when funding is inadequate.[63] Because of the way American communities fund public schools, in combination with the economic extraction segregated Black communities endure, reduced funding for Black schools consistently places Black students at an academic disadvantage compared to white students.[64]

To see what this resource disadvantage actually looks like at Normandy High School, we can look to reporting by St. Louis education reporter Elisa Crouch. She shadowed Normandy High honor student Cameron Hensley for a day in the spring of 2015, a few months shy of the first anniversary of Michael Brown's killing. Cameron remained at Normandy High, although many of his peers had transferred out. According to Crouch, this is what Hensley's day looked like: First period AP English was held in a science lab because the AP English classroom's ventilation system wasn't working and the mildew smell was prominent. The instructor in the room, who was not certified to teach AP English, came and left the classroom randomly throughout the period. The instructor handed Hensley and the one other AP English student a middle school–level worksheet that they completed in five minutes; after this, they were assigned nothing to do for the remaining forty minutes. The next period was jazz band, but there was no instructor or substitute teacher present. Hensley and Crouch headed down to the counselor's office (which Hensley said was the usual pattern since it was common for teachers not to show). Third period, physics, was taught by a permanent substitute who sat in a front corner of the room looking at her computer screen. Other students commented that this teacher "doesn't take attendance. No work at all. No intent to do any work."[65] The next period was precalculus, taught by a retired teacher who Crouch noted "does care and was teaching something."[66] After lunch there was choir and two periods of band. Such was the day in the life of an honor student at Normandy.

Black children in Missouri often receive poor instruction at poorly performing schools in poorly performing districts. In the St. Louis area, nearly one in two Black children attend schools that have been stripped of full accreditation by the state. In stark contrast, only one in twenty-five white students in Missouri live and go to public school in a poorly performing district.[67]

Is it reasonable to expect teenagers confronting this level of neglect and educational malfeasance to persevere, to remain committed to learning? Why have aspirations for the future when the path ahead is overrun by obstacles? The evidence shows that failure to graduate high school, even from schools as brazenly inadequate as Normandy High, increases the chances that a person will track to the school-to-prison pipeline. In the general population, about 18 percent lack a high school diploma. For those who are incarcerated, this number rises to 41 percent. Any high school diploma improves the odds of a student staying out of prison and increases the possibility of a better life for that student.[68]

Even though Michael Brown and his family lived in a town with a predatory and unregulated criminal justice system, his mother held on to the slim hope that if Michael graduated from high school, he would have a better chance. Graduating would improve his odds of avoiding the kind of future contact with the police that fuels the school-to-prison pipeline—and/or a future in which debts, fines, fees, arrest warrants, and the slow violence of economic extraction would overwhelm his day-to-day life.

Witnessing the realities of these odds for her son, I can understand why Leslie McSpadden drew such a swift and sharp connection between them "taking him from her" and how hard she had worked to keep him in school through high school graduation.

VATTER "ROT"

Michael Brown graduated high school and, as frequently mentioned in the media, he was scheduled to start college a week after he was killed.[69] The point was widely broadcast as another instance of individual lost promise. Of course Michael's death by a police bullet for Manner of Walking was a tragic loss for him and for his family. But what exactly was the "promise" of college for him? What kind of college was he going to attend? Michael Brown was headed to Vatterott Education Centers, a for-profit college with fifteen campuses in the Midwest. They specialized in culinary arts, automotive trades, allied health, and music production. Vatterott was perceived as an opportunity for a brighter future, when in fact it, and many other for-profit colleges, was yet another extracting and predatory feature of Black life.[70]

For-profit colleges emerged in the 1990s as an alternative for so-called nontraditional students who have families, jobs, or other responsibilities that make attending a residential, full-time, four-year college impossible. By 2010, the corporations that owned and operated these institutions began to be exposed for generating wild profits, earned not by fulfilling the educational needs of their students, but by exploiting the taxpayer-funded financial-aid system for student loans for private investor gain.

Many for-profit schools deployed aggressive and heavy-handed sales pitches featuring suspiciously exaggerated promises targeted to a vulnerable population. Key to their strategy was pressuring students into enrollment through promises of bright economic horizons and postgraduation career opportunities. Dangling false job placement rates and a fanciful future anchored by a stable, high-paying career was successful in motivating students to take out federally funded loans to pay for tuition. At for-profit colleges, 96 percent of students take out loans and owe an average of $40,000.[71] The healthy profits earned by these schools were almost entirely enabled by government-financed student loans taken out by students because of college sales pitches. Student loans paid to the schools converted to profit for the college owners and simultaneously became an albatross of debt for students. The more debt they could encourage students to take on, the more revenue and profits these schools made.[72]

Also central to the for-profit college business model was the targeting of prospective students who possessed big dreams alongside little to no pathway for upward mobility. Tressie McMillan Cottom describes it this way: "By their own description across various official documents, for-profit colleges rely on prospective students whose aspirations outstrip their available options for mobility."[73] These schools promised to create opportunity that the poverty and substandard school districts extracted. The promise required deception: the schools had to convince prospective students that a degree from the college was the key to higher wages, job prospects, and a secure future.

After receiving many complaints, in 2010 the federal government conducted an undercover investigation of fifteen for-profit colleges and found that all fifteen "made deceptive or otherwise questionable statements."[74] One school told potential students that barbers earned in the range of $250,000 a year (in reality, earnings are in the $35,000–$45,000 range). Another school was discovered to have lied nearly a thousand times about their job-placement rates. As for-profit college reputations suffered, students' degrees from those institutions were likewise tainted, leaving many formerly matriculated or now-graduated students facing a market with few, if any, marketable job skills. The situation left thousands of formerly optimistic students with student-loan due dates with little hope of ever earning enough to pay them. For-profit schools serve 10 percent of all students but account for half of all student loan defaults.[75] Many students with for-profit college degrees had lower earnings than before they enrolled.[76]

Vatterott College, the for-profit school to which Mike Brown was headed, was forced to close all fifteen of its campuses in 2018. Vatterott was cited for fraud, and its accreditation was revoked by the Accrediting Commission of Career Schools and Colleges, which ruled that the "school failed to demonstrate successful student achievement."[77]

Where can you find hungry, even desperate, "prospective students whose aspirations outstrip their available options for mobility"? In Black and Latinx communities. Researchers have found "that for-profit schools cluster in and around Black and Latinx neighborhoods, a stark contrast to their relatively thin presence in predominantly White neighborhoods." Zip codes that are predominantly Black on average host a far greater number of for-profit schools. Majority Black neighborhoods are over 75 percent more likely to have at least one for-profit school than communities that are not predominantly Black. The more densely Black, the greater the concentration of for-profit schools. Some communities are saturated with them.[78]

UNDERSTOOD IN THIS CONTEXT, THE NORMANDY PUBLIC school system was part of a larger system that disproportionately provides substandard education to Black children and preserves school and residential segregation. Black students are contained and consolidated in schools that drain or extract the drive to learn. In the meantime, the children in neighboring white municipalities are protected and provided with valuable educational resources and opportunities. Changes that might disrupt this arrangement are met with what Lawrence called an "atomic explosion"–level response by many white parents. The purpose of the transfer law was to free students enrolled in schools that failed to meet the standards for accreditation, to give them the opportunity to get a decent education. But, when this legal opportunity was seized by Normandy School District families, the new status of "nonaccredited" was created to push them back into Normandy. Vatterott College, and other for-profit schools like it, use a racially targeted extractive business model that preys on the hopes and dreams of young people who see few ways upward and saddles them with debt while offering few if any professional opportunities.

We cannot change what happened to Michael Brown. It can be painful, enraging, and dispiriting to examine up-close the system of indignities, obstacles, disrespect, and culture of containment, extraction, and punishment to which Michael Brown was subjected. But taking a walk in his shoes is a useful way to better understand how systemic factors working together placed him and so many others on a life path mirroring the treacherous, narrow, and unforgiving sidewalk on Canfield Drive where Michael Brown lived and was killed. Ferguson was not an outlier or an exception. Several Black towns in the largely segregated North St. Louis County and other municipalities around the country shared similar practices and conditions: the predatory use of fines and fees, Stop and Frisk, low-ranked schools with few resources, profit-predatory vocational colleges, and more—which together worked to contain, punish, and extract resources from Black people. When we consider what went wrong in Ferguson in the context of other Black towns and neighborhoods facing similar conditions, this gives us the insight and perspective to imagine a more comprehensive, systemic approach to change.

6

HOW WE
BREAK FREE

LEVERAGE POINTS FOR CHANGE

THIS BOOK BEGAN AS A TRAGICOMIC WISH.

Over the years I have spoken publicly on the subject of systemic racism to all kinds of people. My motivation largely derived from a desire to reveal and explain the depths and denial of what Black people confront—and lay bare the mechanisms that keep Black people "caught up in the system." As painful as it can be to be exposed to the staggering evidence of a network of policies and practices written and/or enforced in ways that maximize one's disadvantage, I have also witnessed how bringing it to light carries with it the healing power of recognition and validation. Recognition and validation are acutely important in a social climate that not only produces systemic racism but denies its existence and attempts to invalidate information and analysis that would reveal its impact. Beyond the material force generated by the system, the denial of its existence could be considered a form of racial gaslighting—a coercive effort to get Black people to question their own reality and perceptions.

The denial of systemic racism is not always consciously intended to cause harm. I have found myself in countless social settings in which I have been asked what project I am working on. Once I say "systemic racism," it usually takes only a couple of minutes before some kind of refusal is voiced—from the naïvely hopeful bromides such as "Well, things are getting better, right?" to the more assertive claims that "It's all this talk about race that causes the problem." I learned the hard way that there really isn't anything I could say in those brief social exchanges that would adequately explain the way systemic racism works and its metalevel impact on Black people. These are often frustrating conversations.

After one such event, I went home and half-jokingly said to my husband, "I wish there were a handbook on systemic racism. I could just hand it out and keep moving." "Why don't you write it?" he asked. I demurred, but the seed was planted. I started repeating this idea to friends, other family, students, and colleagues and—almost to a person—they said they would love to have such a handbook. People imagined how valuable such a tract would be in vexing situations where they felt their experiences with systemic racism went unseen, unheard, or rendered illegible. I'd hear things like "I'd give it to my uncle during the holidays!" or "I'd leave it in the mailboxes for my coworkers who keep telling me we live in a colorblind society!"

This book has argued that systemic racism is effective and difficult to see because it relies on an intricate network of policies that together generate metaracism. And this metaracism is obscured by the way we tell stories about racism: stories that focus on individual bad actors or chance encounters, as we saw with Trayvon Martin; or the single-issue approach that hides the multiple interlocking forces that shape the lives of people like Kelley Williams-Bolar; and finally, in the case of Michael Brown and Ferguson, the scapegoat strategy, where mounting evidence of systemic racism meant that the town was painted as an outlier rather than a vividly representative case of the larger set of conditions that shape society as a whole. Each of these stories deflects attention away from the vast interconnections that create systemic racism. For these and other reasons, making the system visible and replacing the paradigm that supports it are critical to the work of dismantling it.

We live in an era when it is almost impossible to avoid being traumatized by footage of police brutality. But before this era, in the times before the ability to produce and share high-quality video footage was in everyone's hands, it was nearly impossible to convince people who were not victims of, bystanders to, or witnesses to the kind of treatment that was going on every day in Black communities. I recall many fruitless conversations that somehow wound up at the pivot: "He must have done *something*." "Something" was the action that justified the beating, choking, and shooting. "Something" was the "evidence" that reinforced the story that the police were justified in their actions and denied that the brutality that we have now captured on video is a systemic feature of racialized policing in this country.

As much as I recoil from watching this footage, the accumulation and circulation of the documentation of police violence targeting Black people has helped change the story many whites and others have about police as a benevolent protective force for everyone. Taking place alongside these widely circulated images have been the tireless, innovative efforts of criminal justice activists, artists, filmmakers, and scholars who have exposed and drawn connections between the gross racial injustices that have defined every aspect of policing. The traumatic footage of Minneapolis officer Derek Chauvin kneeling on George Floyd's neck for nine and a half minutes while he repeatedly said he couldn't breathe, cried out for his mama, and eventually went limp was the tipping point. Many more people began to question the rationale that "He must have done *something*" and replaced it with "*Nothing* justified what I saw." New and compelling information, or the accumulation of observations that successfully challenge the story frame, can alter the meanings we ascribe to what we see. This is what happened during the summer of 2020 in the wake of the murder of George Floyd, when Black Lives Matter protests took place around the country and the world. In fact, some reports indicate that the June 2020 protests represent the largest protests in US history.[1] This sparked a provisional paradigm shift.[2] Maintaining a shift of this magnitude is a formidable challenge under most conditions, but it is especially difficult in the context of sustained backlash and countermovements designed to prevent change.

FINDING LEVERAGE POINTS

No one policy got us here, and no one policy will break us free. At the same time, it is impossible to tackle every single aspect or policy that drives the system all at once. Complex and vast systems are exceptionally difficult if not impossible to capture simultaneously. And, as systems change over time for all kinds of reasons (e.g., activism, adaptation, and other influential factors), there is no one permanent, perfect model that captures all the key elements, interconnections, or outcomes of a system. So where do we look? How do we alter a system so that it creates more of what we want and less of what we don't?

Although each system carries with it its own specific answers, the general advice from systems thinkers is to *find the system's leverage points*. Leverage points are, as Donella Meadows notes, "points of power." They are "places in the system where a small change could lead to a large shift in behavior."[3]

What are the leverage points that can reduce the impact of systemic racism? I am going to focus on three leverage points related to systems thinking: paradigm shifts, system interconnections, and reversing outcomes.

Shifting the Paradigm

Paradigm shifts are crucial for making change on the systems level.

A paradigm is a way of looking at something. It is a framework that contains the basic assumptions and ways of thinking that are commonly accepted. The paradigm we hold shapes the meaning we attach to our observations. The meanings we attach to our observations impact the way we define a problem, and the way we define a problem has an enormous impact on the places we search for causes, how we observe what we find, and the approach we take to solving it. Think about the differences between the ways society framed the crack epidemic in the 1980s in Black communities and the more recent framing of the opioid epidemic. The former was met with criminalization and blame, the latter with a compassionate public health crisis lens.

The most urgent work at hand is to ignite the fundamental paradigm shift necessary for all of us to see systemic racism at work. Thinking systemically is crucial to fueling the profound transformation needed to bring about racial justice in this country.

What does it take to make a paradigm shift? Two habits of mind are especially useful: Question and Challenge. Questioning the status quo and challenging underlying assumptions are essential for creating a paradigm shift that illuminates and effectively dismantles systemic racism. We might ask, what are the current racial frames that drive our understanding about racial inequality today? What do the current stories emphasize? What do they de-emphasize, avoid, or hide? These questions will be disruptive to inherited ideas that hide systemic racism. To interrogate and examine inherited mainstream stories about racism requires active unlearning. The process may take some time, and it might be uncomfortable. It may be difficult to reconcile the stories we've been raised to believe with the realities of systemic racism.

The widely held belief that we live in a functioning meritocracy, for example, surely conflicts with the evidence of a long-standing, ongoing system of deep, racialized educational inequality in America. The pattern of hoarding educational resources in white districts while neighboring Black ones struggle is central to the stories of Michael Brown and Kelley Williams-Bolar; in fact, research shows that this is a national phenomenon. How can we argue that students succeed based on merit when their learning and living environments are so askew? The more you find out about systemic racism, the more shocked you might be about how well its operations and effects have been hidden. As I mentioned earlier, I had a similar experience while researching this book. The invisibility of its effects and metaeffects has been carefully produced for a very long time, so we shouldn't expect to see and digest it all immediately. To shift a paradigm is a process of unlearning and learning, of reflecting, questioning, and sharing—all of which leads to the creation of deeper awareness and recognition.

Making a societal-level paradigm change when so many people and institutions remain invested in the prevailing view requires a concerted effort to reveal the problems with the way things are understood now—not just by asking questions, but by actively challenging unexamined ideas. What are the key problems with the current racial paradigm? What does it fail to reveal or consider? The current racial storytelling frame, for example, is anchored by the deep investment in individualism and colorblindness (an approach that proposes that the only way to end racial discrimination is to eliminate race completely as a metric for evaluating any goal or outcome). How can we keep track of the long history of racism and its current manifestations if we refuse to measure outcomes by race? The dominant story that individuals succeed or fail, win or lose, based only on their own merit, that post–civil rights era American society has leveled the playing field, that we function as a colorblind society and life outcomes are a matter of personal will, grit, and character alone, hides the truths about systemic racism under the façade of equal opportunity.

Another feature in the dominant story is the public overemphasis on individual acts of racism. Individual acts of racism are harmful and worrisome, but they should be distinguished from systemic racism. Systemic racism will not be revealed by constantly lifting up individual stories of discrimination or racist acts characterized as singular events. The system we've created will not be disrupted by the search for guilty individual racists, nor by discarding bad apples, nor by searching for documented proof of stand-alone acts of intentional racism. As laudable as these efforts may appear, defining and then fighting racism this way frames racism as something disconnected from the regular workings of society, when in fact, racism is a problem embedded in how society is organized. This does not mean that individual incidents don't matter, or that we should replace them with elaborate racial systems models exclusively. Instead, we should embed these individual acts in the network of forces that profoundly shape them. The more we are able to make the connections between our individual circumstances and the ways our lives are shaped by systemic racism and the advantages and disadvantages that flow from it, the more clearly we see our relationship to the system itself.

A great deal of energy has gone into making systemic racism invisible. This means it will take considerable effort to bring systemic racism to the center and keep it there. A systems approach to understanding racism profoundly disrupts the notion that racism is solely exhibited by individuals who harbor racist beliefs. This disruption has to be sustained in order to make it stick. So, keep at it! Speak out from a systems point of view, and use it to draw attention to and challenge the failures, contradictions, and irrationalities of the current frame. Share your observations with your communities, social networks, and families. Speak up at school board and town hall meetings. If you're an artist, paint, write poems or songs, make films, write novels that illuminate the unseen aspects of systemic racism.

Collaborate with others and make public space for personal, individual stories told in ways that shed light on the systems that shape them. Inviting others to tell their stories about how their lives have been impacted by systemic racism can help show how systemic racism works in our everyday lives and how it impacts the people we know. This is essential work. In the words of Andre C. Willis, "The ability to name one's circumstances, voice one's experiences and frame subjective conditions is to assert power."[4]

Opening up space for conversations in which shared or disparate experiences can be freely shared challenges existing paradigms and builds a foundation for new ones. In a recent university-based discussion on the important role the government plays in perpetuating systemic racism, I discussed the stark exclusions Black veterans confronted when they attempted to participate in the New Deal G.I. Bill programs that enabled Americans to buy homes with secure, government-backed, low-interest loans. At the reception that followed, a Black medical school dean pulled me aside and shared that after his father had died, he discovered in his father's files a denial letter for a G.I. Bill–related mortgage from well over fifty years ago. He also found the mortgage agreement from a bank that offered his father a mortgage with highly punitive terms and a much higher interest rate than the rate offered by the government-backed loan that his father was denied. The administrator wondered how to calculate the hidden costs and losses that radiated from this racially motivated lending exclusion. The loss of intergenerational wealth and opportunity implicit in the administrator's poignant story is his family's story, it is the story of Black Americans, and it is our collective story.

Identifying System Interconnections

The meat and potatoes of systems thinking is the identification of interconnections that drive impact.

Interconnections are frequently powerful leverage points where significant change might be possible. What are the most powerful interconnections that drive systemic racism in your town, community, or region? Where else can you identify similar drivers? There are many possible answers to these questions, some of which have been taken up by activists, organizations, and municipalities, such as ending police practices like Stop and Frisk, school suspensions, and cash bail. Additional ideas include requiring more equitable funding for public schools, putting a cap on the use of municipal fines and fees, and freeing incarcerated people who are serving longer sentences than would be served for the same crime today.

Researchers readily acknowledge that complex systems are difficult to manipulate; what's more, some leverage points that appear obvious candidates for producing desired changes may have unintended, sometimes opposite, results. The felony job box is a helpful example of this phenomenon. The common hiring practice of conducting a background check or having applicants check a box indicating whether they've been convicted of a felony has weeded out otherwise well-qualified applicants with criminal records from further consideration. This practice, activists and scholars argue, contributes to employment discrimination, giving employers a simple means by which to exclude applicants with criminal records categorically, no matter their relevant qualifications. Ban-the-box laws emerged in response to the mass incarceration explosion that quadrupled the number of incarcerated between 1980 and 2000. The intent was to reduce significant job discrimination and increase callback rates for Black applicants with criminal records.

After ban the box went into effect, research showed that callback rates did increase for Black applicants with records from 8 percent to 10.3 percent but decreased for Black applicants without records from 13.4 percent to 10.3 percent. Researchers posit that the decrease associated with applicants without records could be driven by employers preemptively weeding out young Black men, because they presumed that they might have a criminal record. Devah Pager's research on racism as a barrier to job entry documented how Black job applicant testers in her study were regularly asked, even before submitting an application, whether they had a criminal record. The preexisting association of Black men with crime served perhaps as an invisible, already checked box.[5] This does not mean that ban the box was a failure; it means that sometimes solutions as initially imagined have unintended consequences.

Remember: The devil is in the details! Interconnections are numerous and dynamic. Keep digging.

Reversing Systemic Racism Outcomes

To break free from systemic racism, it helps to know as much as we can about what systemic racism is designed to achieve. One of the most interesting insights of systems thinking is the claim that to figure out what a system is *really* designed to do, one should pay very close attention to the persistent *outcomes*. Sometimes goals and outcomes are aligned. But when they are not, the outcomes that persist over time reveal the actual goals of the system. For example, almost all the explicit goals related to the many policies I researched for this book purported to be race neutral—yet their actual outcomes consistently and over time were shown to contain, extract, and punish Black people disproportionately, and in ways that created metaracism.

Because containment, extraction, and punishment are consistent outcomes of policies that drive systemic racism, focusing on ways to reverse those outcomes could be a strong leverage point for reducing the power of systemic racism. What might such a reversal look like? Containment could be replaced by mobility and access; punishment might be replaced by care and repair; extraction may be replaced by infusion and investment. Defining a new paradigm based on increasing mobility and access, care and repair, infusion and investment would not only interrupt the containment, extraction, and punishment that propel many existing policies, but could also become the foundation of a holistic approach to rebuilding Black lives and a just society. Building a society truly designed to increase mobility and access, care and repair, infusion and investment is aspirational and inspirational. It is a humanizing response to a system based on dehumanization. To implement policies that reverse the outcomes of systemic racism is a reversal of the paradigm that maintains it.

SEEK INSPIRATION

At the beginning of this book, I said that a truthful accounting of systemic racism is painful, daunting, and might feel overwhelming. I suggested that it might provoke intense emotions such as anger, sadness, guilt, or helplessness.

I also said that refusing to confront systemic racism gives it more power, not less.

When I talk with people about systemic racism, probably the single most common question I get asked is, "What can I do?" This isn't a theoretical question; people really do want to know what they can do right away to fix things, make them better. The leverage points for change discussed previously—paradigm shifts, identifying system interconnections, and reversing outcomes—are practical and hopefully generative.

Yet on a deeper level, I fear that the urge to fix something as quickly as possible is motivated less by what it actually takes to end systemic racism and more by wanting to end the discomfort produced by confrontation with the reality of systemic racism. The astonishing breadth, sophistication, and cruelty of the system we've built, what we continue to allow, defend, and deny, are painful to confront. There will be no quick fix. The fact of the matter is that the faster we run from our own discomfort and confusion about systemic racism and what's needed to bring that system to its knees, the longer it will take to break free. We have to learn to deal with the discomfort, the pain, the rage, and the sadness—and find a way to turn it into inspiration.

Transform Discomfort

There were many times I felt a powerful urge to look away from these realities. Some days, I cried while writing this book. Other days, I was filled with anger. On those days, reading and thinking about the details of the system was so overwhelming that I lost access to the words I needed to describe what it feels like to be its target. If I—someone who, for thirty years, has been reading, writing, teaching, and reflecting on Black life in this country—was temporarily paralyzed, how might others feel?

Everyone develops their own strategies for finding inspiration and motivation to make a way through difficult and painful work. I gathered energy by diving into the details of the work with the goal of illuminating the nefarious impact done in the shadows. Finding the devil hiding in the details inspired me to keep going. A deeper understanding of what drives the system enriched my compassion and empathy for those who have been most injured. Black people are significantly over-represented among the people we have unjustly locked up for decades, the kids we have pushed out of school, the jobless, houseless, and hungry, those with addictions whom we treat as criminals, for whom jail beds, not rehab beds, are built. These injustices are minimized and denied. I wanted to be a witness: "Yes, what you're feeling is real. You are not imagining it. The system does contain and punish you; it does extract precious resources and support from your life; it does burden and weigh you down."

Focusing on systemic racism can create discomfort and encourage a mindset that distorts. For example, sometimes the argument that racism is systemic is interpreted to mean that racial discrimination is always involved in every dimension of life at all times, and that it drives all outcomes of all policies and practices. It is common for pushback to rely on this all-or-nothing framework: either racism is at work constantly and everywhere, or it doesn't define the system at all. It should be apparent by now that this is not my argument. Instead, systemic racism works through the combination of policies and practices designed to discriminate and policies used strategically to generate a regularized process of disproportionate negative and discriminatory impact.

Systemic racism is not the only society-wide harm in society, nor is it entirely disconnected from other kinds of discrimination. But it is significant and has important and distinct characteristics that cannot be fully accounted for in the absence of a racially focused examination. Poverty, for example, negatively affects people of all racial backgrounds. And, because many facets of systemic racism are most harshly experienced by poor Black people, and because Black people are disproportionately represented among the poor, racial discrimination is sometimes equated with poverty, the implication being that if we address poverty, racism will solve itself. This assumes that poverty is a race-neutral experience and that class solutions will solve the problems Black people experience.

It is undeniable that the level of poverty we have in the United States today is unconscionable. We should stand united across race and across all group identities to demand policies that lift people up and keep them out of poverty. This includes poor whites who find themselves struggling to survive. That said, class-based solutions cannot substitute for race-based remedies. The idea that racism is a subset of class suggests that poor people across race are facing what amounts to a shared, uniform experience of economic precarity that is not based on or related to race.

Poverty is not a race-neutral category. Being Black and poor carries with it myriad disadvantages of being Black on top of being poor. Being white and poor carries with it the brutality of poverty, experienced in the more favorable context of whiteness.[6] Studies show that the typical Black middle-income family lives in a neighborhood with lower incomes than the typical low-income white family. These results were considered surprising by lead researcher and Stanford professor Sean Reardon; he thought that "comparing people at exactly the same income level would get rid of more of the neighborhood differences than it did."[7] Systemic racism works *across class* through a network of interconnected policies to create racial disadvantages for Black people while providing buffers and advantages for whites across the economic spectrum. This is one of the hard truths we must confront if we hope to break free.

Further, systemic racism *creates* a much larger percentage of Black poor people and targets them—disproportionately—to pay a higher price for being Black and poor, and keeps them poor longer. A 2021 study on the Black-white gap in multigenerational poverty indicates that "Black families experience higher rates of poverty, less upward mobility, and more downward mobility." Black Americans make up 44 percent of those experiencing one generation of poverty while whites comprise 15 percent; Black Americans make up 33 percent of those with two generations of poverty while whites make up only 5 percent.[8] A purely class-focused strategy will not dismantle systemic racism because it does not account for the specific ways that Black communities across economic strata have been consistently and disproportionately targeted for racialized containment, extraction, and punishment and their metaeffects.

My insistence that we look closely at the specific role of systemic racism in society and the devastating harm it does to Black lives may generate difficult feelings and contribute to a belief that this emphasis is divisive. From my point of view, this is another distortion. Racial division results from the perpetuation of systemic racism, not from exposing systemic racism in an effort to break free from it. Figuring out how to become comfortable with the discomfort that fundamental change requires is part of the work.

Courage and Creativity

Courage is that enabling virtue that makes all the other virtues possible.

—Cornel West

Ending systemic racism depends on building communities that value courage and creativity as central to the work of breaking free. The courage and creativity to keep organizing for justice. The creativity and courage needed to fight the latest strategies designed to keep the system of racism in place. Where should we look for inspiration? African American expressive culture is my primary model for courage and creativity in the face of oppression.

What Black people have created in the face of relentless forces designed to crush the human spirit is awe-inspiring. The poetry, dance, song, painting, style, comedy, and storytelling traditions in African American culture are original, and serve as structures of healing and spaces of resistance to oppression. Music like the blues, gospel, hip hop, and jazz has buoyed the spirit and helped people continue on. The term "woke" can be traced to the blues legend Lead Belly, who in a 1938 song advises his listeners to "stay woke" "lest they run afoul of White authority." Some say it originated with an earlier blues artist, Willard "Ramblin'" Thomas, who uses the phrase in "Sawmill Moan," a song historians claim appeared on the surface to be a song about lost love, but in fact was a disguised protest against southern sawmill work conditions.[9] Hip hop artist Kendrick Lamar's 2015 "Alright" was not just an anthem for protesters, a confirmation of how much Black people had to fight for their rights; it was also a powerful affirmation: "Do you hear me, do you feel me? We gon' be alright." Beyonce's 2016 "Freedom," featuring Lamar, is testimony to the legacy of spirituals (with a reference to "Wade in the Water"). The song is a powerful statement against containment ("Freedom, freedom, I can't move") and systems of punishment ("Five-o askin' me what's in my possession"). The chorus elevates and inspires: "I break chains all by myself, won't let my freedom rot in hell, Hey! I'ma keep running cause a winner don't quit on themselves."

Many Black artistic forms, such as quilting, collaging, and sampling, express an extraordinary ability to use that which is left over or discarded to create new forms, and to tell new stories of great imagination and possibility. Black artistic traditions create beauty from the disregarded, to reconnect and repurpose things that have been torn apart and/or thrown away. Collage practices in the hands of Black artists such as Romare Bearden, Faith Ringgold, and Tomashi Jackson help us imaginatively reconstitute and reassemble ourselves. Sampling artists reclaim older sounds and textual patterns as a way to keep musical memory alive and remind us how important our musical ancestors are in building future(s). Black approaches to sound changed the way sampling equipment was made, turning sounds considered undesirable, out of appropriate sonic range, or "in the red" into coveted musical approaches. Improvisation and freestyle are freedom practices, the building blocks of possibility and joy.

I have always been moved and inspired by African American expressive cultures but, now, after researching and writing this book, I appreciate them even *more profoundly* than I did before. Black creativity strengthens and extends the will to create, to innovate, to remake the use of sound, the body, design, and words, and to move freely under conditions of constant containment. The aesthetic priority of making something out of nothing reenergizes the Black community with life, love, and possibility. Black creativity, resistance, and resilience: these are superpowers.

TO BE BLACK IN AMERICA IS TO WITHSTAND NOT ONLY THE sharp violence of the system and its effects, but also to endure the less immediately visible impact of what Arline Geronimus calls "weathering." Weathering is "a stress-related biological process that leaves identifiable groups of Americans vulnerable to dying or suffering chronic disease and disability long before they are chronologically old." The impact of myriad forms of containment, the fragility of constant financial and other types of extraction that devalue Black lives and property, and the constant specter of disproportionately harsh punishment for even the smallest of infractions trigger a set of chronically activated physiological pathways that accelerate long-term "deteriorization and erosion." The impact of exposure to this system of harm shows up on people; it produces differences you can see. Weathering also refers to "strength and endurance"—qualities that Black people have developed to survive systemic racism. At the heart of this kind of weathering are "networks of caring people encompassing both extended family and friends, who do everything they can to support one another."[10] Figuring out how systemic racism works helps us really understand the deteriorization and erosion it causes (the first kind of weathering). It is also a call to invest in the networks of love and care that are the bedrock of strength and endurance, the other kind of weathering.

Systemic racism is very much alive; successful resistance is not inevitable, and justice is not guaranteed. Yet, at the same time, I believe that systemic racism is not inevitable. Resistance is alive, and justice is possible. My plea is for us to work together to break free from the grips of systemic racism. As Lorraine Hansberry reminds us: "This is one of the glories of [humankind], the inventiveness of the human mind and the human spirit: whenever life doesn't seem to give an answer, we create one."

In the sharing and cocreating of communities where we expand, enrich, and rehabilitate one another, we forge the bonds and interconnections of systemic justice.

ACKNOWLEDGMENTS

This has been a collective project that has drawn from the insights and experiences of many. The engaging, generous, and insightful feedback from folks who attended lectures on systemic racism both taught me a great deal and became a source of extraordinary sustenance. After many such presentations, at least one person pulls me aside, lowers their voice, looks me in the eye, and asks: "This is heavy material. What are you doing for self-care?" In these moments, it seems clear that they know from personal experience how much of a chronic stressor systemic racism is for Black people. In the moment, my answers are often deflecting and minimizing: "I am doing ok," "I'm hanging in there!," or "I am still in one piece!" But the regularity of this warm question and heartfelt delivery of concern has itself created a powerful internal echo of affirmation and care. I find myself asking this question of myself: "What are you doing, Tricia, for self-care?" It is as if over vast time and space, folks are sharing and planting the seeds of survival. Thus, I give earnest thanks to many lovely people whom I met yet I cannot name.

This has been a challenging and rewarding project. Throughout the journey, I have been lifted up, productively questioned, and encouraged by so many dear family and friends, research team members, and colleagues, who have helped me stay the course and buoyed my spirit. Whether we talk about the research or plan some sort of escape from it, being together has been very important to me.

I am so grateful to the teams of Brown University undergraduate and graduate student researchers who generously dedicated their extraordinary hearts and minds to the project. Thank you: Mina Asayesh-Brown, Amanda Boston, Aaron Cooper, Clark Craddock-Willis, Emma Dennis-Knieriem, Uwa Ede-Osifo, Charlotte Haq, Tim Ittner, Nnamdi Jogwe, Destiny Jones, Eric Jones, Adeline Mitchell, Dylan Moore, Hannah Pullen-Blasnik, Aida Sherif, Emily Sun, Cat Turner, Naomi Varnis, Susannah Waldman, and Ida Yalzadeh. Special gratitude goes to Sam Rosen, who began working on this project nearly a decade ago as the solo student researcher. Beyond dedicating his excellent research skills to the project for several years, Sam became an invaluable thought-partner.

I am also deeply indebted to the extraordinary staff at the Center for the Study of Race and Ethnicity in America at Brown University for all the collaboration and support over the years, and most especially to current staff members who kept the trains running smoothly while I was on sabbatical writing. Thank you: Trae Alston-Swan, Christina Downs, Stéphanie Larrieux, Caitlin Murphy-Scott, Maggie Murphy, Michael Ruo, and Ellie Winter. In addition to terrific staff, I have been very fortunate to work with wonderful colleagues at Brown University. The faculty and students in my home department of Africana Studies and many colleagues across

Acknowledgments

campus created a dynamic, generative, and supportive environment for this work.

It has been a great pleasure to work with my agent, Tanya McKinnon. She listened carefully and offered unwavering support, valuable insight, and deft guidance every step of the way. Thanks are due to the entire Basic Books team, especially Brian Distelberg and Brandon Proia, for offering thoughtful editorial assistance. Several colleagues spent close and careful time sharing insights, ideas, and excellent suggestions along the way. Thanks to you all, especially to Matt Guterl, Bonnie Honig, and George Lipsitz. I am grateful to the *Du Bois Review*, which offered an opportunity to share an early version of my research on Kelley Williams-Bolar's story.

Many colleagues near and far have created vital bodies of work that have fueled my own thinking on systemic racism over many years, directly and indirectly. I cannot possibly thank them all here, but they include: Michelle Alexander, Andre Banks, Eduardo Bonilla-Silva, Prudence Carter, Kimberlé Crenshaw, William "Sandy" Darity, Angela Davis, Joe Fegan, Skip Gates, Ruth Wilson Gilmore, Lani Guinier, Marc Lamont Hill, Robin D. G. Kelley, George Lipsitz, Donella Meadows, Melvin Oliver, the amazing creative teams at R/GA and Studio Rainwater, Barbara Reskin, Jan Rivkin, Rashad Robinson, Noliwe Rooks, Ryan Senser, Tom Shapiro, and Cornel West.

The love of family and friends holds us together. I am still in one piece because of: Jeremy Berry; TER; Laura and Ken Housman; Thomas Johnson; Marisa Quinn and Jay Sisson; Akua Naru; Ron Aubert; Rick Locke and Zairo Cheibub;

Acknowledgments

Kevin McLaughlin and Ourida Mostefai; Rose Tracy; Coleman Craddock-Willis and Callie Plapinger; Kaleigh and Brian Petrie; Nancy Khalek; Stephanie Bell-Rose; Jason Rose, Evan Rose, Josephine Savannah Rose, and Jasmine Woodard Rose; Lee W-R; Jane Saks; Jennifer DeVere Brody; Jen and Jeremy Sherer; Pam Bradford; Alex Zimmerman; Ashley Baker; Kira Murphy; Kirby Heyward; and my wonderful mother-in-law, Helen Irene Willis. Both of my parents passed away in 2022, but their resilience and courage will continue to inspire me.

Special thanks are due to my brother, Chris Rose, who has been excited about this project from the beginning and has remained a stalwart supporter, critical reader, and ready interlocutor. Very special thanks are due to the indomitable Victoria Lee Hood, who generously devoted her many extraordinary talents to whatever was needed to bring this book into being.

Most of all, my deepest gratitude is reserved for my foundation for everything, my partner in all things, Andre C. Willis. Although I have ample words to describe many things, none adequately captures the impact and power of his love. True to the end.

NOTES

Introduction

1. Eduardo Bonilla-Silva, *Racism Without Racists: Color-Blind Racism and the Persistence of Racial Inequality in America* (Lanham, MD: Rowman & Littlefield, 2018).

2. Lawrence Bobo et al., "From Jim Crow Racism to Laissez-Racism: The Transformation of Racial Attitudes," in *Beyond Pluralism: The Conception of Groups and Identities in America*, edited by Wendy F. Katkin, Ned Landsman, and Andrea Tyree (Champaign: University of Illinois, 1998).

3. "The Wealth Gap Facing Black Americans Is Vast—and Vastly Underestimated," Yale Insights, July 15, 2020, https://insights.som.yale.edu/insights/the-wealth-gap-facing-Black-americans-is-vast-and-vastly-underestimated; "What We Get Wrong About Closing the Racial Wealth Gap—The Samuel DuBois Cook Center on Social Equity," accessed March 31, 2022, https://socialequity.duke.edu/portfolio-item/what-we-get-wrong-about-closing-the-racial-wealth-gap/.

4. Equal Justice Initiative, "Banks Continue to Deny Home Loans to People of Color," Equal Justice Initiative, February 19, 2018, https://eji.org/news/banks-deny-home-loans-to-people-color/; Aaron Glantz and Emmanuel Martinez, "For People of Color, Banks Are Shutting the Door to Homeownership," *Reveal*, February 15, 2018, https://revealnews.org/article/for-people-of-color-banks-are-shutting-the-door-to-homeownership/.

5. Martin Luther King, Jr., "Beyond the Los Angeles Riots," *Saturday Review*, November 13, 1965.

6. Calculated by Google Ngram on March 15, 2023.

7. Luisa Jung, "Big Business Pledged Nearly $50 Billion for Racial Justice After George Floyd's Death. Where Did the Money Go?," *Washington Post*, accessed

March 4, 2023, https://www.washingtonpost.com/business/interactive/2021/george-floyd-corporate-america-racial-justice/.

8. Nick Anderson, "Did Politics Scrub 'Systemic' from AP African American Studies Plan?," *Washington Post*, accessed February 20, 2023, https://www.washingtonpost.com/education/interactive/2023/ap-african-american-studies-controversy/; Dana Goldstein and Stephanie Saul, "The College Board Will Change Its A.P. African American Studies Course," *New York Times*, April 25, 2023, sec. U.S., https://www.nytimes.com/2023/04/24/us/ap-african-american-studies-college-board.html. In April 2023, fewer than three months after the release of the AP course, the College Board announced that it would further modify the course. In a press release entitled "AP African American Studies Scholars to Make Changes to Course," the College Board says that scholars and experts "have decided that they would make changes to the latest course framework during this pilot phase. They will determine the details of those changes over the next few months."

Chapter 1: Caught Up in the System

1. Michelle Alexander, *The New Jim Crow: Mass Incarceration in the Age of Colorblindness* (New York: The New Press, 2012), 90.

2. Rick Perlstein, "Exclusive: Lee Atwater's Infamous 1981 Interview on the Southern Strategy," November 13, 2012, https://www.thenation.com/article/archive/exclusive-lee-atwaters-infamous-1981-interview-southern-strategy/.

3. Barbara Reskin, "The Race Discrimination System," *Annual Review of Sociology* 38, no. 1 (2012): 17–35; Donella H. Meadows and Diana Wright, *Thinking in Systems: A Primer* (White River Junction, VT: Chelsea Green, 2008); Stephen Menendian and Caitlin Watt, "Systems Thinking and Race" (Kirwan Institute, 2008), https://kirwaninstitute.osu.edu/research/systems-thinking-and-race.

4. Reskin, "Race Discrimination System."

5. Meadows and Wright, *Thinking in Systems*.

6. W. M. Byrd and L. A. Clayton, "Race, Medicine, and Health Care in the United States: A Historical Survey," *Journal of the National Medical Association* 93, no. 3, suppl. (March 2001): 11S–34S.

7. "TCF Study Finds U.S. Schools Underfunded by Nearly $150 Billion Annually," The Century Foundation, July 22, 2020, https://tcf.org/content/about-tcf/tcf-study-finds-u-s-schools-underfunded-nearly-150-billion-annually/.

8. Meadows and Wright, *Thinking in Systems*.

9. Reskin, "Race Discrimination System."

10. Psychoanalyst and scholar Joel Kovel is often credited as the first person to coin the term "metaracism." For Kovel, metaracism is not defined as a metaeffect of systemic racism. Rather, he used the term to describe what we might refer to today as colorblind

racism—a new white racial mindset that rejects personal racial prejudice but nonetheless continues to accept a cultural order in which the work of racism is perpetuated. My use of the term "metracism" derives from what systems thinkers consider a primary characteristic of systems: the meta (or more comprehensive or transcending) effects and outcomes (impacts) created by the dynamic interconnections between system elements (or parts). Applying this systems analysis to racism, metaracism is thus understood as a metaeffect of systemic racism. Joel Kovel, *White Racism: A Psychohistory* (New York: Columbia University Press, 1984). For a more contemporary application of Kovel's use of metaracism to examine post-1980s political shifts in racial ideology, see Carter A. Wilson, *Metaracism: Explaining the Persistence of Racial Inequality* (Boulder, Colorado: Lynne Rienner Publishers, Inc., 2015).

11. Joe R. Feagin, *Systemic Racism: A Theory of Oppression* (New York: Routledge, 2006); Paula A. Braveman et al., "Systemic and Structural Racism: Definitions, Examples, Health Damages, and Approaches to Dismantling," *Health Affairs* 41, no. 2 (February 2022): 171–178, https://doi.org/10.1377/hlthaff.2021.01394; Eduardo Bonilla Silva, "Rethinking Racism: Toward a Structural Interpretation," *American Sociological Review* 62, no. 3 (June 1997): 465–480.

12. Anastasia Vikhornova, "What We Can Learn from the History of Systems Thinking," *Systems Thinking for Non-Systems Thinkers* (blog), August 17, 2018, https://medium.com/systems-thinking-for-non-systems-thinkers/what-we-can-learn-from-the-history-of-systems-thinking-79852d8955c4; Robbie W. C. Tourse, Johnnie Hamilton-Mason, and Nancy J. Wewiorski, *Systemic Racism in the United States: Scaffolding as Social Construction* (Cham, Switzerland: Springer, 2018); G. Bellinger, "Systems—A Journey Along the Way," 2004–2005, http://www.systems-thinking.org/systems/systems.htm; Leyla Acaroglu, "Tools for Systems Thinkers: The 6 Fundamental Concepts of Systems Thinking," *Disruptive Design* (blog), March 11, 2021, https://medium.com/disruptive-design/tools-for-systems-thinkers-the-6-fundamental-concepts-of-systems-thinking-379cdac3dc6a; John Powell, "Systems Thinking, Evaluation and Racial Justice," *Philanthropic Initiative for Racial Equity: Critical Issue Forum* 3 (July 2010), https://racialequity.org/wp-content/uploads/2018/11/powell.pdf.

13. "Moving the Race Conversation Forward: How the Media Covers Racism, and Other Barriers to Productive Racial Discourse," https://www.raceforward.org/research/reports/moving-race-conversation-forward.

14. Tresa Baldas, "Detroit Man Settles Race Discrimination Lawsuit, Then Bank Won't Cash His Check," *Detroit Free Press*, accessed March 12, 2023, https://www.freep.com/story/news/local/michigan/detroit/2020/01/23/tcf-bank-race-discrimination-case-sauntore-thomas/4546199002/.

15. Tresa Baldas, "TCF Bank Apologizes for Calling Police on Black Customer Trying to Deposit Checks," *Detroit Free Press*, accessed March 12, 2023, https://www.freep.com/story/news/local/michigan/detroit/2020/01/23/tcf-bank-apology-racial-discrimination-Black/4555125002/.

16. *Teach Us All*, directed by Sonia Lowman, documentary (2017), https://www.youtube.com/watch?v=BElG3joieUE.

17. Mindy Thompson Fullilove, *Root Shock: How Tearing Up City Neighborhoods Hurts America, and What We Can Do About It* (New York: New Village Press, 2016). See also https://encyclopediaofarkansas.net/entries/urban-reneal-7856/.

18. Richard Rothstein, *The Color of Law: A Forgotten History of How Our Government Segregated America* (New York, London: Liveright, 2018).

19. Bill Dedham, "The Color of Money: Home Mortgage Lending Practices Discriminate Against Blacks," *Atlanta Journal-Constitution*, May 1988, https://powerreporting.com/color/.

20. Department of Justice, "Justice Department Secures Agreement with Lakeland Bank to Address Discriminatory Redlining," September 28, 2022, https://www.justice.gov/usao-nj/pr/justice-department-secures-agreement-lakeland-bank-address-discriminatory-redlining; Jeff Goldman, "N.J. Bank Agrees to $13M Settlement After Avoiding Black, Hispanic Customers Seeking Mortgages," nj.com, September 28, 2022, https://www.nj.com/news/2022/09/nj-bank-agrees-to-13m-settlement-after-avoiding-black-hispanic-customers-seeking-mortgages.html.

21. Christine Barwick, "Patterns of Discrimination Against Blacks and Hispanics in the US Mortgage Market," *Journal of Housing and the Built Environment* 25, no. 1 (April 2010): 117–124, https://doi.org/10.1007/s10901-009-9165-x.

22. Ping Cheng, Zhenguo Lin, and Yingchun Liu, "Racial Discrepancy in Mortgage Interest Rates," *Journal of Real Estate Finance and Economics* 51, no. 1 (July 1, 2015): 101, https://doi.org/10.1007/s11146-014-9473-0.

23. George Lipsitz, *How Racism Takes Place* (Philadelphia: Temple University Press, 2011).

24. Elizabeth Korver-Glenn and Junia Howell, "Homes in Black and Latino Neighborhoods Still Undervalued 50 Years After US Banned Using Race in Real Estate Appraisals," *The Conversation*, September 24, 2020, https://theconversation.com/homes-in-Black-and-latino-neighborhoods-still-undervalued-50-years-after-us-banned-using-race-in-real-estate-appraisals-146273; Chenoa Flippen, "Unequal Returns to Housing Investments? A Study of Real Housing Appreciation Among Black, White, and Hispanic Households," *Social Forces* 82, no. 4 (2004): 1523–1551.

25. "TCF Study Finds U.S. Schools Underfunded."

26. Ayelet Sheffey, "For-Profit Schools Target Minority Communities That Typically Owe More Student Debt, Report Says," Business Insider, accessed October 26, 2022, https://www.businessinsider.com/for-profit-schools-target -minority-communities-student-borrower-protection-center-2021-8.

27. Sonali Kohli, "Black Harvard Graduates Have the Same Shot at a Job Call-Back as White State College Grads," Quartz, accessed October 23, 2020, https://qz.com/357445/Black-harvard-graduates-have-the-same-shot-at-a-job -call-back-as-White-state-college-grads/.

28. See Sean F. Reardon, Lindsay Fox, and Joseph Townsend, "Neighborhood Income Composition by Household Race and Income, 1990–2009," *ANNALS of the American Academy of Political and Social Science* 660, no. 1 (July 1, 2015): 78–97, https://doi.org/10.1177/0002716215576104.

29. Reskin, "Race Discrimination System."

Chapter 2: The Devil Is in the Details

1. "Homelessness and Racial Disparities," National Alliance to End Homelessness, accessed July 8, 2023, https://endhomelessness.org/homelessness-in -america/what-causes-homelessness/inequality/. See also Rayshawn Ray and Hoda Mahmoudi, eds., *Systemic Racism in America: Sociological Theory, Education Inequality, and Social Change* (New York: Routledge, 2022), https://www.routledge .com/Systemic-Racism-in-America-Sociological-Theory-Education-Inequality -and/Ray-Mahmoudi/p/book/9781032124940.

2. Rothstein, *Color of Law*; Bruce Mitchell and Juan Franco, "HOLC 'Redlining' Maps: The Persistent Structure of Segregation and Economic Inequality," Database, National Community Reinvestment Coalition (NCRC), March 20, 2018, https://ncrc.org/holc/; Maria Godoy, "In U.S. Cities, the Health Effects of Past Housing Discrimination Are Plain to See," NPR.org, November 19, 2020, https://www.npr.org/sections/health-shots/2020/11/19/911909187 /in-u-s-cities-the-health-effects-of-past-housing-discrimination-are-plain-to-see.

3. Robin Young, "History of Mobility—and Mobility Denied—Told in New PBS Documentary 'Driving While Black,'" WBUR, accessed September 9, 2021, https:// www.wbur.org/hereandnow/2020/10/13/driving-while-Black-documentary; Heather A. O'Connell, "Historical Shadows: The Links Between Sundown Towns and Contemporary Black–White Inequality," *Sociology of Race and Ethnicity* 5, no. 3 (July 1, 2019): 311–325, https://doi.org/10.1177/2332649218761979.

4. Deborah N. Archer, "'White Men's Roads Through Black Men's Homes': Advancing Racial Equity Through Highway Reconstruction," *Vanderbilt Law Review* 73, no. 5 (October 2020): 1259–1330.

5. S. Michael Gaddis, "Discrimination in the Credential Society: An Audit Study of Race and College Selectivity in the Labor Market," *Social Forces* 93, no. 4 (June 1, 2015): 1451–1479, https://doi.org/10.1093/sf/sou111; Devah Pager and Bruce Western, *Race at Work: Realities of Race and Criminal Record in the NYC Job Market*, report released as part of the NYC Commission on Human Rights Conference, December 9, 2005, https://scholar.harvard.edu/files/pager/files/race_at_work.pdf.

6. Darrick Hamilton and William Darity, Jr., "Race, Wealth, and Intergenerational Poverty," *The American Prospect*, August 14, 2009, https://prospect.org/api/content/8dee0485-9542-527a-81ed-5c872600cbd7/; Thomas M. Shapiro, *The Hidden Cost of Being African American: How Wealth Perpetuates Inequality*, electronic resource (New York: Oxford University Press, 2004), https://login.revproxy.brown.edu/login?URL=http://www.brown.eblib.com/EBLWeb/patron/?target=patron&extendedid=P_316388_0; Thomas M. Shapiro, *Toxic Inequality: How America's Wealth Gap Destroys Mobility, Deepens the Racial Divide, and Threatens Our Future* (New York: Basic Books, 2017); Leon Kaye, "Black Families Haven't Benefited from Intergenerational Wealth, but Banks Can Help Narrow the Gap," Triple Pundit, October 13, 2020, https://www.triplepundit.com/story/2020/Black-families-intergenerational-wealth-gap/707026.

7. Douglas A. Blackmon, *Slavery by Another Name: The Re-enslavement of Black People in America from the Civil War to World War II* (New York: Doubleday, 2008).

8. Kriston McIntosh, Emily Moss, Ryan Nunn, and Jay Shambaugh, "Examining the Black-White Wealth Gap," *Brookings* (blog), February 27, 2020, https://www.brookings.edu/blog/up-front/2020/02/27/examining-the-Black-White-wealth-gap/.

9. Lisa Camner McKay, "How the Racial Wealth Gap Has Evolved—and Why It Persists," Federal Reserve Bank of Minneapolis, accessed April 29, 2023, https://www.minneapolisfed.org/article/2022/how-the-racial-wealth-gap-has-evolved-and-why-it-persists; McIntosh, Moss, Nunn, and Shambaugh, "Examining the Black-White Wealth Gap."

10. Leah Douglas, "African Americans Have Lost Untold Acres of Land over the Last Century," *The Nation*, June 26, 2017, https://www.thenation.com/article/archive/african-americans-have-lost-acres/; Andrew W. Kahrl, "Black People's Land Was Stolen," *New York Times*, June 20, 2019, sec. Opinion, https://www.nytimes.com/2019/06/20/opinion/sunday/reparations-hearing.html; Andrew W. Kahrl, *The Land Was Ours* (Chapel Hill: University of North Carolina Press, 2016), https://uncpress.org/book/9781469628721/the-land-was-ours/; Vann R. Newkirk II, "The Great Land Robbery," *The Atlantic*,

September 29, 2019, https://www.theatlantic.com/magazine/archive/2019/09/this-land-was-our-land/594742/.

11. Julian Agyeman and Kofi Boone, "Land Loss Has Plagued Black America Since Emancipation—Is It Time to Look Again at 'Black Commons' and Collective Ownership?," The Conversation, June 18, 2020, https://theconversation.com/land-loss-has-plagued-black-america-since-emancipation-is-it-time-to-look-again-at-black-commons-and-collective-ownership-140514.

12. Douglas, "African Americans Have Lost Untold Acres of Land over the Last Century"; Summer Sewell, "There Were Nearly a Million Black Farmers in 1920. Why Have They Disappeared?," The Guardian, April 29, 2019, https://www.theguardian.com/environment/2019/apr/29/why-have-americas-black-farmers-disappeared.

13. Tom Philpott, "Black Farmers Have Been Robbed of Land. A New Bill Would Give Them a 'Quantum Leap' Toward Justice," Mother Jones (blog), November 19, 2020, https://www.motherjones.com/food/2020/11/Black-farmers-have-been-robbed-of-land-a-new-bill-would-give-them-a-quantum-leap-toward-justice/; Lizzie Presser, "Kicked Off the Land: Why So Many Black Families Are Losing Their Property," New Yorker, 2019, https://www.newyorker.com/magazine/2019/07/22/kicked-off-the-land.

14. Keeanga-Yamahtta Taylor, Race for Profit: How Banks and the Real Estate Industry Undermined Black Homeownership, Justice, Power, and Politics (Chapel Hill: University of North Carolina Press, 2019); Stephen L. Ross and John Yinger, The Color of Credit: Mortgage Discrimination, Research Methodology, and Fair-Lending Enforcement (Cambridge, MA: MIT Press, 2003), http://search.ebscohost.com/login.aspx?direct=true&db=e000xna&AN=78100&site=ehost-live&scope=site&authtype=ip,sso&custid=rock.

15. Debra Kamin, "Black Homeowners Face Discrimination in Appraisals," New York Times, August 27, 2020, sec. Real Estate, https://www.nytimes.com/2020/08/25/realestate/blacks-minorities-appraisals-discrimination.html; Debra Kamin, "Home Appraised with a Black Owner: $472,000. With a White Owner: $750,000," New York Times, August 18, 2022, sec. Real Estate, https://www.nytimes.com/2022/08/18/realestate/housing-discrimination-maryland.html.

16. Dirk Early, Edgar Olsen, and Paul E. Carillo, "Analysis: African-Americans Pay More for Rent, Especially in White Neighborhoods," Chicago Reporter, October 31, 2018, https://www.chicagoreporter.com/analysis-african-americans-pay-more-for-rent-especially-in-White-neighborhoods/.

17. Alexander, New Jim Crow, 98.

18. Alexander, New Jim Crow, 98.

19. M. Marit Rehavi and Sonja B. Starr, "Mandatory Sentencing and Racial Disparity: Assessing the Role of Prosecutors and the Effects of *Booker,*" *Yale Law Journal* 123, no. 1 (October 2013), https://www.yalelawjournal.org/article/mandatory-sentencing-and-racial-disparity-assessing-the-role-of-prosecutors-and-the-effects-of-booker; Jennifer Turner and Jamil Dakwar, *Racial Disparities in Sentencing: Hearing on Reports of Racism in the Justice System of the United States,* American Civil Liberties Union, 2014, https://www.aclu.org/sites/default/files/assets/141027_iachr_racial_disparities_aclu_submission_0.pdf.

20. Ngozi Caleb Kamalu, Margery Coulson-Clark, and Nkechi Margaret Kamalu, "Racial Disparities in Sentencing: Implications for the Criminal Justice System and the African American Community," *African Journal of Criminology and Justice Studies* 4, no. 1 (June 2010): 31.

21. Turner and Dakwar, *Racial Disparities in Sentencing.*

22. Alexander, *New Jim Crow,* 134.

23. Al Baker and Ray Rivera, "Study Finds Street Stops by N.Y. Police Unjustified," *New York Times,* October 26, 2010, sec. New York, https://www.nytimes.com/2010/10/27/nyregion/27frisk.html.

24. "U.S. Department of Education Civil Rights Data Finds Persistent Racial Disparities in School Discipline and Policing," Advancement Project, accessed September 1, 2021, https://advancementproject.org/news/u-s-department-of-education-civil-rights-data-finds-persistent-racial-disparities-in-school-discipline-and-policing/.

25. Kimberlé Crenshaw, Priscilla Ocen, and Jyoti Nanda, "Black Girls Matter: Pushed Out, Overpoliced, and Underprotected," African American Policy Forum, 2015, https://www.aapf.org/blackgirlsmatter.

26. Dedham, "Color of Money."

27. Erin Blakemore, "How the GI Bill's Promise Was Denied to a Million Black WWII Veterans," database, History, June 21, 2019, https://www.history.com/news/gi-bill-black-wwii-veterans-benefits; Mark Boulton, "How the G.I. Bill Failed African-American Vietnam War Veterans," JBHE Foundation, Inc., *Journal of Blacks in Higher Education,* no. 58 (Winter 2007/2008): 4; Jean Folger, "VA Housing Loans and Race: How Racism Impacted Programs to Help Active Members and Vets Get Homes," database, Investopedia, September 21, 2021, https://www.investopedia.com/va-housing-loans-and-race-5077372; Edward Humes, "How the GI Bill Shunted Blacks into Vocational Training," JBHE Foundation, Inc., *Journal of Blacks in Higher Education,* no. 58 (2006): 13.

28. Ira Katznelson, *When Affirmative Action Was White: An Untold History of Racial Inequality in Twentieth-Century America* (New York: W. W. Norton, 2005).

29. Ira Katznelson and Suzanne Mettler, "On Race and Policy History: A Dialogue About the G.I. Bill," *Perspectives on Politics* 6, no. 3 (2008): 519–537.

30. Powell, "Systems Thinking, Evaluation and Racial Justice."

Chapter 3: No Chance Encounter

1. *Rest in Power: The Trayvon Martin Story*, directed by Jenner Furst and Julia Willoughby Nason (Paramount Network, 2018), https://www.paramount network.com/shows/rest-in-power-the-trayvon-martin-story.

2. *Rest in Power.*

3. WhiteHouse.gov, "Video: President Obama on Trayvon Martin Case," *New York Times*, March 23, 2012, sec. U.S., https://www.nytimes.com/video /us/100000001447810/president-obama-on-trayvon-martin-case.html.

4. Kevin Drum, "The Conservative Agenda in the Trayvon Martin Case," *Mother Jones* (blog), accessed August 11, 2021, https://www.motherjones.com /kevin-drum/2012/03/conservative-agenda-trayvon-martin-case/; Jonah Goldberg, "Goldberg: Playing the Race Card Again," *Los Angeles Times*, March 27, 2012, https://www.latimes.com/nation/la-xpm-2012-mar-27-la-oe-goldberg -trayvon-martin-race-20120327-story.html.

5. *Rest in Power.*

6. Sanford, Florida, City-Data.com, https://www.city-data.com/city/Sanford -Florida.html.

7. Angela Onwuachi-Willig, "Policing the Boundaries of Whiteness: The Tragedy of Being 'Out of Place' from Emmett Till to Trayvon Martin," *Iowa Law Review* 102 (n.d.): 73.

8. Colin McArthur and Sarah Edelman, "The 2008 Housing Crisis," Center for American Progress, accessed August 17, 2021, https://www.american progress.org/issues/economy/reports/2017/04/13/430424/2008-housing-crisis/.

9. *Rest in Power.*

10. Lane DeGregory, "Trayvon Martin's Killing Shatters Safety Within Retreat at Twin Lakes in Sanford," *Tampa Bay Times*, accessed August 4, 2022, https:// www.tampabay.com/news/humaninterest/trayvon-martins-killing-shatters -safety-within-retreat-at-twin-lakes-in/1221799/.

11. *Rest in Power.*

12. "Sanford, Florida Population 2022 (Demographics, Maps, Graphs)," accessed August 4, 2022, https://worldpopulationreview.com/us-cities/sanford-fl-population.

13. Douglas S. Massey and Nancy A. Denton, *American Apartheid: Segregation and the Making of the Underclass*, electronic resource (Cambridge, MA: Harvard University Press, 1993), https://login.revproxy.brown.edu/login?url=http://hdl .handle.net/2027/heb.31525.0001.001.

14. Rothstein, *Color of Law*.

15. Cheryl I. Harris, "Whiteness as Property," accessed August 16, 2022, https://harvardlawreview.org/1993/06/whiteness-as-property/; Angie Beeman, Davita Silfen Glasberg, and Colleen Casey, "Whiteness as Property: Predatory Lending and the Reproduction of Racialized Inequality," *Critical Sociology* 37, no. 1 (January 1, 2011): 27–45, https://doi.org/10.1177/0896920510378762.

16. Kamin, "Black Homeowners Face Discrimination in Appraisals."

17. Onwuachi-Willig, "Policing the Boundaries of Whiteness."

18. DeGregory, "Trayvon Martin's Killing Shatters Safety." Amy Green, "Zimmerman's Twin Lakes Community Was on Edge Before Trayvon Shooting," *Daily Beast*, March 28, 2012, https://www.thedailybeast.com/articles/2012/03/28/zimmerman-s-twin-lakes-community-was-on-edge-before-trayvon-shooting.

19. Elena Vesselinov, "Members Only: Gated Communities and Residential Segregation in the Metropolitan United States," *Sociological Forum* 23, no. 3 (2008): 536–555.

20. Lisa Bloom, *Suspicion Nation: The Inside Story of the Trayvon Martin Injustice and Why We Continue to Repeat It* (Berkeley, CA: Counterpoint, 2014).

21. Ian Tuttle, "The Neighborhood Zimmerman Watched," *National Review* (blog), July 22, 2013, https://www.nationalreview.com/2013/07/neighborhood-zimmerman-watched-ian-tuttle/.

22. Chris Francescani, "George Zimmerman: Prelude to a Shooting," Reuters, April 25, 2012, sec. U.S. News, https://www.reuters.com/article/us-usa-florida-shooting-zimmerman-idUSBRE83O18H20120425; Onwuachi-Willig, "Policing the Boundaries of Whiteness."

23. Khalil Gibran Muhammad, *The Condemnation of Blackness: Race, Crime, and the Making of Modern Urban America*, electronic resource (Cambridge, MA: Harvard University Press, 2011), https://login.revproxy.brown.edu/login?url=https://ebookcentral.proquest.com/lib/brown/detail.action?docID=3301129; Blackmon, *Slavery by Another Name*; Alexander, *New Jim Crow*; Elizabeth Hinton, Cindy Reed, and LeShae Henderson, *An Unjust Burden: The Disparate Treatment of Black Americans in the Criminal Justice System* (New York: Vera Institute of Justice, 2018), https://storage.googleapis.com/vera-web-assets/downloads/Publications/for-the-record-unjust-burden/legacy_downloads/for-the-record-unjust-burden-racial-disparities.pdf.

24. Nazgol Ghandnoosh, "Race and Punishment: Racial Perceptions of Crime and Support for Punitive Policies," Sentencing Project: Research and Advocacy for Reform, 2014, https://www.sentencingproject.org/reports/race-and-punishment-racial-perceptions-of-crime-and-support-for-punitive-policies/.

25. R. Richard Banks, Jennifer L. Eberhardt, and Lee Ross, "Discrimination and Implicit Bias in a Racially Unequal Society," *California Law Review* 94, no. 4 (2006): 1169–1190, https://doi.org/10.2307/20439061.

26. Ghandnoosh, "Race and Punishment"; John Smiley Calvin and David Fakunle, "From 'Brute' to 'Thug': The Demonization and Criminalization of Unarmed Black Male Victims in America," *Journal of Human Behavior in the Social Environment* 26, nos. 3–4 (2016): 350–366, https://doi.org/10.1080/10911359.2015.1129256; Jennifer L. Eberhardt et al., "Seeing Black: Race, Crime, and Visual Processing," *Journal of Personality and Social Psychology* 87, no. 6 (2004): 876–893, https://doi.org/10.1037/0022-3514.87.6.876.

27. "Portrayal and Perception: Two Audits of News Media Reporting on African American Men and Boys," accessed July 21, 2023, https://www.opensocietyfoundations.org/publications/portrayal-and-perception-two-audits-news-media-reporting-african-american-men-and-boys; Jennifer Carlson, "Moral Panic, Moral Breach: Bernhard Goetz, George Zimmerman, and Racialized News Reporting in Contested Cases of Self-Defense," *Social Problems* 63, no. 1 (2016): 1.

28. Franklin D. Gilliam and Shanto Iyengar, "Prime Suspects: The Influence of Local Television News on the Viewing Public," *American Journal of Political Science* 44, no. 3 (2000): 560–573, https://doi.org/10.2307/2669264; Alexander, *New Jim Crow*.

29. "Transcripts of Calls in the George Zimmerman Case," accessed March 30, 2023, http://law2.umkc.edu/faculty/projects/ftrials/zimmerman1/zimcalls.html.

30. Rene Lynch, "Trayvon Martin Shooting: George Zimmerman Dreamed of Being a Cop," *Los Angeles Times*, March 20, 2012, https://www.latimes.com/nation/la-xpm-2012-mar-20-la-na-nn-george-zimmerman-trayvon-martin-20120320-story.html.

31. Bloom, *Suspicion Nation*.

32. Lynch, "Trayvon Martin Shooting."

33. "Race and Punishment: Racial Perceptions of Crime and Support for Punitive Policies," Sentencing Project, accessed August 4, 2022, https://www.sentencingproject.org/publications/race-and-punishment-racial-perceptions-of-crime-and-support-for-punitive-policies/.

34. Digital Risk, https://digitalrisk.mphasis.com/home.html. In 2013 Mphasis acquired Digital Risk.

35. Richard Luscombe, "George Zimmerman: A Wannabe Cop 'Sick and Tired' of Criminals, Court Hears," *The Guardian*, July 12, 2013, https://www.theguardian.com/world/2013/jul/12/george-zimmerman-trayvon-martin-murder-trial.

36. Victoria Bell, "The White to Bear Arms: How Immunity Provisions in Stand Your Ground Statutes Lead to an Unequal Application of the Law for Black Gun Owners," *Fordham Urban Law Journal* 46, no. 4 (2019): 902–941; LaKerri R. Mack and Kristie Roberts-Lewis, "The Dangerous Intersection Between Race, Class and Stand Your Ground," *Journal of Public Management and Social Policy* 23, no. 1 (May 2016): 15; Giffords Law Center, "'Stand Your Ground' Kills: How These NRA-Backed Laws Promote Racist Violence," Giffords Law Center to Prevent Gun Violence: Southern Poverty Law Center, July 2020, https://www .splcenter.org/sites/default/files/_stand_your_ground_kills_-_how_these _nra-backed_laws_promote_racist_violence_1.pdf.

37. Molly Jackman, "ALEC's Influence over Lawmaking in State Legislatures," *Brookings* (blog), December 6, 2013, https://www.brookings.edu/articles /alecs-influence-over-lawmaking-in-state-legislatures/. "Stand Your Ground States 2023," Wisevoter, accessed July 15, 2023, https://wisevoter.com/state-rankings /stand-your-ground-states/.

38. Giffords Law Center, "'Stand Your Ground' Kills."

39. Bell, "The White to Bear Arms."

40. Bell, "The White to Bear Arms"; Mack and Roberts-Lewis, "The Dangerous Intersection Between Race, Class and Stand Your Ground."

41. John K. Roman, "Race, Justifiable Homicide, and Stand Your Ground Laws: Analysis of FBI Supplementary Homicide Report Data," Urban Institute, July 2013; American Bar Association, *National Task Force on Stand Your Ground Laws: Report and Recommendations*, American Bar Association, September 2015, https://www.americanbar.org/content/dam/aba/administrative /diversity/SYG_Report_Book.pdf; Giffords Law Center, "'Stand Your Ground' Kills"; Sarah Childress, "Is There Racial Bias in 'Stand Your Ground' Laws?," *Frontline*, July 31, 2012, https://www.pbs.org/wgbh/frontline/article /is-there-racial-bias-in-stand-your-ground-laws/.

42. Ta-Nehisi Coates, "Trayvon Martin and the Irony of American Justice," *The Atlantic*, July 15, 2013, https://www.theatlantic.com/national/archive/2013/07 /trayvon-martin-and-the-irony-of-american-justice/277782/.

43. Mark Follman and Lauren Williams, "Actually, Stand Your Ground Played a Major Role in the Trayvon Martin Case," *Mother Jones* (blog), July 31, 2013, https://www.motherjones.com/politics/2013/07/stand-your-ground-george -zimmerman-trayvon-martin/.

44. John Paul Wilson, Kurt Hugenberg, and Nicholas O. Rule, "Racial Bias in Judgments of Physical Size and Formidability: From Size to Threat," *Journal of Personality and Social Psychology* 113, no. 1 (2017): 59–80.

45. Bloom, *Suspicion Nation*.

46. US Department of Education, "An Overview of Exclusionary Discipline Practices in Public Schools for the 2017–18 School Year," US Department of Education Office of Civil Rights, June 2021, https://www2.ed.gov/about/offices/list/ocr/docs/crdc-exclusionary-school-discipline.pdf; Libby Nelson, "The Hidden Racism of School Discipline, in 7 Charts," *Vox*, October 31, 2015, https://www.vox.com/2015/10/31/9646504/discipline-race-charts; Emily Arcia, "Variability in Schools' Suspension Rates of Black Students," *Journal of Negro Education* 76, no. 4 (2007): 597–608; Russell Skiba et al., "Race Is Not Neutral: A National Investigation of African American and Latino Disproportionality in School Discipline," *School Psychology Review* 40, no. 1 (2011): 85–107; Russell J. Skiba, Mariella I. Arredondo, and Natasha T. Williams, "More Than a Metaphor: The Contribution of Exclusionary Discipline to a School-to-Prison Pipeline," *Equity and Excellence in Education* 47, no. 4 (October 2, 2014): 546–564, https://doi.org/10.1080/10665684.2014.958965.

47. Hilary Lustick, "'Restorative Justice' or Restoring Order? Restorative School Discipline Practices in Urban Public Schools," *Urban Education* 56, no. 8 (October 1, 2021): 1269–1296, https://doi.org/10.1177/0042085917741725; Skiba et al., "Race Is Not Neutral"; Lindsay Leban and Marlow Masterson, "The Impact of Childhood School Suspension on Dropout and Arrest in Adolescence: Disparate Relationships by Race and Adverse Childhood Experiences," *Criminal Justice and Behavior* 49, no. 4 (August 28, 2021), https://doi.org/10.1177/00938548211041387.

48. John M. Wallace, Jr., et al., "Racial, Ethnic, and Gender Differences in School Discipline Among U.S. High School Students: 1991–2005," *Negro Educational Review* 59, nos. 1–2 (Spring/Summer 2008): 47–62; Crenshaw, Ocen, and Nanda, "Black Girls Matter."

49. Francis L. Huang, "Do Black Students Misbehave More? Investigating the Differential Involvement Hypothesis and Out-of-School Suspensions," *Journal of Educational Research* 111, no. 3 (May 2018): 284–294, https://doi.org/10.1080/00220671.2016.1253538.

50. La Vonne Neal, Audrey Davis McCray, and Gwendolyn Webb-Johnson, "The Effects of African American Movement Styles on Teachers' Perceptions and Reactions—La Vonne I. Neal, Audrey Davis McCray, Gwendolyn Webb-Johnson, Scott T. Bridgest, 2003," accessed March 2, 2022, https://journals.sagepub.com/doi/abs/10.1177/00224669030370010501?journalCode=seda.

51. Crenshaw, Ocen, and Nanda, "Black Girls Matter."

52. "U.S. Department of Education Civil Rights Data Finds Persistent Racial Disparities in School Discipline and Policing," Advancement Project, accessed August 15, 2021, https://advancementproject.org/news/u-s

-department-of-education-civil-rights-data-finds-persistent-racial-disparities -in-school-discipline-and-policing/; Department of Education, "Overview of Exclusionary Discipline Practices in Public Schools."

53. Amity L. Noltemeyer et al., "Relationship Between School Suspension and Student Outcomes: A Meta-Analysis," *School Psychology Review* 44, no. 2 (April 2015): 224–240, https://doi.org/10.17105/spr-14-0008.1.

54. Janet E. Rosenbaum, "Educational and Criminal Justice Outcomes 12 Years After School Suspension," *Youth and Society* 52, no. 4 (May 2020): 515–547, https://doi.org/10.1177/0044118X17752208.

55. Elise Swanson, Heidi H. Erickson, and Gary W. Ritter, "Examining the Impacts of Middle School Disciplinary Policies on Ninth-Grade Retention," *Educational Policy* 35, no. 6 (September 1, 2021): 1014–1041, https://doi .org/10.1177/0895904819843600.

56. Bloom, *Suspicion Nation.*

57. Jerry L. Rushton, Michelle Forcier, and Robin M. Schectman, "Epidemiology of Depressive Symptoms in the National Longitudinal Study of Adolescent Health," *Journal of the American Academy of Child and Adolescent Psychiatry* 41, no. 2 (February 1, 2002): 199–205, https://doi.org/10.1097/00004583-200202000-00014.

58. Jeffrey H. Lamont et al., "Out-of-School Suspension and Expulsion," *Pediatrics (Evanston)* 131, no. 3 (2013): 3: e1000–1007, https://doi.org/10.1542/peds.2012-3932.

59. Paul J. Hirschfield, "Preparing for Prison? The Criminalization of School Discipline in the USA," *Theoretical Criminology* 12, no. 1 (February 1, 2008): 79–101, https://doi.org/10.1177/1362480607085795; Thomas Mowen and John Brent, "School Discipline as a Turning Point: The Cumulative Effect of Suspension on Arrest," *Journal of Research in Crime and Delinquency* 53, no. 5 (August 1, 2016): 628–653, https://doi.org/10.1177/0022427816643135; Skiba, Arredondo, and Williams, "More Than a Metaphor"; Julie Gerlinger, "Exclusionary School Discipline and Neighborhood Crime," *Socius* 6 (January 1, 2020): 1493–1509, https://doi.org/10.1177/2378023120925404; Julie Gerlinger et al., "Exclusionary School Discipline and Delinquent Outcomes: A Meta-Analysis," *Journal of Youth and Adolescence* 50, no. 8 (August 1, 2021): 1493–1509, https://doi.org/10.1007 /s10964-021-01459-3.

60. Rosenbaum, "Educational and Criminal Justice Outcomes."

61. Jordan T. Camp and Christina Heatherton, eds., *Policing the Planet: Why the Policing Crisis Led to Black Lives Matter* (London, New York: Verso, 2016), https://login.revproxy.brown.edu/login?URL=http://search.ebscohost.com /login.aspx?direct=true&scope=site&db=nlebk&db=nlabk&AN=1053730; Bernard E. Harcourt, *Illusion of Order: The False Promise of Broken Windows Policing* (Cambridge, MA: Harvard University Press, 2001).

62. Jamie Amemiya, Elizabeth Mortenson, and Ming-Te Wang, "Minor Infractions Are Not Minor: School Infractions for Minor Misconduct May Increase Adolescents' Defiant Behavior and Contribute to Racial Disparities in School Discipline," *American Psychologist* 75, no. 1 (January 2020): 23–36, https://doi.org/10.1037/amp0000475.

63. "U.S. Census Bureau QuickFacts: United States," accessed February 5, 2021, https://www.census.gov/quickfacts/fact/table/US/RHI825219.

64. "In Trayvon Martin's Hometown, Police Policy Is 'Stop and Frisk on Steroids,'" The Takeaway, WNYC Studios, accessed August 15, 2021, https://www.wnycstudios.org/podcasts/takeaway/segments/in-trayvon-martin-hometown-police-employ-stop-and-frisk-on-steroids-policy.

65. Conor Friedersdorf, "The City Where Blacks Suffer Under 'Stop and Frisk on Steroids,'" *The Atlantic*, May 30, 2014, https://www.theatlantic.com/national/archive/2014/05/where-Blacks-suffer-under-stop-and-frisk-on-steroids/371869/.

66. "In Trayvon Martin's Hometown, Police Policy Is 'Stop and Frisk on Steroids.'"

67. Friedersdorf, "City Where Blacks Suffer Under 'Stop and Frisk on Steroids.'"

68. Susan A. Bandes et al., "The Mismeasure of *Terry* Stops: Assessing the Psychological and Emotional Harms of Stop and Frisk to Individuals and Communities," *Behavioral Sciences and the Law* 37, no. 2 (March 2019): 176–194, https://doi.org/10.1002/bsl.2401.

69. "In Trayvon Martin's Hometown, Police Policy Is 'Stop and Frisk on Steroids.'"

70. Alexandra Natapoff, *Punishment Without Crime: How Our Massive Misdemeanor System Traps the Innocent and Makes American More Unequal* (New York: Basic Books, 2018), 11. Contact with the misdemeanor system is not only a feature of disadvantage; it generates disadvantage (10–11).

Chapter 4: Stealing Education

1. Michael O'Malley, "Did the Punishment Fit the Crime When Akron Mother Was Jailed for Sending Her Kids to a Suburban School?," Cleveland.com, 2011, https://www.cleveland.com/metro/2011/02/did_the_punishment_fit_the_cri.html.

2. "Readers React to the Williams-Bolar Case," *Akron Beacon Journal*, February 2, 2011, sec. A.

3. Pauline Lipman, *The New Political Economy of Urban Education: Neoliberalism, Race, and the Right to the City*, The Critical Social Thought Series (New York: Routledge, 2011).

4. Facebook, Inc., "Support Kelley Williams-Bolar," 2011.

5. Ed Meyer and Carol Biliczky, "Kelley Williams-Bolar Leaves Jail but Public Outcry Escalates," *Akron Beacon Journal*, 2011, https://www.amren.com /news/2011/02/kelley_williams/.

6. Change.org, "Gov. John Kasich: Pardon Kelley Williams-Bolar—She Shouldn't Go to Jail for Protecting Her Kids," Change.org, 2011, https://www .change.org/p/gov-john-kasich-pardon-kelley-williams-bolar-she-shouldnt-go -to-jail-for-protecting-her-kids.

7. Marcia Alesen Dawkins, "A Mind Is a Terrible Thing to Waste— Except in Ohio?," *Diverse: Issues in Higher Education*, March 15, 2011, https://www.diverseeducation.com/home/article/15090356/a-mind-is-a -terrible-thing-to-waste-except-in-ohio; Michael Lomax, "The Root: The Akron Mom Is Like You and Me," NPR, February 17, 2011, https://www.npr .org/2011/02/17/133833901/the-root-the-akron-mom-is-like-you-and-me?ps=rs.

8. Jamilah King, "Theft Charge Dismissed Against Ohio Mom Kelley Williams-Bolar," ColorLines, 2011, https://www.colorlines.com/articles/theft -charge-dismissed-against-ohio-mom-kelley-williams-bolar.

9. County of Summit, "Page of Prosecutor, Sherri Bevan Walsh," Prosecutor— County of Summit, Ohio, accessed October 30, 2011, https://prosecutor.summitoh .net/pages/About-Prosecutor-Sherri-Bevan-Walsh.html (page taken down).

10. Tina Kaufman, "Analysis: Williams-Bolar for the Record," *Akron News Now.Com*, 2011 (site discontinued).

11. Lipsitz, *How Racism Takes Place*, 6. See also page 37 for discussion on the effects of concentrated poverty and race.

12. Thomas Shapiro, *The Hidden Cost of Being African American* (New York: Oxford University Press, 2004); Ira Katznelson, *When Affirmative Action Was White: An Untold History of Racial Inequality in Twentieth-Century America* (New York: W. W. Norton, 2006).

13. Salary.com, "Teacher Aide Salary in Akron, Ohio," accessed October 31, 2022, https://www.salary.com/research/salary/benchmark/teacher-aide-salary/akron-oh.

14. State of Ohio Adult Parole Authority, Columbus, Ohio, "Minutes of the Special Meeting of the Adult Parole Authority," July 20, 2011.

15. Megan Cottrell, "The Shocking Statistics on Child Poverty," Change.org, 2010, accessed August 2011 (site discontinued).

16. Department of Numbers, "Akron, Ohio Unemployment," accessed October 31, 2022, https://www.deptofnumbers.com/unemployment/ohio/akron/.

17. Randy Tucker, "Workplace Equality for Blacks Remains Elusive," *Dayton Daily News*, 2011, https://www.daytondailynews.com/news/local /workplace-equality-for-blacks-remains-elusive/YC9bBYRXojQaCYB1W244xI/.

18. City-data.com, "Akron, Ohio Neighborhood Map—Income, House Prices, Occupations—List of Neighborhoods," 2012, https://www.city-data.com/nbmaps/neigh-Akron-Ohio.html.

19. Bob Jones, "Study Shows Akron Blacks Are Excluded from Economic Opportunity," News 5 Cleveland News, November 2, 2018, https://www.news5cleveland.com/news/local-news/akron-canton-news/study-shows-akron-Blacks-are-excluded-from-economic-opportunity.

20. Niche.com, https://www.niche.com/places-to-live/copley-township-summit-oh/residents/. Niche is a school and neighborhood demographics search site.

21. City-data.com, "Akron, OH (Ohio) Houses and Residents," 2012, https://www.city-data.com/housing/houses-Akron-Ohio.html.

22. City-data.com, "Akron, OH Neighborhood Map—Income, House Prices, Occupations—List of Neighborhoods," https://www.city-data.com/nbmaps/neigh-Akron-Ohio.html. There are a few exceptions to this pattern of greater racial concentration than overall population ratios warrant. So, for example, Downtown, East Akron, and Elizabeth Part Valley are around 60/40, Black-white areas.

23. Copley Township, "Demographics," accessed October 30, 2022, https://www.copley.oh.us/217/Demographics.

24. Seyma Bayram, "The Failed Akron Innerbelt Drove Decades of Racial Inequity. Can the Damage Be Repaired?," accessed November 12, 2022, https://www.beaconjournal.com/in-depth/news/2022/02/03/akron-innerbelt-history-racial-inequity-Black-history-urban-renewal-ohio/9033520002/.

25. Bayram, "Failed Akron Innerbelt."

26. "50 Years After Akron Riots, Healing Racial Divide Is an Ongoing Project," Akron Beacon Journal, accessed November 12, 2022, https://www.beaconjournal.com/story/news/local/2018/07/17/50-years-after-akron-riots/10546412007/.

27. Ed Meyer, "Prosecutor Says AMHA Tenant, Father Schemed to Get Girls in Copley Schools," Ohio.com, 2011, http://www.ohio.com/news/pair-accused-of-lies-1.201124 (site discontinued).

28. Public School Review, "Schumacher Community Learning Center (2022–23 Ranking)—Akron, OH," accessed November 3, 2022, https://www.publicschoolreview.com/schumacher-community-learning-cent-profile; Public School Review, "Litchfield Middle School (2022–23 Ranking)—Akron, OH," accessed November 2, 2022, https://www.publicschoolreview.com/litchfield-middle-school-profile/44313.

29. Public School Review, "Copley-Fairlawn City School District (2022-23)—Akron, OH," accessed November 3, 2022, https://www.publicschoolreview.com/ohio/copley-fairlawn-city-school-district/3904998-school-district.

30. EdBuild, "Fault Lines: America's Most Segregating School District Borders," accessed July 3, 2021, https://edbuild.org/content/fault-lines.

31. National Center for Education Statistics, "The Condition of Education—Preprimary, Elementary, and Secondary Education—Finances—Public School Revenue Sources—Indicator April (2020)," accessed February 12, 2021, https://nces.ed.gov/programs/coe/indicator_cma.asp.

32. Alvin Chang, "More Affluent Neighborhoods Are Creating Their Own School Districts," Vox, April 17, 2019, https://www.vox.com/2019/4/17/18307958/school-district-secession-worsening-data.

33. Michael E. Bell and Charlotte Kirschner, "Effective Property Tax Rates," A Reconnaissance of Currently Available Measures of Effective Property Tax Rates (Lincoln Institute of Land Policy, 2008), https://www.jstor.org/stable/resrep18265.4.

34. EdBuild, "Fault Lines."

35. "TCF Study Finds U.S. Schools Underfunded."

36. EdBuild, "Fault Lines."

37. Gary Orfield, Susan E. Eaton, and the Harvard Project on School Desegregation, Dismantling Desegregation: The Quiet Reversal of Brown v. Board of Education (New York: New Press, 1996); Janelle Scott and Jennifer Jellison Holme, "Public Schools, Private Resources: The Role of Social Networks in California Charter School Reform," 2002, https://gspp.berkeley.edu/faculty-and-impact/publications/public-schools-private-resources-the-role-of-social-networks-in-california.

38. Robert B. Reich, "Secession of the Successful," New York Times, January 20, 1991, sec. Magazine, https://www.nytimes.com/1991/01/20/magazine/secession-of-the-successful.html.

39. Robert Frederick Hill III, "An Historical Analysis of Policy Decisions and the Fiscal Equity of School Funding in Ohio: 1980–2003" (PhD diss., College of Education, Ashland University, 2008).

40. Sandra K. McKinley, "Litigation and Other Considerations in School Finance Reform in Ohio," Forum on Public Policy 2, no. 2 (2006): 441–454.

41. "School Funding Matters," accessed July 15, 2011, http://www.schoolfundingmatters.org/content/FundingToday.aspx.

42. "Ohio's Current School Funding System," n.d., http://www.tpspc.org/meeting_info/flyers/OhiosSchoolFundingSystem.pdf.

43. "Ohio's Current School Funding System."

44. Scott Piepho, "Five Inconvenient Facts About the Kelley Williams-Bolar Case," *Fairlawn-Bath Patch*, 2011.

45. Brian Poe, "Mother Jailed for School Fraud, Flares Controversy," NPR, 2011, https://www.npr.org/2011/01/28/133306180/Mother-Jailed -For-School-Fraud-Flares-Controversy.

46. Lisa Flam, "Ohio Mom Jailed for Lying About Kids' School Residency," *AolNews*, 2011, accessed March 2011, http:/ www.aol.com/2011/01/26/ohio -mom-kelly-williams-bolar-jailed-for-lying-about kids-scho/ (site discontinued).

47. Lipsitz, *How Racism Takes Place*, 35.

48. Jessica Trounstine, *Segregation by Design: Local Politics and Inequality in American Cities* (New York: Cambridge University Press, 2018).

49. Edward Zigler, Katherine W. Marsland, and Heather Lord, *The Tragedy of Child Care in America* (New Haven, CT: Yale University Press, 2009), 12.

50. Dorothy Roberts, *Torn Apart: How the Child Welfare System Destroys Black Families—And How Abolition Can Build a Safer World* (New York: Basic Books, 2022).

51. LaToya Baldwin Clark, "Family | Home | School," *Northwestern University Law Review* 117, no. 1 (2022): 1.

52. Patricia Hill Collins, *Black Sexual Politics: African Americans, Gender, and the New Racism* (New York: Routledge, 2004); Dorothy E. Roberts, *Killing the Black Body: Race, Reproduction, and the Meaning of Liberty* (New York: Pantheon Books, 1997).

53. Julia S. Jordan-Zachery, *Black Women, Cultural Images and Social Policy* (New York: Routledge, 2008), 29.

54. Martin Gilens, *Why Americans Hate Welfare: Race, Media, and the Politics of Antipoverty Policy*, Studies in Communication, Media, and Public Opinion (Chicago: University of Chicago Press, 1999); Kaaryn Gustafson, "The Criminalization of Poverty," *Journal of Criminal Law and Criminology* 99, no. 3 (August 1, 2009): 643; Ange-Marie Hancock, *The Politics of Disgust: The Public Identity of the Welfare Queen* (New York: NYU Press, 2004); Dorothy Roberts, *Shattered Bonds: The Color of Child Welfare*, reprint edition (New York: Civitas Books, 2003); Julie Anne White, "The Hollow and the Ghetto: Space, Race, and the Politics of Poverty," *Politics and Gender* 3, no. 2 (2007): 271–280.

55. Wahneema Lubiano, ed., *The House That Race Built: Original Essays by Toni Morrison, Angela Y. Davis, Cornel West, and Others on Black Americans and Politics in America Today*, reprint edition (New York: Vintage, 1998); Roberts, *Killing the Black Body*.

56. Andrea Canning and Leezel Tanglao, "Ohio Mom Kelley Williams-Bolar Jailed for Sending Kids to Better School District," ABC News, 2011, https:// abcnews.go.com/US/ohio-mom-jailed-sending-kids-school-district/story ?id=12763654.

57. Leah Faw and Huriya Jabbar, "Poor Choices: The Sociopolitical Context of 'Grand Theft Education,'" *Urban Education* 55, no. 1 (January 1, 2020): 3–37.

58. County of Summit, "Page of Prosecutor, Sherri Bevan Walsh."

59. Author interview with David Singleton, November 14, 2022.

60. Melanie Eversley, "Ohio Governor Reduces Mom's Charges to Misdemeanors," *USA Today*, 2011.

Chapter 5: Manner of Walking Along Roadway

1. Aubrey Bryon, "In Much of Ferguson, Walking in the Street Remains the Only Option," Strong Towns, accessed October 21, 2022, https://www.strong towns.org/journal/2018/2/19/ferguson-sidewalks-mike-brown-decline.

2. Colin Gordon, *Citizen Brown: Race, Democracy, and Inequality in the St. Louis Suburbs* (Chicago: University of Chicago Press, 2019).

3. Gordon, *Citizen Brown*, 5.

4. Jelani Cobb, "What I Saw in Ferguson," *New Yorker*, August 14, 2014, https://www.newyorker.com/news/news-desk/saw-ferguson.

5. Shelby Steele and Eli Steele, *What Killed Michael Brown?*, Prime Video, accessed August 19, 2022, https://www.amazon.com /Killed-Michael-Brown-Shelby-Steele/dp/B09TKTGKXM/ref=sr_1_6?crid =33TTFCR2VB6YV&keywords=michael+brown&qid=1660919574&sprefix =michael+brown%2Caps%2C66&sr=8-6.

6. Aaron Miguel Cantú, "How the Mainstream Media Helped Kill Michael Brown," Truthout, accessed September 18, 2022, https://truthout.org/articles /how-the-mainstream-media-helped-kill-michael-brown/.

7. Mark Peters, "Police: Officer Wasn't Aware Michael Brown Was Suspect in Alleged Robbery—WSJ," accessed March 31, 2023, https://www .wsj.com/articles/police-name-darren-wilson-as-officer-in-ferguson-missouri -michael-brown-shooting-1408108371.

8. Peters, "Police: Officer Wasn't Aware Michael Brown Was Suspect in Alleged Robbery—WSJ."

9. *Investigation of the Ferguson Police Department*, justice.gov/sites/default/files /opa/press-releases/attachments/2015/03/04/ferguson_police_department _report.pdf.

10. Matthew Pratt Guterl, "Why Darren Wilson Is Driving You Mad," *The Guardian*, November 30, 2014, sec. Opinion, https://www.theguardian.com /commentisfree/2014/nov/30/darren-wilson-ferguson-retirement-fear.

11. Molly Hennessy-Fiske, "Walking in Ferguson: If You're Black, It's Often Against the Law," *Los Angeles Times*, March 5, 2015, sec. World and

Nation, https://www.latimes.com/nation/la-na-walking-Black-ferguson-police
-justice-report-20150305-story.html.

12. Natapoff, *Punishment Without Crime.*

13. Hennessy-Fiske, "Walking in Ferguson"; Brentin Mock, "In Ferguson,
Walking While Black Was a Crime," Grist, March 4, 2015, https://grist.org/cities
/in-ferguson-walking-while-Black-was-a-crime/.

14. United States Department of Justice, *Department of Justice Report Regarding
the Criminal Investigation into the Shooting Death of Michael Brown by Ferguson,
Missouri Police Officer Darren Wilson* (Washington, DC: Department of Justice,
2015), 2.

15. United States Department of Justice, *Department of Justice Report*, 6.

16. Angela LaScala-Gruenewald, Katie Adamides, and Melissa Toback, "New
York's Ferguson Problem—How the State's Racist Fee System Punishes Poverty,
Lacks Transparency, and Is Overdue for Reform," No Price on Justice Coalition,
Fines and Fees Justice Center, September 4, 2020, https://finesandfeesjustice
center.org/articles/new-yorks-ferguson-problem/; Catherine E. Lhamon et al.,
"Targeted Fines and Fees Against Communities of Color," United States Commis-
sion on Civil Rights, Fines and Fees Justice Center, September 2017, https://fine
sandfeesjusticecenter.org/articles/targeted-fines-fees-against-communities-color/.

17. Radley Balko, "Opinion: How Municipalities in St. Louis County,
Mo., Profit from Poverty," *Washington Post*, September 3, 2014, https://www
.washingtonpost.com/news/the-watch/wp/2014/09/03/how-st-louis-county
-missouri-profits-from-poverty/; Elizabeth Jones, "Racism, Fines and Fees and the
US Carceral State," *Race and Class* 59, no. 3 (January 1, 2018): 38–50, https://doi
.org/10.1177/0306396817734785; Kathryn Zickuhr, "Applying a Racial Equity
Lens to Fines and Fees in the District of Columbia," D.C. Policy Center, April 22,
2019, https://www.dcpolicycenter.org/publications/racial-equity-fines-fees/.

18. Blake Ellis and Melanie Hicken, "The Secret World of Government Debt
Collection," CNN Money, February 17, 2015, https://money.cnn.com/interactive
/pf/debt-collector/government-agencies/index.html.

19. Torie Atkinson, "A Fine Scheme: How Municipal Fines Become Crushing
Debt in the Shadow of the New Debtors' Prison," *Harvard Civil Rights–Civil Liberties Law Review* 51 (2016): 189.

20. Sian Miranda Sing ÓFaoláin, *NOLA Shakedown: How Criminalizing
Municipal Fines and Fees Traps Poor and Working Class Black New Orleanians
in Poverty*, New Orleans Workers' Center for Racial Justice, September 2019,
https://www.nolashakedown.org/report.

21. United States Department of Justice, *Department of Justice Report.*

22. United States Department of Justice, *Department of Justice Report*, 12.

23. United States Department of Justice, *Department of Justice Report*, 10.

24. United States Department of Justice, *Department of Justice Report*, 42.

25. United States Department of Justice, *Department of Justice Report*, 43.

26. United States Department of Justice, *Department of Justice Report*, 42.

27. United States Department of Justice, *Department of Justice Report*, 3.

28. Jodi Rios, *Black Lives and Spatial Matters: Policing Blackness and Practicing Freedom in Suburban St. Louis* (Ithaca, NY: Cornell University Press, 2020), 86.

29. Rios, *Black Lives and Spatial Matters*, 80.

30. Rios, *Black Lives and Spatial Matters*, 92, 97.

31. Rios, *Black Lives and Spatial Matters*, 87.

32. Rios, *Black Lives and Spatial Matters*, 99.

33. Teresa Mathew, "St. Louis County Is Profiting Off the 'Muni Shuffle' Long After Ferguson Protests," The Appeal, accessed October 23, 2022, https://theappeal.org/st-louis-county-fines-and-fees-ferguson/.

34. Meadows and Wright, *Thinking in Systems*, 39.

35. United States Department of Justice, *Department of Justice Report*, 4.

36. United States Department of Justice, *Department of Justice Report*, 74.

37. "Why Did Ferguson Erupt? The Answer Depends on Your Race," NBS News, August 22, 2014, https://www.nbcnews.com/feature/in-plain-sight/why-did-ferguson-erupt-answer-depends-your-race-n186031.

38. Topher Sanders, Kate Rabinowitz, and Benjamin Conarck, "Walking While Black," ProPublica, November 16, 2017, https://www.propublica.org/series/walking-while-black.

39. Natapoff, *Punishment Without Crime*.

40. United States Department of Justice, *Department of Justice Report*, 44.

41. Carla O'Connor, "The Premise of Black Inferiority: An Enduring Obstacle Fifty Years Post-*Brown*," *Teachers College Record* 108, no. 14 (December 1, 2006): 316–336, https://doi.org/10.1177/016146810610801417; Michael E. Ruane, "A Brief History of the Enduring Phony Science That Perpetuates White Supremacy," *Washington Post*, April 30, 2019, https://www.washingtonpost.com/local/a-brief-history-of-the-enduring-phony-science-that-perpetuates-white-supremacy/2019/04/29/20e6aef0-5aeb-11e9-a00e-050dc7b82693_story.html.

42. Jake Halpern, "The Man Who Shot Michael Brown," *New Yorker*, August 3, 2015, https://www.newyorker.com/magazine/2015/08/10/the-cop.

43. "2023 Q1 State Unemployment by Race and Ethnicity," Economic Policy Institute, accessed July 17, 2023, https://www.epi.org/indicators/state-unemployment-race-ethnicity/.

Notes to Chapter 5

44. Devah Pager and Bruce Western, *Race at Work: Realities of Race and Criminal Record in the NYC Job Market*, Schomburg Center for Research in Black Culture, 2005, https://scholar.harvard.edu/files/pager/files/race_at_work.pdf.

45. Steele and Steele, *What Killed Michael Brown?*

46. Rios, *Black Lives and Spatial Matters*, 91.

47. Stephen Portnoy and Stephanie Wash, "A Different Look at Ferguson's Michael Brown Just Days Before His Death," ABC News, accessed October 25, 2022, https://abcnews.go.com/US/fergusons-michael-brown-days-death/story?id=25077435.

48. *NYC Epicenters 9/11→2021½*, directed by Spike Lee (HBO Documentary Films, 2021), accessed July 17, 2023, https://www.google.com/search?q=Spike+Lee+NYC+Epicenters&rlz=1C5CHFA_enUS835US835&oq=Spike+Lee+NYC+Epicenters&aqs=chrome..69i57.5111j0j7&sourceid=chrome&ie=UTF-8.

49. Rios, *Black Lives and Spatial Matters*.

50. Matt Barnum, "Normandy High, by the Numbers: Inside Michael Brown's School, a Snapshot of Staggering Inequality," accessed October 25, 2022, https://www.the74million.org/article/normandy-high-by-the-numbers-inside-michael-browns-school-a-staggering-snapshot-of-inequality/.

51. 2014 MSIP5 District/Charter APR Summary Report—Public, https://apps.dese.mo.gov/MCDS/Reports/SSRS_Print.aspx?Reportid=1a22f906-d154-446f-87a7-9cf506487852. Found on the State of Missouri, Districts, Charters and Schools website: https://apps.dese.mo.gov/MCDS/home.aspx. See also Nikole Hannah-Jones, "The Problem We All Live With—Part One," *This American Life*, July 31, 2015, https://www.thisamericanlife.org/562/the-problem-we-all-live-with-part-one; Nikole Hannah-Jones, "School Segregation, the Continuing Tragedy of Ferguson," ProPublica, accessed September 5, 2022, https://www.propublica.org/article/ferguson-school-segregation?token=Tu5C70R2pCBv8Yj33AkMh2E-mHz3d6iu.

52. Rios, *Black Lives and Spatial Matters*, 114.

53. "Stanton Lawrence: How Missouri Killed the Normandy School District," *Diane Ravitch's Blog* (blog), June 22, 2014, https://dianeravitch.net/2014/06/22/stanton-lawrence-how-missouri-killed-the-normandy-school-district/.

54. Editorial Board, St. Louis Post-Dispatch, "Missouri Student Transfer Bill Needs Simple Tuition Fix," *St. Louis Post-Dispatch*, February 23, 2015, sec. Editorial, https://www.stltoday.com/opinion/editorial/editorial-missouri-student-transfer-bill-needs-simple-tuition-fix/article_d24e82a1-fe57-589f-81aa-2368a8c81460.html.

55. Nikole Hannah-Jones, "How School Segregation Divides Ferguson—and the United States," *New York Times*, December 19, 2014, sec. Sunday Review, https://www.nytimes.com/2014/12/21/sunday-review/why-are-our-schools -still-segregated.html.

56. Hannah-Jones, "The Problem We All Live with—Part One."

57. Hannah-Jones, "The Problem We All Live with—Part One."

58. Hannah-Jones, "The Problem We All Live with—Part One."

59. Editorial Board, *St. Louis Post-Dispatch*, "Missouri Transfer Bill Needs Tuition Fix."

60. Elisa Crouch, "Politics and Turmoil Surrounding School Transfers Intensifies," *St. Louis Post-Dispatch*, June 23, 2014, sec. News, https://www.stltoday .com/news/local/education/politics-and-turmoil-surrounding-school-transfers -intensifies/article_3d02ae9e-3c3a-50cf-9f3b-cc6835a1d588.html.

61. Prudence L. Carter et al., eds., *Closing the Opportunity Gap: What America Must Do to Give All Children an Even Chance* (New York: Oxford University Press, 2013).

62. Julien Lafortune, Jesse Rothstein, and Diane Whitmore Schanzenbach, "School Finance Reform and the Distribution of Student Achievement," *American Economic Journal: Applied Economics* 10, no. 2 (April 2018): 1–26, https:// doi.org/10.1257/app.20160567; C. Kirabo Jackson, Rucker C. Johnson, and Claudia Persico, "The Effects of School Spending on Educational and Economic Outcomes: Evidence from School Finance Reforms," *Quarterly Journal of Economics* 131, no. 1 (February 1, 2016): 157–218, https://doi.org/10.1093/qje/qjv036.

63. Linda Darling-Hammond, "Unequal Opportunity: Race and Education," *Brookings* (blog), 1998, https://www.brookings.edu/articles/unequal-opportunity -race-and-education/; Frank Gettridge, "Why Are Schools That Predominately Serve Black and Brown Students Consistently Underfunded?," *The Hechinger Report*, October 17, 2019, https://hechingerreport.org/opinion-why-are-schools -that-predominately-serve-Black-and-brown-students-consistently-underfunded/.

64. Carl Bankston III and Stephen J. Caldas, "Majority African American Schools and Social Injustice: The Influence of De Facto Segregation on Academic Achievement," *Social Forces* 75, no. 2 (December 1, 1996): 535–555, https://doi .org/10.1093/sf/75.2.535. See also Noliwe Rooks, *Cutting School: Privatization, Segregation, and the End of Public Education* (New York: New Press, 2017).

65. Elisa Crouch, "A Senior Year Mostly Lost for a Normandy Honor Student," *St. Louis Post-Dispatch*, May 3, 2015, sec. News, https://www.stltoday.com /news/local/education/a-senior-year-mostly-lost-for-a-normandy-honor-student /article_ce759a06-a979-53b6-99bd-c87a430dc339.html.

66. Hannah-Jones, "The Problem We All Live with—Part One."

67. Hannah-Jones, "The Problem We All Live with—Part One"; John Eligon, "In Missouri, Race Complicates a Transfer to Better Schools: [National Desk]," *New York Times*, Late Edition (East Coast), August 1, 2013, sec. A, https://www.nytimes.com/2013/08/01/us/in-missouri-race-complicates-a-transfer-to-better-schools.html.

68. Caroline Wolf Harlow, *Education and Correctional Populations*, US Department of Justice, Bureau of Justice Statistics, Special Report, April 15, 2003, https://bjs.ojp.gov/content/pub/pdf/ecp.pdf.

69. Catherine E. Shoichet, "Missouri Teen Shot by Police Was Two Days Away from Starting College," CNN, August 12, 2014, https://www.cnn.com/2014/08/11/justice/michael-brown-missouri-teen-shot/index.html.

70. Celeste Bott, "Vatterott Immediately Closes All Campuses," STLtoday.com, accessed September 6, 2022, https://www.stltoday.com/news/local/education/vatterott-immediately-closes-all-campuses/article_4c0ea18a-3feb-5e51-bc78-5d1e6f3d6831.html; "Vatterott College System Closes All 15 Campuses," AP News, April 29, 2021, https://apnews.com/article/us-news-mo-state-wire-education-us-department-of-education-st-louis-71a07fb863bf4e459a7f1c2417cb1ecd.

71. James Surowiecki, "The For-Profit-School Scandal," *New Yorker*, October 26, 2015, https://www.newyorker.com/magazine/2015/11/02/the-rise-and-fall-of-for-profit-schools; Ayelet Sheffey, "For-Profit Schools Target Minority Communities That Typically Owe More Student Debt, Report Says," Business Insider, accessed October 26, 2022, https://www.businessinsider.com/for-profit-schools-target-minority-communities-student-borrower-protection-center-2021-8.

72. James Surowiecki, "The Rise and Fall of For-Profit Schools," *New Yorker*, October 26, 2015, https://www.newyorker.com/magazine/2015/11/02/the-rise-and-fall-of-for-profit-schools.

73. Tressie McMillan Cottom, *Lower Ed: The Troubling Rise of For-Profit Colleges in the New Economy* (New York: New Press, 2018).

74. Surowiecki, "The For-Profit-School Scandal."

75. Howard Gold, "Who's at Fault for Student-Loan Defaults?," University of Chicago Booth School of Business, accessed October 26, 2022, https://www.chicagobooth.edu/review/whos-fault-student-loan-defaults.

76. Bourree Lam, "Most For-Profit Students Wind Up Worse Off Than if They Had Never Enrolled in the First Place," *The Atlantic*, June 1, 2016, https://www.theatlantic.com/business/archive/2016/06/for-profit-earnings/485141/.

77. Celeste Bott, "Vatterott Immediately Closes All Campuses," STL today.com, accessed September 6, 2022, https://www.stltoday.com/news/local/education/vatterott-immediately-closes-all-campuses/article_4c0ea18a-3feb-5e51-bc78-5d1e6f3d6831.html.

78. Sheffey, "For-Profit Schools Target Minority Communities That Typically Owe More Student Debt, Report Says"; Aarthi Swaminathan, "For-Profit Colleges Target Minority Areas Across America, Study Argues," accessed October 26, 2022, https://finance.yahoo.com/news/predatory-for-profit-colleges-target-minority-areas-study-150406599.html.

Chapter 6: How We Break Free

1. Larry Buchanan, Quoctrung Bui, and Jugal K. Patel, "Black Lives Matter May Be the Largest Movement in U.S. History," *New York Times*, July 3, 2020, sec. U.S., https://www.nytimes.com/interactive/2020/07/03/us/george-floyd-protests-crowd-size.html.

2. Rebecca Morin, "Survey: Higher Percentage in US Agree Black People Face Discrimination," accessed March 28, 2023, https://www.usatoday.com/story/news/politics/2020/06/08/survey-higher-percentage-us-agree-Black-people-face-discrimination/3143651001/.

3. Meadows and Wright, *Thinking in Systems*, 146.

4. Andre C. Willis, "Obama's Racial Legacy: The Power of Whiteness," *Critical Philosophy of Race* 5, no. 2 (2017): 183–197, https://doi.org/10.5325/critphilrace.5.2.0183.

5. Devah Pager, *Marked: Race, Crime, and Finding Work in an Era of Mass Incarceration* (Chicago: University of Chicago Press, 2007).

6. Shannon Sullivan, *Good White People: The Problem with Middle-Class White Anti-Racism*, SUNY Series, Philosophy and Race (Albany: State University of New York Press, 2014).

7. David Leonhardt, "Middle-Class Black Families, in Low-Income Neighborhoods," *New York Times*, June 24, 2015, sec. The Upshot, https://www.nytimes.com/2015/06/25/upshot/middle-class-Black-families-in-low-income-neighborhoods.html.

8. Scott Winship, Christopher Pulliam, Ariel Gelrud Shiro, Richard V. Reeves, and Santiago Deambrosi, "Long Shadows: The Black-White Gap in Multigenerational Poverty," *Brookings* (blog), June 10, 2021, https://www.brookings.edu/research/long-shadows-the-Black-White-gap-in-multigenerational-poverty/.

9. Aja Romano, "A History of 'Wokeness,'" October 9, 2020, Vox, https://www.vox.com/culture/21437879/stay-woke-wokeness-history-origin-evolution

-controversy; Bloomberg, "Here's Where 'Woke' Comes From," *Arkansas Democrat Gazette*, 2:17, https://www.arkansasonline.com/news/2023/jan/08/heres-where-woke-comes-from/.

10. Arline T. Geronimus, *Weathering: The Extraordinary Stress of Ordinary Life in an Unjust Society* (New York: Little, Brown Spark, 2023).

INDEX

Index

Index

Index

Index

Index

Index

Index

North Sacramento, 186–187
North St. Louis County
   municipal fines and fees in, 181–183
   racial composition of, 181–182
   See also Ferguson
NSD. *See* Normandy School District
nuclear families, 156
NYC Epicenters 9/11→2021½
   (documentary), 194
NYPD. *See* New York Police Department

Obama, Barack, 81–84
Ohio, property tax school funding in,
   147–154. *See also specific locations*
Ohio Department of Education, 131,
   149–150
Ohio Supreme Court, 147–148, 161–162
open enrollment, 149–152, 162
opioid epidemic, 216
opportunity gaps, school performance
   gaps as, 202
oppression, resistance to, 228–231
opt-out loophole, 150–153, 157–158, 162
order-maintenance offenses, 121–122,
   170–171, 187
ordinances, municipal, 170–173. *See also*
   fines and fees
O'Reilly, Bill, 81
outcomes, system
   adaptation of policies to achieve same,
     72–77
   criteria for identifying, 32–33, 36
   definition of, 32
   leverage points for reversing, 222–223
   system goals aligned with, 222–223

Pager, Devah, 222
paradigms
   definition of, 216
   importance of shifting, 214–220
PBS *Frontline*, 107
People (magazine), 85
personal responsibility, 187–193
photographs
   of Brown, 193
   of Williams-Bolar, 128

plea bargains, 159–160
POA. *See* power of attorney
Poe, Brian, 152–153
police
   containment through strategies of,
     62–63
   harassment by, 168–173
   implicit bias in, 96
   punishment through strategies of, 69
   racial profiling by, 118–123, 168–170
   response to Ferguson protests,
     166–167
   response to Martin's murder, 79–80,
     102–103
   Stand Your Ground laws on, 104–105
   unjustified use of force by, 189
   visibility of violence by, 12, 168,
     213–214
   See also specific locations and policing
     strategies
policies and practices driving systemic
   racism, 57–77
   adaptation of, 72–77
   current status of, 10–11
   interconnections among, 58–62
   overview of, 19–20
   race-neutral language of, 29–30, 62,
     74, 222
   in wealth gap, 10–11
   See also specific policy areas
poverty
   in Copley Township, 139
   intergenerational, 65, 227
   in Normandy, 195
   role of systemic racism in, 226–227
   in St. Louis County, 181–182
power of attorney (POA), grandparent,
   155–156
predatory lending, 45–46, 73
Price, Deborah, 133
prison. *See* incarceration
profiling. *See* racial profiling
property seizures, 66
property tax school funding, 144–154
   interconnections with other issues, 35
   Ohio Supreme Court on, 147–148

Index

Index

Index

Index

Index

intergenerational, 28, 65, 220
size of, 65
weathering, 230–231
"welfare queens," 156–157
Wellston School District, 196–197
West, Cornel, 228
West Akron, 137–144
  public housing in, 154–155
  residential segregation in, 137–141
  schools in, 141–144
  See also Williams-Bolar, Kelley
What Killed Mike Brown? (documentary),
  191–192
white Americans
  assumption of innocence of, 96,
    99–100
  historical vs. modern racism of, 8–12
  liberal, 9–12
  in middle class, 76
  on racial equality, 8
  on racial tensions, 186
  unemployment rates of, 139, 190
white flight, 90–91, 138, 141
white homogeneity, 91–92
whiteness
  as American identity, 83
  economic value of, 92
Williams-Bolar, Kelley, 127–162
  career of, 138–139
  clemency for, 160–161
  evidence against, 132
  felony charges against, 127–134,
    158–161
  media coverage of, 128, 133, 135, 157
  motivations of, 129–130, 134–137,
    141–142
  moving to Copley as option for,
    154–156
  myth of Black criminality and,
    156–158
  overview of story of, 21–23
  property tax school funding and,
    144–154
  remorse of, lack of, 158–160

residency of, 130–131
residential segregation and, 137–141
vs. school system, as criminal,
  130–137
sentencing of, 127, 132, 157–158
single-issue interpretations of,
  132, 161
supporters of, 132–134, 136, 160–161
time served in prison, 127, 131–132
Willis, Andre C., 219
Wilson, Darren, 163–209
  on Brown's strength, 169
  myth of Black criminality and, 169
  on personal responsibility, 189–191
  police lies about actions of, 22, 166
  See also Brown, Michael
wokeness, 14, 228
women, Black, as single mothers, 156–157
work. *See* employment

zero-tolerance policies
  of police, 119
  of schools, 48, 59, 116
Zigler, Edward, 155
Zimmerman, George, 79–125
  beliefs about Black criminality, 94,
    97–99, 101–103, 123
  career of, 101–102
  encounter with Martin described
    by, 102
  initial lack of charges against, 80,
    102–103
  911 calls by, 80, 94, 97–99, 102, 109
  overview of story of, 21–23
  role in neighborhood watch, 88, 94
  self-defense claims of, 80, 84, 111
  as vigilante vs. hero in media, 84
  See also Martin, Trayvon
Zimmerman, George, trial of, 124–125
  Martin's character in, 124–125
  myth of Black criminality at, 99
  silence about racism at, 83
  Stand Your Ground in, 107–109, 124
  verdict in, 108–109

277

Tricia Rose is Chancellor's Professor of Africana Studies and the director of the Center for the Study of Race and Ethnicity in America at Brown University. The author of three books, including the foundational, award-winning scholarly analysis of hip hop *Black Noise* and its sequel, *The Hip Hop Wars*, Rose has received fellowships from the Ford and Rockefeller Foundations, and her research has been funded by the Mellon and Robert Wood Johnson Foundations.